OTHER BOOKS IN THIS SERIES:

Bruce H. Wilkinson
Executive Editor

Paula A. Kirk
Editor

Calvin W. Edwards
General Editor

Walk Thru the Bible Ministries
Atlanta, Georgia

Zondervan Publishing House
Grand Rapids, Michigan

Family Walk Again
Family, Friends, Self-esteem, and 49 Other Weekly Readings
for Your Family Devotions
Copyright © 1993 by Walk Thru the Bible Ministries
All rights reserved

Published by Zondervan Publishing House

Requests for information should be addressed to:
Walk Thru the Bible Ministries   or   Zondervan Publishing House
4201 North Peachtree Road   Grand Rapids, MI 49530
Atlanta, GA 30341–1207

Library of Congress Cataloging-in-Publication Data

Family Walk Again: family, friends, self-esteem, and 49 other weekly readings
for your family devotions / Walk Thru the Bible Ministries, Atlanta, GA
    p. cm.
    ISBN 0-310-54581-1
    1. Family—Prayer-books and devotions—English. 2. Devotional calendars.
3. Bible—Devotional use. I. Walk Thru the Bible (Educational Ministry).
BV255.F3343   1993
249—dc20   93—18803
                                                                CIP

Cover and interior design by Michelle Beeman
Cover photo by FPG International.
Cartoons by Martha Campbell

Printed in the United States of America

96 97 / DH / 5

Dedication

When I think of families who are spiritually consistent, Biblically faithful, and outstanding leaders in the business community, there is one that is always on my list. Mrs. Pauline Myers, and her late husband Stanley, through their Christian walk, their children, and their business were living out a Biblical "family walk" long before we put ink on paper. We therefore dedicate *Family Walk Again* to Mrs. Pauline Myers for her contribution to strengthening Christian families through the example of her own.

Bruce H. Wilkinson

ACKNOWLEDGMENTS

Family Walk Again: Family, Friends, Self-esteem, and 49 Other Weekly Readings for Your Family Devotions is the third compilation of topical studies from *Family Walk,* a devotional guide published monthly by Walk Thru the Bible Ministries. We are grateful to everyone in Walk Thru the Bible's Specialized Publishing Group who worked so faithfully on this devotional guide during the past 10 years, from those on the leadership and sales teams right down through all the support and production staff.

Special thanks for great ideas and exceptionally fine work on this book go to our *Family Walk* editorial assistant, Robyn Holmes, and designer, Michelle Beeman. May their investment of time, talent, and exceptional teamwork make a lasting difference in families who read this book.

INTRODUCTION

Family Walk Again is carefully designed to help parents train their children to apply biblical truths to everyday situations. With this book, parents have a tool to open communication about the vital issues families face today and to find the answers in God's Word.

Family Walk Again will help you and your children establish the Scriptures as your foundation for living in this chaotic and insecure world. As you discover practical applications for family problems in *Family Walk Again,* your child will see the Bible in a new light. No longer will the Bible simply be a book of exciting stories about things that happened long ago. Instead, your children will see the Bible as a vital resource for a happy and successful life. As you and your children grow spiritually and become confident in God's love, you will become more secure as a family.

We at Walk Thru the Bible Ministries are pleased to join with Zondervan Publishing House to make this Bible reading guide available to you. The common purpose of our ministries is to help Christians become grounded in the Scriptures.

Bruce H. Wilkinson
President and Executive Editor

How to Get the Most Out of *Family Walk Again*

Family Walk Again is arranged by topics for you and your children to explore together each week. You can start with the first topic or just jump in at any point in the book. Simply put a check in the accompanying box to keep your place.

Day One of each topic brings your family a definition of the topic and a key Bible verse. The primary Scripture portion for Day One is the key verse, and we encourage you and your children to read it aloud several times and perhaps even memorize it. Use the cartoon as a discussion starter or just have a good laugh together.

Days Two–Five are divided into these three sections:

> **An opening story** helps your family focus on the question for the day.

> **Take a Look** guides you to a passage in God's Word that gives insight into the biblical answer to the day's question. Let your children find the passage in their Bibles and read the selection aloud. Or let them read the verse that is printed in italic type. Encourage your children to mark that verse in their own Bibles and reread it at some point during the day.

> **Take a Step** reveals useful ways you can practice what you learn. Through discussion about the Scripture you read, references back to the opening story, and concrete action your family can take, Take a Step is designed to generate conversation about the issues young people face today.

We encourage you to be sensitive to your children's needs and questions. Stop at any point to discuss what you're reading and how it relates to your situation. Spiritual growth is a process that takes place over time. *Family Walk Again*, if used consistently, is a tool that will give your family and its individual members opportunities to prepare for the challenges that will come your way.

WALK THRU THE BIBLE MINISTRIES

Walk Thru the Bible Ministries (WTB) began in the early 1970s in Portland, Oregon, when a young teacher named Bruce Wilkinson developed an innovative way of teaching surveys of the Bible. By enabling people to actively participate in the learning process through memorable hand signs, the Word of God came alive for them and lives were changed.

From these small beginnings emerged the multifaceted Bible-teaching outreach that Dr. Wilkinson officially founded as a nonprofit ministry in 1976. In 1978 WTB moved to its current home in Atlanta, Georgia. Since then, WTB has grown into one of the leading Christian organizations in America with an international ministry extending to 30 countries representing 22 languages. International branch offices are located in Australia, Brazil, Great Britain, Singapore, and New Zealand.

By focusing on the central themes of Scripture and their practical application to life, WTB has been able to develop and maintain wide acceptance in denominations and fellowships around the world. In addition, it has carefully initiated strategic ministry alliances with more than one hundred Christian organizations and missions of wide diversity and background.

WTB has four major outreach ministries: seminars, publishing, leadership training, and video training curricula. Since it began its seminar ministry two decades ago, WTB has instructed more than one million people worldwide through seminars taught by more than two hundred highly qualified, well-trained teachers. People of all ages and religious persuasions have developed a deeper understanding of the Bible through these unique Old and New Testament surveys, and many have come to know Christ in a new and more personal way.

WTB's publishing ministry began in 1978 with the launching of *The Daily Walk* magazine. Since then, WTB Publishing has continued to develop additional publications that enable individuals, families, and churches to maintain a regular, meaningful habit of daily devotional time in the Word of God. The publications include *Closer Walk, Family Walk, LifeWalk, Quiet Walk,* and *Youthwalk*. WTB is one of the largest publishers of devotional magazines in the Christian community. The third strategic ministry of WTB is the training of Christian leaders and communicators. Launched in the late 1980s, the Applied Principles of Learning (APL) training conference for teachers, pastors, and parents has rapidly become the most widely used interdenominational teacher training program in North America. Dozens of certified WTB instructors regularly conduct this life-changing course in schools, churches, businesses, and colleges. In addition, WTB's Leadership Dynamics curriculum is an integral part of the regular and ongoing discipleship training in hundreds of churches.

The newest ministry of WTB is the Video Training curriculum. In just a few short years, the WTB creative team has developed a number of leading video courses that have enjoyed widespread distribution. *The Seven Laws of the Learner,* featuring Dr. Bruce H. Wilkinson, focuses on the needs of the student and helps teachers learn to communicate in the most effective and compelling manner possible. *The Seven Laws of the Teacher,* featuring Dr. Howard G. Hendricks, equips church school teachers, parents, and others to effectively prepare and teach Bible lessons that capture attention and change lives. *Master Your Money,* a six-part presentation by Christian financial planner Ron Blue, trains people to maximize their effectiveness as stewards of God's resources. Thousands of churches use these and other fine WTB videos with their congregations each year.

WTB has had a consistent history of strategic ministry from its beginning. The organization strives to help fulfill the Great Commission in obedience to the Lord's call. With this mission in mind, WTB lives out its commitment to excellence with the highest standards of ethical conduct and integrity, not only in the ministry but also in its internal operational policies and procedures. No matter what the ministry, no matter where the ministry, WTB focuses on the Word of God and encourages people of all nations to grow in their knowledge of Him and in their unreserved obedience and service to Him.

For more information about Walk Thru the Bible's publications, videos, or seminars in your area, write to Walk Thru the Bible Ministries, 4201 North Peachtree Road, Atlanta, Ga 30341–1207 or call (404) 458-9300.

CONTENTS

MERCY

*T*hough William Shakespeare died in 1616, he is still considered one of the greatest writers of all time. As you read this quotation from his play *The Merchant of Venice*, can you discover our topic for the week?

> *The quality of mercy is not strain'd,*
> *It droppeth as the gentle rain from heaven*
> *Upon the place beneath. It is twice bless'd:*
> *It blesseth him that gives and him that takes.*
> *'Tis mightiest in the mightiest: it becomes*
> *The throned monarch better than his crown. . . .*
> *But mercy is above this sceptred sway,*
> *It is enthroned in the hearts of kings,*
> *It is an attribute to God himself;*
> *And earthly power doth then show likest God's*
> *When mercy seasons justice.*

◆ LOOKING AT MERCY

Shakespeare squeezed a lot of information about mercy into those lines! Can you pick out his statements that say . . .

1. Both the giver and the receiver of mercy are blessed.
2. Mercy is more becoming to a king than even his crown.
3. By His very nature God is merciful.
4. We act like God when we show both justice and mercy.

Mercy is **compassion in action toward those who are in trouble or despair.** God provides the supreme example of mercy.

● KEY VERSE ON MERCY

For the Lord your God is a merciful God; he will not abandon or destroy you or forget the covenant with your forefathers (Deuteronomy 4:31).

▲ LOOKING AHEAD

See if you can match these verses to three of Shakespeare's statements about mercy: (1) Matthew 5:7; (2) Daniel 9:9; (3) James 3:17.

ANSWERS: (1) "It blesseth him . . . . "
(2) "It is an attribute . . . ."
(3) "It droppeth . . . ."

"Mom's cool. She makes me eat spinach, but she lets me put chocolate syrup on it."

Real love will find a way to forgive

"**L** ook," Beth said defiantly, "I've forgiven Stacia for what she said about me. But there's no way I'm going to help her now that she's in trouble."

Beth was still upset because Stacia had spread an ugly rumor about her a week ago. Even though the rumor was untrue, it still hurt. So Beth thought she had a right to be mad.

"But Beth," Connie pleaded, "you're the only one who can help her. You told me you know she couldn't have taken that money out of Mr. Lasko's desk drawer because you saw her in the library that period. But you won't stand up for her! How can you say you've forgiven her if you won't show a little mercy when she really needs your help?"

Q

How can I show mercy?

A

I show mercy when I forgive others who have hurt me.

PARENT
Discuss with your children recent situations in which you've tried to deal with them mercifully. Did they realize what you were doing? How did they feel about your action?

◆ **TAKE A LOOK / Nehemiah 9:7, 9, 11, 15-17, 21-33**

All people need forgiveness, because all have sinned. And God will forgive us because of His merciful love—if we ask Him.

About 444 B.C., Nehemiah led a group of Israelites from Babylon, where they had been held captive, to their home city of Jerusalem. Because they wanted to honor God, they read His Word often, thinking back over their nation's history. As they did, a very important truth dawned on them. Read how Nehemiah led the people in prayer in Nehemiah 9:7, 9, 11, 15-17, 21-33.

What do you think they discovered about God?

▲ **TAKE A STEP**

When the people of Nehemiah's day reviewed their past, they discovered that, even though they had been held captive for many years in a pagan land, God's mercy and forgiveness still remained. And even though their nation had stubbornly and continually disobeyed God (verse 29), He still loved them. Their eyes were opened to the great truth that . . .

"In your great mercy you did not put an end to them or abandon them, for you are a gracious and merciful God" (Nehemiah 9:31).

Beth said she had forgiven Stacia, yet she refused to show mercy by helping her out of a tough situation.

Do you think Beth had truly forgiven? What would you say to help Beth understand the true meaning of forgiveness?

Are you willing to forgive people who have hurt you? How do you show mercy?

Rick fought back his tears, fearing that once again he wouldn't be able to move his hands away before Phil's quick, hard slap hit him again. "Why did I ever get myself involved in a game of slapjack," he asked himself, "especially with mean old Phil?"

Rick felt the eyes of his classmates on him. His face was flushed with embarrassment. He slowly stretched out his red, throbbing hands again.

Smack! This slap was the hardest. Rick couldn't hold his tears back any longer. He rubbed his hands and sobbed.

"Ready to give up now?" Phil jeered. "Say 'mercy' or put your hands out again!"

Rick shook his head. "Chicken!" Phil laughed cruelly. "That's all you are—a chicken."

◆ TAKE A LOOK
1 Peter 2:24; Romans 5:8; Ephesians 2:4-5

Phil enjoyed seeing Rick in painful misery, so he forced him to play strictly by the rules of the game and beg for mercy. But if Phil was truly merciful, he wouldn't have treated Rick so unkindly.

As humans, we need God's mercy. But God isn't a heavenly bully who makes us perform certain deeds to earn His mercy. No, God is merciful to us because He loves us.

But we must also realize that God's loving mercy does not cancel out His justice. He doesn't ignore sin or its deadly penalty. God requires a perfect sacrifice for the sins of the world. That requirement was met when Jesus died on the cross in our place, for our sins.

Jesus' death was the greatest demonstration of God's mercy for us. Want proof? Have different family members read 1 Peter 2:24; Romans 5:8; Ephesians 2:4-5; and Titus 3:4-5.

▲ TAKE A STEP
He saved us, not because of righteous things we had done, but because of his mercy (Titus 3:5).

Mercy is a wonderful blessing from God to us. But God does not promise mercy or acceptance to anyone who refuses to acknowledge Jesus Christ as Savior.

If you haven't done so, now is the time to put your trust in Christ for your salvation. God is waiting to show you mercy by forgiving your sins and giving you new life!

God's mercy is free, but it cost a great price

Q

Why does God show mercy?

A

God shows mercy because He loves us.

Each day gives proof that God is merciful

Q

What are some other ways God shows mercy?

A

Mercy is seen in the everyday blessings of God in my life.

PARENT
These ideas will help you start your list: food in the kitchen, a comfortable home, parents, brothers and sisters, the Bible . . . keep thinking!

*T*he mountains glistened in their blanket of winter snow. The late afternoon sun emphasized their proud majesty. The fresh mountain air mingled with the aroma of the stew simmering on the fireplace of the old cabin.

"I love it up here," Charles said, holding his new bride close. "In the summer it's so green, and the water's great for swimming and fishing. In the autumn, the colors are more brilliant here than anywhere else on earth. And in springtime, every tree and flower gives fresh testimony to the beauty of nature."

Karen was quiet, thinking about what Charles was saying. They looked at each other, smiled, and started praying together, praising God for the beauty around them . . . for each other . . . for the provisions of life . . . even for the fact that the sun would come up tomorrow. They thanked God for all His good gifts, for they knew that when they looked at them, they saw His mercy.

◆ TAKE A LOOK
Psalm 23:6; 108:4; Lamentations 3:22-23

If you had been at the cross when Jesus died, you could not have seen a more merciful sight. Even so, as Charles and Karen realized, God demonstrates mercy in a thousand other ways as well. And He does it every day.

Not all of the verses below include the word *mercy*, but they do describe God's mercy. On the lines at the right, jot down a few words describing ways God shows mercy:

This verse . . .	describes God's mercy as:
Psalm 23:6	
Psalm 108:4	
Lamentations 3:22-23	
Joel 2:13	
Micah 7:18	

▲ TAKE A STEP
The Lord is good and his love endures forever (Psalm 100:5).

God's mercy endures forever, too—each day brings evidence of that.

You can appreciate the evidences of God's mercy in your life. Divide into two teams, get pencil and paper, and a timer. Take three minutes to list everything you see that shows God has been merciful to you. The team with the most items gets to lead the family in a prayer of thanks!

But Dad, it's not fair! You and Mom let Michael get away with murder."

"Hold on, Kyle," Mr. Harrison cautioned. "It's not as simple as you think. Your mother and I have our reasons."

"He ought to get what's coming to him," Kyle muttered.

"All right, son, if that's the way you feel . . . " his father said as he stood up and reached for the paddle.

Kyle stepped back, looking surprised. "What are you going to do—spank him?"

"First, I'm going to spank you. Since you feel it's so important that I give Michael what he deserves, I guess you expect me to do the same to you. Remember yesterday afternoon when I told you to clean the garage? Instead you went to Brad's house. So I have to punish you for not obeying me perfectly."

"Okay, okay," Kyle nodded slowly. "I see what you mean. Just forget I said anything . . . please?"

◆ TAKE A LOOK
Luke 6:35; Romans 15:1, 7-9; James 2:12-13; 3:17

Mr. Harrison had his reasons for showing mercy to Kyle's brother. But Kyle wanted to see pure justice—until he realized how that affected him!

We've learned a lot about God's mercy toward us. But the flip side of that truth is that God expects His children—those who have received His mercy—to show mercy to others as well:

"Be merciful, just as your Father is merciful" (Luke 6:36).

According to James 2:12-13, why is it so important to be merciful? Look for practical ways to put mercy into action in these verses: Luke 6:35; Romans 15:1, 7-9; James 3:17.

▲ TAKE A STEP

Think of someone you know who has hurt you; are you bitter about it?

Think of someone who is different; do you look the other way?

Think of someone who is spiritually or physically needy; do you consider yourself too busy to help?

Those people need your mercy. Ask God in prayer right now to help you give it. Then look for opportunities for God to answer your prayer!

God wants me to be as merciful as He!

Q

Why should I show mercy to others?

A

Mercy is expected of God's children because He has been so merciful to us.

PARENT
Discuss mercy and justice with your older child. Why is it sometimes not "merciful" simply to let an offender off with no punishment or corrective action?

MIND

*T*hough we talk about it several times a day, other people may wonder if we ever use it! What is "it"? Our mind!

Read these common expressions and you'll discover that one little word covers a lot of territory!

"You're driving me out of my *mind!*"

"She has a right to change her *mind.*"

"His *mind* is out in left field."

"I can't make up my *mind.*"

"He really let her have a piece of his *mind!*"

"His *mind* is in the gutter."

"My *mind* is playing tricks on me."

"I couldn't sleep because my *mind* was racing."

See if you can come up with three more ways to use that word!

◆ LOOKING AT YOUR MIND

How does a thought get started inside the brain? Nobody really knows. But we do know that human beings have **the ability to reason, judge, learn, think logically, and be aware of themselves.** These functions of the brain are known as the mind.

Each human has been equipped by the Creator with a mind, a will, and emotions. According to this week's key verse, why do you think God made you that way?

"What a day! A million things on my mind, and not one of them turned up on the test."

● KEY VERSE ON MIND

Jesus replied, "Love the Lord your God with all your heart and with all your soul and with all your mind. This is the first and greatest commandment" (Matthew 22:37-38).

▲ LOOKING AHEAD

Learn an important difference between God's mind and the human mind by reading 1 Samuel 15:29. What would happen if God changed His mind as often as people do?

I *just won't go back—ever! I hate it!" At Jeffrey's startling announcement, Dad peered over the morning paper, Mom sat with her coffee cup in front of her mouth, and his sister Teresa nearly choked on her waffle.*

Since kindergarten Jeffrey had never liked school. But now that he was in the tenth grade, everyone thought he had finally accepted the fact that he would be in school at least two more years—and probably six.

Jeff's mom reassuringly said, "But you've got to finish school, honey. You need—"

"But Mom," Jeff interrupted, "I get so tired of people making fun of what I believe. If I mention God, they look at me like I'm an idiot. Yesterday Mr. Kramer told me there wasn't any room for God in the scientific process. I asked him if he could prove that, but he just got mad. I'll never think the way he thinks I should think."

◆ TAKE A LOOK / 2 Corinthians 4:4; 10:3-5

Researchers tell us most people use only a small percentage of their brain's capacity. But when our minds are stretched, when we use them to explore truths about God and His creation, they can give us great satisfaction.

The human mind does have limitations. The apostle Paul points out the major weakness of the human mind:

> *How unsearchable [God's] judgments, and his paths beyond tracing out! Who has known the mind of the Lord? Or who has been his counselor? (Romans 11:33-34).*

God is infinite; He knows no boundaries. But our minds *do* have limits. Because we are human, we can never fully understand God or His creation with our minds.

Our minds are also limited because of Satan's attacks. Read 2 Corinthians 4:4 to learn why unbelievers are willing to leave God out of their thoughts. And in 2 Corinthians 10:3-5, you'll find two ways for believers to win the battle for their minds.

▲ TAKE A STEP

Jeff determined not to let the world's thinking affect his mind. Have *you* done that?

According to 2 Corinthians 10:5, you can do two things to protect your mind. Discuss what you think it means to "demolish arguments" and "take captive every thought to make it obedient to Christ." Close in prayer that God will give you strength to put that verse to work!

Who will win the battle for your mind?

What are the limits of the human mind?

The mind cannot know everything about God or His creation.

Some people are really "Bent Out of Shape!"

Q

What is a depraved mind?

A

A mind is depraved when it continually ignores God's truth and concentrates on evil instead.

At last—the big city! Clifford had dreamed of this place, read books about it, looked at pictures, studied maps. The massive skyscrapers, busy sidewalks, and bustling crowds were so unlike anything he had ever seen in the small town where he grew up. Now, on tour with his high school drama club, he could soak up the excitement of big city life for one whole week.

But it wasn't long before Clifford saw a different side of the city. Next to the glamour of the buildings, hotels, and museums, Clifford saw the squalor of neglected slums, trash rotting on the sidewalks, and homeless people.

From his seat on a bus, he saw prostitutes standing on street corners, young men openly dealing drugs, pornography shops advertising "adult" books and magazines, and movie marquees with titles that embarrassed him.

"How can people in their right minds get involved in all this stuff?" Clifford thought to himself. "Can't they see that it's totally gross?"

◆ TAKE A LOOK / Romans 8:5-8; 1:18-32

What Clifford saw on the city streets doesn't make a pretty picture. But these revolting things were just as much the product of the human mind as were the beautiful buildings and the inspiring works of art he saw that week.

The Bible says each person is either *for* God or *against* Him. And so our minds are too. Romans 8:5-8 and 1:18-32 show clearly where a mind that's controlled by the sinful nature will end. First read the verses in chapter 8. Then, as someone slowly reads verses 18-28 in chapter 1, jot down the words or phrases you hear describing the steps that ultimately lead to a depraved mind (verse 28).

▲ TAKE A STEP

Since they did not think it worthwhile to retain the knowledge of God, he gave them over to a depraved mind (Romans 1:28).

A depraved mind is so twisted in its thought processes that it actually approves of any and every kind of sin. (Some of those evils are listed in the verses you just read.)

What things did Clifford see on the city streets that demonstrated depraved minds at work? Think about evidence you've seen of the work of depraved minds in your city. How does that make you feel? How do you think it makes God feel?

What was that you said?" Greg asked his friend Sandy. "I couldn't hear you over the roar of your engine."

"I just said, 'Can't you watch where you're going!' I was yelling at that idiot in the car ahead." Sandy grimaced as he realized what he'd said. "Oops. There I go again. I wonder if I'll ever learn."

"I know what you mean." Greg replied. "When I accepted Jesus as my Savior, I still had to deal with my old ways of talking and acting. But as I began to read the Bible, I realized that most of the things I used to think about didn't please God at all. The more I read, the more I saw things from His point of view. It almost seemed as though I began to think like He did."

"That's how it is with me now," Sandy replied slowly. "When I read the Bible, I feel like God is washing my mind and throwing away the trash. Pretty soon my friends in the old neighborhood won't recognize me." Then he paused: "But that's the way it's supposed to be, isn't it?"

◆ **TAKE A LOOK / Ephesians 4:22–5:7**

Sandy truly wanted his life to please God. He sensed the Holy Spirit working to change his sinful thought patterns and habits. But even as a "baby Christian," he realized that accepting Christ as Savior doesn't mean instant maturity. It's a change that comes gradually as a person's mind is cleaned up, changed, and renewed by God's Spirit and His Word.

Paul put it this way in his letter to the Romans: *Do not conform any longer to the pattern of this world, but be transformed by the renewing of your mind (Romans 12:2).*

Ephesians 4:22–5:7 describes the kind of life a believer who has a "new attitude of mind" can enjoy. Divide into two teams, and when you come to verse 25 have one group list the *do's* and the other team the *don'ts* described here.

▲ **TAKE A STEP**

A person who comes to know Christ as Savior can have his mind reprogrammed so that he will think and behave in a way that pleases God. This inner transformation depends on time spent reading, studying, and obeying God's Word in the power of the Holy Spirit.

Spend a quiet moment thinking about how obeying God's Word has changed you. Then share your thoughts with the rest of your family.

Set your mind on things above

Q

How can I "reprogram" my mind to please God?

A

The mind can be renewed when I obey God's Word in the Spirit's power.

PARENT
Is your home free of "mental garbage"? Evaluate the programs you and your child watch on TV, the books and magazines you read, the music you allow to flood your mind.

When is it wise to have a one-track mind?

Q

How can I love God with all my mind?

A

A mind fully focused on God desires to make choices that please Him.

Wow, I sure learned a lot," Rodney said as he and his dad left the auditorium. I can hardly wait to graduate."

Rodney and his dad had attended a Career Night at school. As an honor student Rodney was enthusiastic about his job prospects for the future.

"Dad, I know I can get a scholarship to a good college. I ought to be making top bucks before I'm 30."

When his dad didn't reply, Rodney continued, bubbling over with ideas about his future. "I'll be able to buy a neat car, take super vacations, and do just about anything I want. I'm not bragging, but the doors are wide open for people with brains who are willing to work."

Rodney paused for breath, noticing his dad's silence. "Uh—isn't that right, Dad?" he asked.

"Yes, you're right, son. We've talked before about how God has given you a bright, quick mind. I've even heard you say that you wonder why he picked you. Now I hear you planning to use that mind completely for your own benefit. I just wonder if you've forgotten the number-one commandment."

◆ TAKE A LOOK
Colossians 3:2, 17; 2 Corinthians 10:5

Rodney knew exactly what his dad meant by the "number-one commandment." As a young boy, he had memorized this verse:

"Love the Lord your God with all your
heart and with all your soul and with all
your strength and with all your mind"
(Luke 10:27).

His dad's comments made Rodney think about what loving God really means. Jesus told His questioners that the most meaningful way to show their love for God was with their whole selves—with everything in them. Your emotions, your soul, your physical strength, and your intellect should all be focused on demonstrating *your* love for God.

But Rodney wondered, "How can I specifically use my mind to love the Lord?" Colossians 3:2, 17; 2 Corinthians 10:5; Philippians 4:8; and Psalm 26:1-8 might help him—and you—answer that question.

▲ TAKE A STEP

Choosing a career path in order to serve God and others—instead of yourself—is one way you can love God with your mind. If you were Rodney, what kind of career would you choose that would demonstrate love for God?

JESUS

Matt's hand shot up from where he sat in the back of the room. "Wait a minute!" Matt exclaimed. "My history teacher says people just got all excited over Jesus' teachings and started making up stories about His life, and that's how we got the Bible. What if he's right?"

Matt was the skeptic in the youth group. He enjoyed the social activities, but at the Sunday night study he often raised questions that Scott—the youth leader—sometimes found difficult to answer. It was a game for Matt; he just liked to cause trouble.

But this time, Matt seemed sincere. His voice wasn't argumentative, and instead of the other kids rolling their eyes and sighing—the usual response to his questions—they perked up: Matt was serious!

"Why is this Person who lived 2,000 years ago so important?" he asked. "And how can He really be alive today? I don't understand it."

◆ LOOKING AT JESUS

At school you may have read Greek myths about "gods" who walked the earth disguised as men and women. Maybe you were surprised at how sinfully and violently they acted. Those "gods" were ungodly! And they were not real people either.

Or teachers may tell you that Jesus is only one among many religious leaders whose teachings guide people to a better life. But Jesus is more than a mythical god or a great moral teacher. **Jesus is God Himself**—as He claimed when He said:

● KEY VERSE ON JESUS

"I and the Father are one" (John 10:30).

▲ LOOKING AHEAD

This week we'll discover how Jesus is unique—totally different from all other religious leaders.

The story of Jesus is found in Matthew, Mark, Luke, and John. If you read Mark 1–3 today, two more chapters on each of the next five days, and chapters 14–16 on the sixth day, you'll read through the shortest gospel in one week. Why not start tonight!

"You'll like this book. It's all about imaginary people."

Look at His life and let it speak for itself

How do we know that Jesus is really God?

A

Jesus' life demonstrated that His claim to be God is true.

PARENT
Josh McDowell has several books and tapes presenting the evidence for the deity of Christ. Check your church library or Christian bookstore.

S *cott was startled by Matt's sincere question. Maybe this was the opportunity he'd been praying for. It seemed Matt was really seeking answers; he wanted to know who Jesus was.*

"Matt, none of us can ever completely understand all there is to know. But I believe the Bible contains satisfying answers. And if you're willing to look into it honestly, study it carefully, and think about it objectively, you'll learn who Jesus really is. But is there a specific question bothering you?"

"Well," Matt began hesitantly, "I know Jesus was a real, historical person. But how do we know He's really God?"

◆ TAKE A LOOK / John 10:30-33 (also read Mark 4–5)

How can we, who live 2,000 years after Christ, really know He is God? Let's look at some evidence.

First, Jesus Himself stated that He was God. He referred to Himself by names and titles that showed Him to be equal with God. He did things only God can do. He never claimed to be merely a prophet or a teacher; He claimed to be God.

Everyone who hears about Jesus must decide what to believe about Him. As you look up the following verses, match the verse on the left with its description on the right:

This verse shows . . .
1. John 10:30-33
2. Mark 2:5-7
3. John 9:37-38
4. Exodus 3:14; John 8:58-59

. . . Jesus is God because He:
a. accepted worship reserved for God.
b. claimed to be equal with God.
c. forgave sins.
d. used one of God's Old Testament names for Himself.

▲ TAKE A STEP

Jesus' claims cannot be ignored. There are only three possibilities: (1) Jesus was a lying imposter, so His teachings are untrue; (2) He was crazy and His claims were wrong, so His teachings should be ignored; or (3) He was and is who He claimed to be, so His teachings should have top priority in our lives.

Which do you believe, and why? What other evidence can you find in Mark chapters 1–5 that Jesus was indeed God in the flesh?

ANSWERS: 1–b; 2–c; 3–a; 4–d.

*T*he Sunday night youth meeting really came to life. Matt's questions started the whole group buzzing excitedly about Jesus.

"Most of you have heard about Jesus since you were babies," Scott explained. "So now you don't even think about what you're hearing. But when you hear with your head and your heart, you begin to understand that Jesus wasn't just another prophet strolling around in sandals.

"Can you imagine what it must have been like back then—no radio, no TV, no newspapers? But news about Jesus spread like wildfire! Think about the miracles. Suppose you had been the lame man . . . imagine how you would have felt if your daughter was raised from the dead. No one had ever seen anything like it!"

"Yeah," Matt interrupted, "when you put it like that, it's not so hard to see why the crowds followed Jesus."

◆ **TAKE A LOOK / Mark 6:30-56**
(also read Mark 6–7)
Jesus is not walking around today, preaching and teaching as He did so many years ago. But His 33 years on earth still make an impact on our world.

As you think back on what you've learned so far, try to picture Jesus as a real person. What do you suppose He wore? What did He look like? How did He talk?

As you read Mark 6:30-56, visualize yourself as part of the crowd of 5,000 people . . . or one of the disciples in the boat . . . or a sick person brought to Him in one of the villages. Have each family member describe what happened and how he or she felt after meeting Jesus.

▲ **TAKE A STEP**
Two phrases in the passage you just read describe why the crowds followed Jesus:
They all ate and were satisfied (Mark 6:42).
All who touched him were healed (Mark 6:56).
Unlike anyone they had known, Jesus met people's needs. He gave them inner peace and freedom from sin's guilt as well.

People who lived in Jesus' day weren't all that different from people living today; everyone has needs. And Jesus' power to meet those needs hasn't changed, either. Have each person share a special need he's experiencing right now, and pray for one another that Jesus will meet those needs.

He meets needs as no one else can!

Q

Why did people follow Jesus?

A

Jesus met people's needs during His earthly life, and He can meet my needs too.

Your choice about Jesus counts— forever

After the meeting broke up, Matt couldn't wait to get home and start reading. By Thursday night, questions were leaping into his mind. There was only one thing to do—call Scott!

"Hey, Scott, one thing in Mark really confuses me. Why did all those people want to kill Jesus? He loved everybody, so what did He do to make people so angry?"

Scott was excited. He wasn't accustomed to having kids call with questions like that, so he wanted to answer it carefully.

"It's like this, Matt," he said after a pause. "Jesus did the same thing to the religious leaders that He does to people today. He threatened their way of life. They knew that if they acknowledged Him, they'd have to admit they were wrong about Him, and their lives would change."

"Yeah," Matt's voice came slowly. "If I read much more about Jesus, I might have to change too. . . . "

◆ TAKE A LOOK / Mark 8:27-38 (also read Mark 8–9)

When you find out who Jesus is and what He claims, you must accept Him or reject Him. As you've already seen in Mark, many people accepted Jesus, and even gave up their homes, families, and businesses to follow Him. People from every walk of life and with every level of intelligence were transformed by His touch.

Even so, the religious leaders rejected Jesus. They realized He might very well be the promised Messiah—the One sent by God to save His people. But the leaders had wealth and authority they didn't want to give up. You'll find another reason why they didn't want to follow Jesus in Mark 8:27-38.

▲ TAKE A STEP

Knowing Jesus involves commitment. And it takes an entire lifetime. Jesus' followers made that commitment . . . and the world was changed. The Jewish religious leaders refused to believe . . . and they ultimately lost their nation and the opportunity to spend eternity with God.

As Scott explained to Matt, Jesus still makes that same demand:

"If anyone would come after me, he must deny himself " (Mark 8:34).

If you were Scott, what would you tell Matt next? What decision does Matt face now?

Q

Why did the religious leaders hate Jesus?

A

They did not want to follow Him or commit their lives to Him.

*T*he youth group met again the following Sunday. "I'm sure by now you realize what a special man Jesus was," Scott began enthusiastically.

"Special? That's an understatement!" Matt's tone of voice told everyone something was different about him. "I've been reading in Mark this week, and I'm kind of mad at myself for believing what my teachers told me without investigating it for myself. I can't wait to tell you guys what's happened."

Matt continued, "You see, Thursday night I was talking to Scott. I told him I could see that Jesus really is who He claimed to be—He really is God. And when I finished reading, I also knew that Jesus is alive today. But Scott asked me what I was going to do about it. Anyway, after we talked some more I asked God to forgive my sins. Scott and I prayed together, and I accepted Jesus as my Savior!"

◆ TAKE A LOOK / Mark 8:31-38 (also read Mark 10–11)

Matt couldn't contain His excitement. He realized that Jesus is God, and that He came to earth to save people from the consequences of sin. Christ's death paid the price; His resurrection proved that the payment had been accepted by God, and that Jesus was in fact God Himself!

Christians use phrases like *being born again*, *getting saved*, *being converted*, *accepting Christ*, and *becoming a believer* to describe what happened to Matt. Regardless of the words, when you hear Jesus' claims, you have a decision to make. The only two choices really are these:

(1) Either Jesus Christ is God Himself who died for you and rose again in triumph; or

(2) He is just another man—a liar or a lunatic—and you can live as you please.

Becoming a Christian means trusting in Jesus alone for eternal life and committing yourself to follow Him daily. Jesus explained what that means in Mark 8:31-38.

▲ TAKE A STEP

This week, you've seen the evidence about Jesus. If you've come to believe He is God, and that He died for your sins, there's only one thing to do: Confess your need for Him, turn from your sins, and commit yourself to follow Him.

Have you made that response? Does your everyday life show it?

Christ's claims call for commit-ment

Q

Is Jesus really who He claimed to be?

A

Jesus deserves my complete and lifelong commit-ment because He truly is God.

QUIET TIME

*T*he gang from "Peanuts" was at it again. But this time they actually had a chance to win. The batter popped a fly, and the team yelled, "It's going right to Lucy! Catch it, Lucy! Catch it!"

And what happened? Lucy just stood there. "What kind of out-fielder are you?" Charlie Brown shouted. "What do you want them to do, come out here and hand you the ball? What in the world made you miss that one?"

Lucy looked at him calmly and settled the argument with her reply: "I was having my quiet time!"

◆ LOOKING AT QUIET TIME

Few people would think of having a "quiet time" while playing baseball. But Lucy's experience does show that having a quiet time is a very personal, individual experience . . . a time that should be free of distractions such as high fly balls!

As a child of God, the most important thing you can do is to know and love the Lord. Since the best way to get to know anyone is to spend time with that person, a believer should have a "quiet time" to get to know God—**spending time regularly alone in God's presence.**

This week's key verse explains why:

● KEY VERSE ON QUIET TIME

You have made known to me the path of life; you will fill me with joy in your presence (Psalm 16:11).

"I thought we came here to get away from the phone."

▲ LOOKING AHEAD

Having a quiet time every day is probably the most important habit a Christian can develop. More than anything else having a quiet time alone with God will help you grow as His child.

According to John 17:3, God wants His children to _____ Him. Think of three things you could do to get to know another person well. Would doing those same three things help you know God better?

Colin went to Sunday school and worship service nearly every week. But when it came to the lessons and sermons, the words went in one ear and out the other while he daydreamed or made plans for the week.

One Sunday Colin's teacher asked the kids to write down what they thought it meant to be a Christian. Then he asked, "How does being a Christian affect the way you live?" and, "How many meals do you skip each day?"

"What do my eating habits have to do with being a Christian?" Colin thought. He wrote "none" on his paper.

When Colin heard the fourth question, the teacher's point hit home: "How many days a week do you feed your spirit in a quiet time alone with God?" Colin had to write the same answer he had for question number three.

◆ TAKE A LOOK
Luke 8:19-21; John 10:3-5, 27; Romans 8:14
Most of us eat meals every day. But how many days a week do we skip the opportunity to feed on God's Word? Spending time reading God's Word and praying is your opportunity to feed your spirit and to hear God speak to you through His Word, the Bible. That's a wonderful privilege for God's children!

But we have a responsibility to listen as God speaks to us. And that takes time and effort. After you read Luke 8:19-21; John 10:3-5, 27; and Romans 8:14, complete this sentence: The fact that I can hear God speaking through His Word is an evidence that I _____

_____ .

▲ TAKE A STEP
Hearing God's voice through His Word indicates that you truly belong to Him. Jesus said, *"My sheep listen to my voice; I know them, and they follow me"* (John 10:27).

One way to find out how carefully you listen to the Lord is to answer the last question Colin answered in his Sunday school class: "I spend _(minutes/hours)_ each week having a quiet time."

If your answer is zero like Colin's, or even 15 or 30 minutes a week, you're cheating yourself! We'll find out tomorrow how to change that.

But don't wait till then to spend some moments alone with your Lord. Tonight before you go to bed, go to a quiet place and pray for a few minutes. Thank God for ten things He gave you today.

Is your spiritual diet balanced?

Why should I have a quiet time?

A

Quiet times help me grow spiritually as God speaks to me through His Word.

PARENT
Guard your family members' quiet times by keeping them free of interruptions. Perhaps your whole family could arrange to have individual quiet times simultaneously, but in different rooms.

Is your quiet time #1 on today's "To Do" list?

Q

How can I start having a quiet time?

A

Quiet times can become a natural part of my daily routine when I make them my top priority.

Donna, you'll make yourself sick if you don't slow down. You can't survive on five hours' sleep!"

"Oh, Mom, please quit worrying," Donna replied curtly. She jogged to her room, dropped her books, and sprawled across the bed.

It did seem as though she wasn't getting much sleep these days. But there was so much to do! Cheerleading practice after school, church or school activities almost every night, then a couple of hours of homework after she finally got home about 9:30. She almost never turned off her light before midnight. Six A.M. rolled around awfully fast, but the bus came at 7:30, and she needed that much time to shower, dress, and do her hair.

"I don't have any time for myself anymore," Donna griped to herself as she lay in bed. Then an inner voice reminded her, "No, and you don't seem to have any time for the Lord, either."

◆ **TAKE A LOOK / Mark 1:21-35**

As you read Mark 1:21-35, you'll realize that a high-pressure lifestyle didn't originate in the 20th century.

It didn't take long for news about Jesus to spread, and people came from near and far to seek His help. His days became increasingly hectic as the people constantly pressed around Him.

As you read the account of one of Jesus' demanding days, notice what He did early the next morning (v. 35).

▲ **TAKE A STEP**

Very early in the morning, while it was still dark, Jesus got up, left the house and went off to a solitary place, where he prayed (Mark 1:35).

Can you find great guidelines in that verse for your own quiet time? Notice that Jesus met His Father at a specific time and place away from distractions and interruptions.

If you make your daily meeting with God a top priority, you'll discover that He is never too busy to meet with you. Perhaps you'd like to make that commitment now. Write this prayer on an index card, filling in the blanks: "Father God, with Your help, I will meet with You each day _(where?)_ , _(when?)_ , from _____ to _____ ."

What should you do if you don't have time for a quiet time?

Darrin, will you be quiet and listen!" the youth leader snapped. But it was too late: Stephen—who was trying to share a serious problem—walked out.

Darrin's face flushed red with embarrassment. "But Tom, I was only trying to help," he blurted.

"I know that," Tom replied. "But Stephen was trying to be serious. We needed to listen, not make wisecracks."

Tom put his hand on Darrin's shoulder. "Look, I don't mean to be sharp with you. But there's an art to listening. If you're talking all the time or planning what you're going to say next, other people will sense that you're not really interested in what they're saying. The important thing is to concentrate on who's talking, not on yourself. And that takes practice."

◆ **TAKE A LOOK** / Jeremiah 15:16; Proverbs 3:5-6

Darrin's embarrassing experience illustrates how important it is to listen. That's also true of your daily meeting with the Lord. Too often we think of devotional times as an opportunity to tell God all our problems, and *we* do all the talking. But a quiet time should be a spiritual mealtime, an opportunity to take in nourishment from God's Word:

When your words came, I ate them; they were my joy and my heart's delight, for I bear your name, O Lord God Almighty (Jeremiah 15:16).

▲ **TAKE A STEP**

One effective way of hearing the truth in God's Word is to divide your quiet time into three main segments: the *preparation*, the *passage*, and the *plan*.

PREPARATION involves *purifying* your heart and *presenting* yourself to the Lord. How do Psalm 46:10 and 1 John 1:9 help us prepare ourselves?

Next, read the *PASSAGE* you've chosen for the day. In a notebook, rewrite the passage in your own words. Next write down any *promises* you can claim. Then write out the *principles* you are instructed to obey.

Finally, *PLAN* specifically how you will put the truth into practice. Close with a *prayer* of commitment.

As a family, practice this method by using Proverbs 3:5-6 in your individual quiet times today. Then regroup and discuss what you learned from God's Word—and what you'll do about it.

Listen to what God has to say, and plan to obey

Q

What should I do during my quiet time?

A

Quiet times are most helpful when I prepare myself, carefully read a Bible passage, then plan to obey.

PARENT
You and your spouse will benefit from reading the same Bible passages in your individual quiet times, then discussing what you learn.

Can you hear your Master's voice?

George Müeller has inspired many by his determination to live according to God's Word. This passage from his autobiography shows us the source of his spiritual strength:

"The most important thing I had to do was to give myself to the reading of the Word of God. . . . Not the simple reading of the Word of God so that it only passes through my mind just as water runs through a pipe, but considering what I read, pondering over it, and applying it to my heart. To meditate on it, that thus my heart might be comforted, encouraged, warned, reproved, instructed. . . . and brought into communion with the Lord."

◆ TAKE A LOOK
Matthew 24:10-13, 23-26; John 10:1-10, 27-30

Q

What will having a quiet time do for me?

In our world many people are saying, "Follow me." If you want to please God, you must learn to distinguish His voice from all the other voices clamoring for attention.

Having a quiet time helps you learn how to identify God's "voice." As you read His Word, learn His promises, and find out what He wants you to do, you begin to know His character. And when you know God that well, you will not be easily deceived by false teachings. (Who do you suppose is behind these teachings?)

A

Quiet times will help me recognize God's voice.

In Matthew 24, Jesus described what would be happening on earth before His return. Verses 10-13, 23-26 warn against false teachers who will appear. After you read those verses, turn to John 10:1-10, 27-30 to see why it's important to know the Father's voice.

▲ TAKE A STEP

As the time of the Lord's return draws closer, there will be many more false teachers. But if you are God's sheep and have learned to know His voice, you have this promise from Him:

"They will never follow a stranger; in fact, they will run away from him because they do not recognize a stranger's voice" (John 10:5).

Have you ever heard about anyone who claimed to be a "god," or taught a way to God that was different than what the Bible says? Would you listen to that person? Now think about the voices you do listen to—the TV shows and movies you watch, the music you enjoy, the friends you hang out with. Are their voices influencing you for good or for bad?

DISCIPLINE

Maybe it's a teacher filling out a detention notice. Or Mom sending you to your room when all your friends are playing outside. It may be Dad's firm hands gripping your shoulders. Or even a few well-placed swats with a paddle.

It may mean no dessert, no phone privileges, no car, or no TV. Maybe it means having to miss an activity you had looked forward to, or being sent to bed immediately after dinner.

It may come with soft, sad words of love and concern. It may include tears or angry voices. You may hear phrases like: "I'm sorry I have to do this," or "This hurts me as much as it does you."

Sometimes you may talk your way out of it; sometimes you make it worse by resisting. But if you are—or were—an ordinary kid, you can identify with at least one of those situations. Because sometime in your life, you experienced discipline.

◆ LOOKING AT DISCIPLINE

Many people believe discipline only means punishment. But discipline is more than punishment. Discipline involves **consistent training over a long period of time.** Its purpose is to produce mental, physical, or spiritual strength and godly character.

Our English word *discipline* comes from the Latin word *discipulus*, which means pupil or learner. Someone who needs discipline is someone who needs to learn something. And as God's children, we all have something to learn.

● KEY VERSE ON DISCIPLINE

Our fathers disciplined us for a little while as they thought best; but God disciplines us for our good, that we may share in his holiness (Hebrews 12:10).

▲ LOOKING AHEAD

As God's children, it's important that we recognize and learn from His loving discipline.

After you read Hebrews 12:5-6, tell about a time when you were disciplined. Can you understand now how that discipline helped you in the long run?

"Do you realize I can't see the TV from here?"

Love means a spanking when you need it

Q

Why does God discipline His children?

A

Discipline is one way God lovingly trains me to be the best I can be.

PARENT
Dr. James Dobson's excellent book, DARE TO DISCIPLINE, gives helpful guidance in this area.

My parents won't let me do anything," Austin complained.

"Aw, come on," Joey grinned. "Your folks don't seem so mean."

"But what about all the chores I have to do? Even when I come in after running track, I still have to take out the garbage and wash my own clothes. Then on Saturdays I have to sweep the carport or cut the grass. If I don't, Dad takes away privileges."

"Hey, if my dad would restrict me once in a while, at least I'd know he cared."

"Yeah," Austin said slowly. He thought about how Joey's dad always had some excuse for missing Joey's games . . . how the two of them never did anything together. "You're right, Joey. But there are times I wish my folks didn't care quite so much!"

◆ TAKE A LOOK / Hebrews 12:5-11

Because Joey was rarely disciplined, he wondered if his father even loved him.

The writer to the Hebrews says parents correct their children out of love to train them to live properly. In the same way, God disciplines *His* children for *their* eternal benefit. God's discipline may seem tough, but He always has our best interests at heart. You'll see why as you read Hebrews 12:5-11.

▲ TAKE A STEP

People often think of discipline as punishment. But training and correction are forms of discipline too. Punishment should be used only for willful disobedience.

God is always training His children to be the best they can be. He knows that . . .

No discipline seems pleasant at the time, but painful. Later on, however, it produces a harvest of righteousness and peace for those who have been trained by it (Hebrews 12:11).

Sometimes God disciplines us because of sin in our lives; other times He does it to develop our character.

On a sheet of paper make four columns. In the first, write your family's rules for behavior. In the second, write the reason for each rule. The third column is for appropriate rewards for obedience, and the final column is for punishments for disobedience. Now everyone knows!

Be sure and post your list in a prominent place where the entire family can see it.

*I*t just makes me sad . . . and confused," Carla sighed to her grandmother. "Ever since Ken lost his leg in the accident, he's been angry at God and bitter toward everyone else. He keeps saying he didn't deserve such an awful punishment. Is he right, Grandma? Did God punish Ken?"

Carla's grandmother just shook her head. "Poor dear," she said softly, thinking of Ken. "God does discipline people. But not every tragedy is a punishment. In Ken's case, his own choice led to his accident. He was warned not to use that chain saw, but he did anyway. He had that accident because he was inexperienced and hasty."

Grandma paused, then continued, "I do know one thing: God loves Ken and will use his suffering to make him a stronger person spiritually. That is, if Ken will let God work in his life."

◆ TAKE A LOOK / John 9:1-6

Yesterday when you read Hebrews 12:5-11, you learned that God disciplines *every one* of His children. Not just some, or a few, or most, but *every single one!* It's a sign you're His child.

During Bible times, people often believed that if someone was sick or handicapped, God was judging that person's sin. Even Jesus' disciples were confused about this. Once they asked Jesus whose sin caused a certain man's blindness. Jesus' answer in John 9:1-6 helps us to understand how God can use tragedies for His glory.

▲ TAKE A STEP

Christians may experience hardships and trials in life

. . . because of our own carelessness, as in Ken's case;
. . . because Satan attacks us, as in Job's troubles;
. . . because of the sinful world we live in;
. . . because God is directly disciplining us and
    training us to obey and trust Him totally.

Though we may never know **why** we experience such tragedies, we can still benefit from them by drawing closer to God and by letting Him use them for good, as He promises:

We know that in all things God works for the good of those who love him, who have been called according to his purpose (Romans 8:28).

What if Ken asked you whether you thought God was punishing him—what would you tell him? What Bible verse would you give Ken to remind him that God is working?

Life is simply one lo-o-o-ng lesson!

Q

Are trials and tragedies God's punishment?

A

Discipline in the form of trials and tragedies can draw me closer to God.

God's children are all in school together

Cal couldn't believe it. Here he was in the principal's office with his parents, the teacher, and the principal! He'd never made below a B in conduct, but now, out of the blue, this teacher had given him an F. It was crazy! He hadn't done anything wrong.

Well, maybe he'd acted up a little bit, but surely not enough to get an F! "If this keeps me from playing spring football," he thought rebelliously, "I'll quit school."

After the principal had listened to everyone, he turned to Cal. "Well, you have created quite a stir by constantly challenging your teacher's authority, both in the way you acted and by what you said in class. That's unacceptable, Cal, so the F will stand. But you will benefit from it if you learn how to relate properly to those in authority over you. One day you'll have a boss to deal with, and bosses don't fool around. Now go on back to class, and don't let this happen again."

Q

What should I learn when I am disciplined?

◆ **TAKE A LOOK / James 2:23**

Cal hadn't thought his behavior was all that bad. But now he realized that what he thought was funny was in fact disrespectful. As he considered the principal's advice, he determined to learn from this experience.

We can learn how to benefit from discipline by looking at the lives of people who were "trained" by God. *Abraham* was tested when told by God to sacrifice his son Isaac. *Job* faced trials when his family and possessions were destroyed. *David* was disciplined after his sin with Bathsheba when his sons rebelled against him. *Paul* suffered with a persistent physical problem. As you read the verses below, you'll see what they learned from discipline:

Discipline can teach me to trust in God's power if my attitude is right.

Verse:	Person:	Result of discipline:
James 2:23	_____	_____
James 5:11	_____	_____
Psalm 51:10-12	_____	_____
2 Corinthians 12:7-10	_____	_____

▲ **TAKE A STEP**

God disciplines His children so they can see His power displayed in their lives. As Jesus said to Paul:

"My power is made perfect in weakness"
(2 Corinthians 12:9).

What could Cal learn from his experience? How important was his attitude about being disciplined? How's *your* attitude?

How many times have I told you not to leave your bike in the driveway?" Mr. Landrum yelled at nine-year-old Tommy. "Now go to your room. And you may not ride your bike again for one week."

Tearfully Tommy tried to protest, "But Dad, I didn't." "You heard me," his father raged. "Now go!" Later that evening Mrs. Landrum mentioned that Tommy had been sick and had stayed inside all day. Mr. Landrum realized that he had angrily blamed Tommy for something he hadn't done.

* * *

2. "Oh, I'll double up on my devotions in the morning," Alana thought as she picked up her latest Nancy Drew mystery. "I won't be able to sleep until I find out how this ends."

* * *

3. "I know I don't really need this," Mrs. Graham said as she picked up her third piece of fudge, "but chocolate is so yummy!"

◆ **TAKE A LOOK / 1 Corinthians 6:20; James 1:19-20; Ephesians 5:15-16**

Indulge yourself! Pamper yourself! That's the message of the world. But God's Word teaches us that "self" should not be the center of a Christian's life. We are to be disciplined in all areas of our lives by bringing them under the control of the Holy Spirit, who lives within us.

Read these verses, then match each with one of the three situations above: (a) 1 Corinthians 6:20; (b) James 1:19-20; (c) Ephesians 5:15-16 and 2 Timothy 2:15.

(Answers: 1-b, 2-c, 3-a)

▲ **TAKE A STEP**

The apostle Paul sometimes compared Christians to athletes competing for a grand prize or to soldiers in a battle zone. Both jobs require excellent training, self-discipline, and tip-top physical condition. He says,

Everyone who competes in the games goes into strict training. They do it to get a crown that will not last; but we do it to get a crown that will last forever (1 Corinthians 9:25).

Think about the areas of discipline we've mentioned today: temper, time, thoughts, tongue, and body. Are you having a problem with one or more of these? How are you going to bring them under control? What areas of your life need self-discipline?

Personal pain can result in personal gain

Q

What areas of my life need self-discipline?

A

Discipline is needed in every area of my life if I want to grow.

PARENT
Two other areas that require discipline are money management and TV viewing. Discuss with your child how these two "appetites" can be controlled in light of 1 Corinthians 6:12.

GOODNESS

This week, keep your antennas out and listen for the words "good" and "goodness." If you can, jot down the different ways the words are used. Here's a list of sentences to get you started. After reading them, how would you define goodness?

"Surely goodness and love will follow me all the days of my life" (Psalm 23:6).
"Now kids, be good and mind your manners."
"Mmmm, Mmmm good!"
"Look, Dad, I made a really good grade."
"He's off to a good start in the race."
"Have I got some good news for you!"
"He's done his good deed for the day."
"Thanks for inviting me over. I had a good time."
"For goodness' sake!"
"The ball is between the uprights—the kick is good!"

◆ LOOKING AT GOODNESS

It's a bit hard to define a word with so many uses! People use *good* or *goodness* to describe warm, fuzzy feelings, perfect behavior, or anything nice. But goodness as God sees it is something far more important. In fact, it's one of the Spirit-empowered character qualities He desires to see in His children's lives.

"You're making Uncle Don a squash casserole? Is that what you call a good deed?"

● KEY VERSE ON GOODNESS
The fruit of the Spirit is . . . goodness (Galatians 5:22).

▲ LOOKING AHEAD
The Bible uses *good* or *goodness* to describe the people whose **noble, godly character leads them to help others actively.**

Our good character should result in doing good. Brainstorm five "good deeds" you might do for another Christian, then five "good deeds" for someone who isn't a believer (yet). Now do one of each today!

Do you think you'll go to heaven when you die?" David had to ask 20 people that question as an assignment for a course on religion. With each one he grew more disappointed; it seemed no one knew for sure!

One man responded, "I've lived a good life. I haven't done anything really bad and I've done my share of good deeds. I'm better than most people, so I guess I'll make it."

Another said, "I provide for my family. I think it's important to take care of your loved ones."

But most people said something like this: "I try to keep the Ten Commandments and live a good life."

◆ **TAKE A LOOK / Romans 3:20-26; 4:1-5**

If people try to do their best, won't God let them into heaven?

Most of the world's religions teach that a person gets to heaven by doing good works. But none of them explains *how many* good works one must do, or *how good* one must be. So a person who believes good works pave the way to heaven can never be sure he has done enough!

Though the Bible does teach that we should do good works, it's not to earn our way to heaven. The only way to get to heaven is by trusting in Jesus Christ.

[God] saved us, not because of righteous things [good deeds] we had done, but because of his mercy (Titus 3:5).

Using Abraham, the founder of the Jewish nation, as an example Paul taught this truth to the believers at Rome. In Romans 3:20-26 and 4:1-5 he explains what good works can and cannot do.

▲ **TAKE A STEP**

No matter how much good a person does or how hard he or she tries to keep God's law, that's not the way into heaven. God's entrance requirement is to trust Jesus Christ as your Savior. That's why God sent His Son to die for us.

If you have all done that, close your family time with a prayer of thanksgiving for your salvation and your eternal home in heaven.

If you or someone in your family has not yet trusted Jesus Christ as your Savior you can do that right now. Read Romans 3:23; 6:23; 5:8; and 10:9-10, 13. Then acknowledge to God in prayer that you are a sinner, and ask Him to come into your life and make you His child.

Are you hoping your good deeds outweigh the bad?

Q

Can I get into heaven by being good?

A

Goodness won't get me to heaven; only faith in Christ and His "good work" on the cross can do that.

Faith without works isn't really faith at all

Q

What do good works have to do with my faith?

A

Goodness should result from my relationship with God as I put my faith into action.

I really enjoy working at the shelter two nights a week," Shaun told his friend Marty as they drove downtown. "There are some neat folks there. You'd be amazed at what some of them have been through. I wanted you to see it for yourself." Shaun pointed to the large, old hotel that served as the shelter for the homeless.

"But I'm just a college student," Marty protested. "What can I do?"

"You've got two ears and a heart. Many of them need somebody to listen—somebody who'll care. They need to be accepted as individuals, not as homeless bums. Just listen to them. Share God's love with them. It's not like you're just doing your good deed for the day; your whole perspective on things will change. And you'll soon find you're receiving a whole lot more than you're giving."

◆ **TAKE A LOOK / Ephesians 2:8-10; James 2:14-26**

In working with homeless and hurting people, Shaun was in fact doing a good deed. But he wasn't trying to earn "brownie points" for heaven. Instead, he saw it as an opportunity to help the helpless and demonstrate God's love for them.

Shaun knew that good works are important in a Christian's life. Good deeds put faith into action, provide evidence to unbelievers that God loves them and that He's actively involved in His children's lives. The Bible says,

Live as children of light (for the fruit of the light consists in all goodness, righteousness and truth) (Ephesians 5:8-9).

You'll see the part goodness plays in the Christian life by reading Ephesians 2:8-10 and James 2:14-16.

▲ **TAKE A STEP**

A person's good works will not open the door to heaven. But goodness—often in the form of good works—is an important characteristic of a Christian's life.

Reread the italicized verses we've included on the pages for Day One, Day Two, and today. Which verse tells you that goodness is a natural response of being a child of God? Could you say that's true in your life?

Involve your entire family in planning a good deed that will help a needy person experience God's loving care and compassion. Ask your pastor to suggest someone in your area who needs help.

Mrs. O'Reilly is nice, isn't she?" Carrie commented to her friend Pamela as they waved to the older woman. "Sometimes I wonder how anybody can be that good."

"What do you mean?" Pamela asked.

"She spends a lot of time doing good things," Carrie explained. "She's a volunteer at the nursing home, she goes to all her grandkids' ball games, and she works in the church. One time when my mom was real sick, she brought us a whole dinner—even dessert! It seems like goodness just oozes out of her. When I'm around her, I feel like she really loves me, like she's really interested in me. And I'm not even her grand-child!"

"Yeah, I know what you mean now," Pamela replied. "I think it's because she goes to church so much. You can't be around her very long before she mentions God—not in a pushy way, but in a natural way, like He's a part of her or something. She's different!"

◆ **TAKE A LOOK / Galatians 5:13-26**

Pamela and Carrie weren't Christians, so they misunderstood why Mrs. O'Reilly was so genuinely interested in them. But they were right in sensing that the love and acceptance she showed them was a natural part of her character. Mrs. O'Reilly saw every ordinary relationship as an opportunity to let God work through her. Like the godly woman described in this verse, she was . . .

well known for her good deeds, such as bringing up children, showing hospitality, washing the feet of the saints, helping those in trouble and devoting herself to all kinds of good deeds (1 Timothy 5:10).

See if you can discover the source of her ability to live the "good life" in Galatians 5:13-26.

▲ **TAKE A STEP**

People who knew Mrs. O'Reilly experienced an overflow of goodness that came from the Holy Spirit, who controlled her life from within.

How can you be controlled by the Spirit? It's a matter of your will. Do you *want* to know and obey God more than anything else? Then confess your sins, ask God to cleanse you, and ask Him to fill you with His Spirit (see Ephesians 5:18).

Would anyone describe you the way Pamela and Carrie described Mrs. O'Reilly? If not, what can you do about that?

If the Holy Spirit's inside, goodness shines out

Q

Where do I get the power to be good?

A

Goodness is a natural quality of my life when I am controlled by the Holy Spirit.

Meditate and celebrate God's goodness to you!

Q

What is the right response to God's goodness?

A

Goodness originates in God Himself, so my good works should bring glory to Him.

As you read these verses from Psalm 145, underline the ways David says we should respond to God's goodness:

"One generation will commend your works to another; they will tell of your mighty acts.

They will speak of the glorious splendor of your majesty, and I will meditate on your wonderful works.

They will tell of the power of your awesome works, and I will proclaim your great deeds.

They will celebrate your abundant goodness and joyfully sing of your righteousness.

The LORD is gracious and compassionate, slow to anger and rich in love.

The LORD is good to all; he has compassion on all he has made.

All you have made will praise you, O LORD; your saints will extol you" (vv. 4-10).

◆ TAKE A LOOK
Nehemiah 9:25, 35; Psalm 23:6; 31:19-20; 69:16

This week we've seen that God's plan for His children is to "do good works" (Ephesians 2:9)—not to earn entrance to heaven, but to demonstrate His love to others.

Now like David, who wrote the words of the psalm above, we also want to think about God's goodness. As you read Nehemiah 9:25, 35; Psalm 23:6, 31:19-20, 69:16; Romans 15:14; Titus 3:4-5; and Hebrews 6:5, write the appropriate reference beside the phrase describing an aspect of God's goodness to us:

God's goodness in giving me:	. . . is described in:
His Word	_____
Salvation	_____
Material blessings	_____
Safety from enemies	_____
Eternal life with Him	_____
Knowledge about Him	_____
Love, mercy, answered prayer	_____

▲ TAKE A STEP
No matter what your menu, have a "Valentine/ Thanksgiving Dinner." As you eat, have each person share things about God that they are most thankful for today (put Psalm 145 to work!).

After dinner, make a Valentine's card for God, listing those things on it. Close with a prayer of thanks for God's goodness.

GUILT

*F*rank had heard that Allan had become a real troublemaker. But when Allan asked him to stay over Friday night, he thought it would be a great chance to renew their friendship.

Now it was Monday, and Frank couldn't get the weekend out of his mind. For one thing, Allan hadn't said his parents would be gone. Frank kept thinking about what he'd done Friday night with Allan and two other guys. Where in the world did Allan get such a dirty video movie? Frank wished he'd never seen it. And he could hardly bear to think about what they'd done at the school before they watched it.

Frank tried to shake the thoughts out of his mind. But what if his parents found out what he had done? What if some other kids heard about it and told the principal? Frank felt sick.

◆ LOOKING AT GUILT

Frank definitely has a bad case of the "guilts." And if you're honest, you'll admit you recognize that feeling—an inner uneasiness that gnaws at the mind and upsets the stomach.

When a person breaks a law—whether it's a civil or moral law—he is guilty. The Bible calls such wrongdoing "sin." Guilt is **the legal and moral condition that results from wrongdoing**. The feeling that condition produces is also called *guilt*.

As far as God's law is concerned, everyone is guilty. Why? Because everyone has sinned; no one has kept God's law perfectly.

● KEY VERSE ON GUILT

For all have sinned and fall short of the glory of God (Romans 3:23).

▲ LOOKING AHEAD

When you've done something wrong, it's a fact that you are guilty —whether you *feel* guilty or not. But, like Frank, most of us *do* feel guilty when we do wrong.

Another way to describe Frank is to say he has a "guilty conscience." After you've read Romans 2:14-15, tell how you think God uses a person's conscience.

"I guess today separated the wheat from us chaff . . ."

"And the sentence of this court is . . ."

Frank couldn't concentrate on his classwork. A battle raged in his mind as he tried to rationalize what he'd done Friday night.

"Everybody does stuff like that. Most guys never get caught. They won't find out who shot off the fire extinguishers in the school. Sure, we had a close call when the security guard came by, but we didn't get caught." Frank's mind replayed the scene.

"Oh, it was just a prank, was it?" his conscience interrupted. "Don't fool yourself! You're guilty. They could send you to the detention center! That'll look great on your record."

"What a mess! What'll I do?" Frank wondered.

◆ TAKE A LOOK / Romans 3:9-23

Frank knew he had broken the law when he and Allan sneaked into the school and sprayed some fire extinguishers in the hallways. And he knew if he got caught he couldn't claim that Allan made him do it, or that he didn't know better. He was responsible. He was guilty. He would have to pay the price.

Some of us may go through life without committing a crime or breaking the laws of our country or state. But no one goes through life without breaking God's laws.

Sin isn't a popular idea. But the Bible says we have all sinned. We are all guilty. And the penalty for sin is death.

We cannot truly understand why Jesus came into the world until we first understand that we are legally guilty before God. And there's no way we can defend ourselves or pay for our own sin. Reading Romans 3:9-23 will help you understand that truth.

▲ TAKE A STEP

The Bible says every person is guilty of breaking God's law. Paul quoted from the Book of Psalms when he wrote to the Romans:

"There is no one righteous, not even one" (Romans 3:10).

But some people are declared "Not guilty" as far as God is concerned. The Bible calls those people *righteous* or *just*, because their sins have been removed and they have been given Christ's righteousness.

What must a person do in order for that to happen? Reread Romans 3:21-22 to find out. Then ask yourself, "Have I received the righteousness of God? Have I put my trust in Jesus Christ for my salvation?"

Q

What does it mean to be legally guilty?

A

Guilt means that I—like everyone else—have broken God's law.

For the past few days the thought of eating made Frank sick. And he'd been praying more than he had in a long time. He realized that praying only when you're desperate isn't exactly the best way to pray, but he had to do something!

"Oh, Lord," he whispered, "please don't let anybody find out about what we did. I'll never do anything that dumb again. Please don't let my parents find out."

By Wednesday night, no one had accused Frank of the vandalism. He was beginning to think he could just forget all about it. But unexpectedly his dad called him into the den. As he walked in, Frank's mind was churning again: "Does he know? Is he giving me a chance to confess? What if he doesn't know? What should I do?"

◆ **TAKE A LOOK / 2 Samuel 13:1-20***

As we've learned, guilt is the legal status or condition of someone who has broken the law—either a government law or God's moral and spiritual law. But Frank's story shows us that someone who does something wrong usually *feels* guilty too. He or she may experience fear, dread, depression, and unhappiness, or may even be physically affected with nausea and sleeplessness.

But such guilt feelings can't always be trusted. Some people who *are* guilty of sin *don't* feel guilty. And others may *feel* guilty about a particular sin when they didn't commit it. The story of Amnon and his half-sister Tamar in 2 Samuel 13:1-20 illustrates this. Which person was truly guilty of sin? Which person do you think felt guilty?

▲ **TAKE A STEP**

Tomorrow we'll find out what a person who is truly guilty of a specific sin can and should do. And on Day Five we'll talk about getting rid of false guilt feelings that cause us to condemn ourselves. But first it's important to realize that our feelings don't always tell us the truth about guilt. The Word of God can tell us the truth about our sin:

Through the law we become conscious of sin (Romans 3:20).

Why then is it so important to know God's law? Together, try to decide which of God's laws helped Frank know he was truly guilty (see Exodus 20). What do you think he should do now?

***Note to parent:** Read today's Scripture yourself before reading it to your children. If you have young children, you may simply want to explain the story to them and focus on Tamar and Amnon's reactions after the sin (verses 17-19).*

Guilt is a fact, not just a feeling

Q

Will a person who sins always feel guilty?

A

Guilt usually causes sadness and uneasiness, but some ignore these warning signs and continue to sin.

Deal with your sin and your guilt will go

*F*rank recalled the time he had to return some stolen candy when he was six. That had been tough, but telling his folks about Friday night was a thousand times worse. He'd do anything to make it up to them, and he'd never do anything like that again.

But it was so hard! Frank had nearly died when his dad called him into the den, but it was only to help him move the couch. Then Frank had tried—and failed—to tell his parents at dinner. Now his parents were in the family room, and he was trying to get the nerve to go in and tell them. He knew he'd have to pay for what he had done, but anything would be worth getting rid of this guilt!

Finally, he did it. As his parents listened to his stumbling, tearful confession, he saw the hurt in their eyes. But when he finished, a huge weight lifted from his heart—especially after his dad stood and gave him a long, hard hug.

Q

How can I get rid of my guilt?

A

Guilt is removed forever when I accept Jesus' death on the cross.

◆ TAKE A LOOK / Romans 5:12-19

At the moment Jesus died on the cross, He paid the death penalty for our sins *once and for all.* Paul explains it this way:

[Jesus] was delivered over to death for our sins and was raised to life for our justification (Romans 4:25).

As you read Romans 5:12-19, remember that *righteous* and *justified* are legal terms that mean "no longer guilty."

▲ TAKE A STEP

Accepting Jesus' payment for sin involves what the Bible calls *repentance.*

Repentance means that you recognize your sin, turn away from it, and commit yourself anew to Jesus as Lord.

When you accept Jesus as your Savior, God declares you "not guilty." And that is how God looks at you.

But even after you become a Christian you will still sin. When that happens, you need to take those same steps of repentance for each specific sin, so there won't be any barriers between you and God.

In the opening story can you find the steps of repentance that Frank followed? Should he have done anything else? Share a time when you were called on to confess a sin to your parents or others. Did you truly repent?

*I*t hadn't been easy, but with his dad beside him, Frank confessed his part in the vandalism to the principal, who suggested an alternative to reporting him to the police. Frank spent the next three months working with the janitorial staff after school. He'd come to appreciate how hard it was to clean the school, even without gobs of fire extinguisher foam everywhere!

But Frank still couldn't erase what he'd seen on that video from his mind. He and his folks had prayed together about that too, and he had confessed it to God. But Frank still felt guilty about watching it. He felt he'd done something for which God would never forgive him. Sometimes he wondered if these awful feelings of guilt would ever end!

◆ TAKE A LOOK
Romans 8:1, 33; Ephesians 1:7-8

When Jesus died on the cross, He settled the problem of our guilt. He took away the punishment for all our sins—past, present, and future. But as God's children we still sometimes sin, putting a barrier between us and our holy God.

To restore our relationship with God we must admit our sin and turn from it:

If we confess our sins, he is faithful and just and will forgive us our sins and purify us from all unrighteousness (1 John 1:9).

A Christian who sins should feel sincerely sorry. But once you've confessed your sin, turned away from it, and asked God to forgive you, continuing to feel guilty shows you really don't believe God. You're still trying to solve your sin problem by yourself—and that just won't work.

Paul understood that God does not want us to feel condemned for sins He has already forgiven. Read Romans 8:1, 33; Ephesians 1:7-8; and Colossians 1:13-14, 2:13-14, and 3:1-3 so you will understand that too.

▲ TAKE A STEP

If we have sincerely repented God doesn't want us to mope around feeling guilty about a sin He has already forgiven. But He does want us to try to fix any physical or emotional damage our sin might have caused for others, as Frank did at the school.

However, other kinds of sins affect only the sinner, as when Frank watched the X-rated movie. What would you advise Frank to do? Can you think of some other things that fall into that category?

The truth is what God says, not how you feel

Q

How can I deal with guilt feelings?

A

Guilt feelings fade away when I believe what God says about forgiveness.

PARENT
Think of some situations in which people need to make restitution for their sins, and others in which the one sinning must live with the consequences. Pose them to your children and discuss what they would advise.

MARTYRS

* * * * * * * * * * * * * * * * *

*T*he Christians knew their cave hiding place had been discovered. Soon the Roman guards would charge in and arrest them, accusing them of treason for worshiping God rather than Caesar. The Christians knew the soldiers would be violent, yet they remained calm. A teenage boy quoted a letter from the apostle Peter:

"If you suffer as a Christian, do not be ashamed, but praise God that you bear that name" (1 Peter 4:16).

In the 1970s, Ugandan believers entered their church to worship God despite their dictator's threats that Christians would be killed if they assembled to worship. As they gathered, military guards watched quietly. Then they opened fire as the minister read these words of Jesus:

"Blessed are you when people insult you, persecute you and falsely say all kinds of evil against you because of me. Rejoice and be glad, because great is your reward in heaven . . . " (Matthew 5:11-12).

◆ LOOKING AT MARTYRS

At different times in history, Christians have faced severe persecution. Some have even died rather than deny their Lord.

The word *martyr* simply means a witness, and every Christian is in fact a witness. But in the early church the possibility of dying for Christ's sake was very real. And so *martyr* came to mean **a person whose witness for Christ led to death.**

● KEY VERSE ON MARTYRS

Which of the two passages above do you think makes the best Key Verse for the week—1 Peter 4:16 or Matthew 5:11-12?

▲ LOOKING AHEAD

The Bible says a lot about standing up—and suffering—for your faith. In Hebrews 11:32-39 you'll find a list of some unnamed Old Testament martyrs. Which of their qualities did God commend (praise)?

"I was doing okay 'til I stuck my neck out on 'guillotine.' "

King Henry VIII of England claimed to be a Christian, but in many cases he made laws that went against God's law. He also demanded that all his religious and political advisers agree with him. Those who chose to obey God rather than the king were often killed.

John Fisher, a close friend of the king, chose God's law above Henry's, and was sentenced to die. On the day of his execution, he asked to be brought his best clothes.

"This is my 'wedding day,' " he explained, "and I ought to dress as if for a holiday."

Carrying his New Testament, he was led to the execution platform. There he prayed, "Lord, grant that I may find some word of comfort so that I may glorify You in my last hour."

The first words he saw as he opened the Scriptures were these: "Now this is eternal life; that they may know you, the only true God, and Jesus Christ, whom you have sent" (John 17:3).

"That will do," he said. "Here's learning enough to last me to my life's end."

Within minutes, John Fisher was dead.

◆ TAKE A LOOK
Acts 6:8–7:2, 51-60; John 15:18-19, 22

Fisher was executed in 1535, one of many martyrs throughout history who died rather than deny their faith in God. Still, it may seem puzzling that Christians should be killed simply because their views are different from those of the government.

You'll learn the reason when you read the story of Stephen, the first Christian martyr, in Acts 6:8–7:2, 51-60. If you have trouble finding the reason there, Jesus' words in John 15:18-19, 22 will be helpful.

▲ TAKE A STEP

The godly witness of martyrs like John Fisher and Stephen threatened wicked people and convicted them of sin. Jesus said:

"If I had not come and spoken to them, they would not be guilty of sin. Now, however, they have no excuse for their sin" (John 15:22).

Do you know people who are so committed to Christ that they are not afraid to share their faith boldly with others, or to speak out against situations that dishonor God? Share one or two accounts of Christian bravery with the family. Ask God to use you in that way too—no matter what it may cost you.

When it comes to my Lord, there's no compromise

Q

Why are Christians sometimes persecuted?

A

Martyrs are persecuted because they are unwilling to compromise with the world.

PARENT
Browse in your church library or Christian bookstore for biographies of Christian martyrs—if you want some challenging reading!

When earthly life ends, eternal life has just begun

*J*ustin knew what the Roman judge would say, but it didn't matter—he and his friends would not deny their Lord.

"We will not sacrifice to idols," he said boldly. "God says we are to have no other gods before Him. That is the first of His commandments."

The judge stared at the men with a frown of anger. "You think you know the truth. If I have you beaten and beheaded, do you believe you will then go to heaven?"

"I do not believe it—I know it," Justin said.

Then the judge passed sentence: "Let those who will not obey the emperor and sacrifice to the gods be scourged and put to death in accordance with the law."

◆ TAKE A LOOK
Matthew 10:28; 28:20; John 15:18; Acts 5:29

A similar story may be happening somewhere in the world right now. Or it may happen to you one day. It *did* happen to Justin in Rome 1,826 years ago. Why are martyrs like Justin willing to die?

Reason One: They are sure of heaven. They know life on earth is temporary, and that heaven— eternal life with Jesus Himself—is the next step.

Reason Two: They are convinced they must obey God's Word rather than compromise with the world.

Reason Three: Jesus Himself set the example by being totally faithful to God. And as followers of Christ, martyrs are willing to walk the same path, if necessary.

Read Matthew 10:28; 28:20; John 15:18; Acts 5:29; 2 Corinthians 5:8; and 1 Peter 4:13-14. Two of those verses support each of the three reasons above. Can you match them?

▲ TAKE A STEP

Are you just as convinced of those three reasons as a martyr might be? If you're not, read this passage aloud:

> For I am convinced that neither death nor life, neither angels nor demons, neither the present nor the future, nor any powers, neither height nor depth, nor anything else in all creation, will be able to separate us from the love of God that is in Christ Jesus our Lord (Romans 8:38-39).

Are you that convinced? Close in prayer for one another, asking God to strengthen your confidence in that truth.

Q

Why are martyrs willing to die?

A

Martyrs are willing to die because they know that what they believe is true.

ANSWERS
Reason One—
Matthew 10:28; 2
Corinthians 5:8.
Reason Two—
Matthew 28:20;
Acts 5:29. Reason
Three—John 15:18;
1 Peter 4:13-14.

A s a missionary in Colombia, Chet Bitterman worked to translate the Bible into unwritten native languages. That way God's love for them could be explained in their own tongue, and they could come to know Jesus.

But on March 7, 1981, Chet was kidnapped. Christians everywhere prayed for his release, but after 48 days his kidnappers killed him.

Some of the letters Chet wrote while he was held prisoner were featured in newspapers around the world. In one he wrote, "I continue finding much to make me happy, especially from the Scriptures."

Chet Bitterman had not lived in vain. Through his death, millions of people saw firsthand what it means to be a committed Christian.

◆ TAKE A LOOK / Matthew 10:16-20; Luke 21:12-19
From the time he put his trust in Christ until the day he died, Chet took God's Word seriously. As a student, he memorized large portions of Scripture. His last memory project was learning the entire book of 1 Peter.

Letters Chet wrote during his captivity mentioned specific Bible references, which journalists reprinted in their stories. A verse he quoted in his last letter to his wife clearly shows that he found his strength—and peace—in knowing that the Lord was with him:

We live by faith, not by sight. . . . So we make it our goal to please him, whether we are at home in the body or away from it (2 Corinthians 5:7-9).

Jesus knew that His followers would suffer tremendous persecution, and that some would even die. As you read Matthew 10:16-20 and Luke 21:12-19, look for Jesus' specific instructions for those most difficult times.

▲ TAKE A STEP
You may never be faced with the possibility of losing your life for Christ. But that possibility seems to become more real each day. Look through the newspaper for articles about Christians who are suffering for their faith around the world. Does their reliance on God and His Word shine through?

Determine today to begin storing God's Word in your heart, as Chet Bitterman did. Begin with one or two verses that show how it will be there whenever you need His strength. You will be surprised at how God will use those verses to remind you about His love.

Store the Scriptures in your heart

Q

Where do martyrs get their strength?

A

Martyrs find strength from God's Word and from the indwelling Holy Spirit.

Heaven is just a stone's throw away

Q

What can I learn from the lives of martyrs?

A

Martyrs' lives teach me that God is faithful to His children.

Frustrated from his day at school, Bob swung the front door open and nearly collided with his dad.

"How was your day, Bob?" Mr. Collins asked absent-mindedly.

"It was horrible! You always tell me people will respect me because I'm a Christian and stand up for what I believe. But that sure isn't what happened today!"

"What happened?"

"Johnny and Thad wanted to look in Mrs. Cabot's drawer at the test we're having Monday, and I told 'em it wasn't right. Well, they didn't do it, but they made sure all their friends knew what I said. Everybody gave me the silent treatment. A few guys called me 'goody-goody Christian,' and nobody, absolutely nobody, sat at my lunch table. It was like I had the plague!"

◆ TAKE A LOOK
Revelation 12:11; 1 Peter 2:20-21; Psalm 112:7-8

What can we learn from the lives of martyrs like Stephen, Peter, Paul, Justin, John Fisher, Chet Bitterman, and thousands of others who have died as witnesses for Jesus Christ? We can learn these facts of the faith:

1. We may suffer—even die—just as Christ our Master did.
2. Our faith in Christ is worth dying for.
3. God's Word stored in our hearts can prepare us and comfort us in any situation—even persecution.
4. Through His indwelling Spirit, God gives us grace and strength when we face fearful situations.

Now read these Bible verses, and match them with the four facts above: (a) Revelation 12:11; (b) 1 Peter 2:20-21; (c) Psalm 112:7-8; and (d) Psalm 119:11 and 1 Peter 3:15-16.

▲ TAKE A STEP
When Paul and Silas were arrested, severely beaten, thrown into a cell, and had their feet put in stocks, they responded by . . .

Praying and singing hymns to God (Acts 16:25).

Try to imagine yourself in that situation. Honestly now—how do you think you would have responded?

Close your family time by selecting and singing a hymn or a praise song that would encourage you if you were in a similar situation.

HEALTH

*R*ecently, the American Medical Association surveyed numerous physicians across the country. The doctors were asked, "In an average week, what percentage of your patients have needs that you are qualified to treat with your medical skills?"

The average reply was 10 percent! In other words, 90 percent of all the people who see a doctor really don't have a problem that can be treated medically. Even so, they are ill; they suffer real pain, but it may not be caused by a physical problem.

The survey also asked what the doctors did for these patients. Most said they prescribed tranquilizers. When asked what they would like to do for them, the doctors said they would like to spend an hour a week talking to these patients about their lives, their families, and their jobs.

It's clear that health involves a lot more than just your body!

◆ LOOKING AT HEALTH

For many centuries, doctors have assumed that curing illness would restore the sick person to perfect health. But today we know that being well means a lot more than simply not being sick.

True health is **wholeness at all levels of life—spiritual, emotional, and physical.** Proverbs 3:7-8 explains that your relationship with God has a lot to do with your physical health.

● KEY VERSE ON HEALTH

Do not be wise in your own eyes; fear the Lord and shun evil. This will bring health to your body and nourishment to your bones (Proverbs 3:7-8).

▲ LOOKING AHEAD

This week we'll do our part to help you become a healthier, happier family.

For starters, would you say you get too much or not enough physical exercise? To warm up for your week on health, do ten jumping jacks, five sit-ups, and run in place for one minute. Now read 1 Timothy 4:8. What does Paul say about "spiritual exercise"?

"But that's not the trouble spot!"

I'm sick and tired of being sick and tired!

Q

Is good health more than not being sick?

A

Health involves knowing you are loved and accepted by God and other people.

Stella always seemed to have fun. She had such a knack for making people laugh that her teachers and classmates enjoyed having her around. And yet, nobody seemed to want Stella as a special friend. As time went on, she felt lonelier and lonelier and began to withdraw into herself.

By the time she was 14, Stella hated to get up in the mornings. She stared into the mirror as she scrubbed her face, but instead of seeing all her good points, Stella focused only on the trouble spots. "Ugly, ugly, ugly! Twenty pounds too fat, shiny braces, pimples. And frizzy red hair. Why was I even born?"

One morning Stella woke up with severe stomach pains that didn't get any better as the week went on. In fact, months went by and the pains grew worse. But medical tests revealed nothing wrong. Stella looked—and felt—sicker than ever.

◆ TAKE A LOOK / Matthew 9:9-12

Why do you think Stella felt so sick? Her story shows that being "healthy" is not simply being free of disease. Many things contribute to your good health, such as feeling good about yourself, understanding your emotions, and knowing that you belong to a group of people who care about you.

Jesus is often called the Great Physician, but curing diseases was not the only healing He did. Can you discover why the person whose story is told in Matthew 9:9-12 also needed to be "healed"?

▲ TAKE A STEP

No doubt Matthew's party was impressive; many important people of Jerusalem were there. And probably none of the guests was actually ill. So, when Jesus was asked why He spent time with such "sinners," why do you suppose He answered this way:

"It is not the healthy who need a doctor, but the sick. But go and learn what this means: 'I desire mercy, not sacrifice' " (Matthew 9:12-13).

Unlike Matthew's friends and Stella's teachers and classmates, Jesus saw people not as they appeared to others, but as they really were inside.

What "sickness" did Jesus see in Matthew and his friends? How did Jesus' acceptance of Matthew help in his healing? Think together about what you could do as a Christian to bring healing to someone like Stella.

Doctors have found seven key "ingredients" to the recipe of good health. The more of these habits a person develops, the healthier he or she will become.

Have your family members state honestly if each statement below is true or false about them. (Be careful not to criticize or make fun of anyone!) Ready? True or false . . .

1. I exercise moderately and regularly.
2. My weight is normal for my age and height.
3. I eat a balanced breakfast every day.
4. I eat three meals regularly with no snacks between meals.
5. I normally sleep 7-8 hours a night.
6. I avoid alcoholic beverages.
7. I do not smoke.
8. I eat all kinds of fruits and vegetables.

◆ TAKE A LOOK / 1 Corinthians 6:19-20; 9:24-27; 1 Timothy 4:8

There's one in every crowd—a "health nut" who works out, jogs, or does aerobic exercises every day; runs in marathons; gulps vitamins and refuses to consume caffeine, sugar, or red meat; and has a near-perfect body.

Then there are people whose exercise schedule includes "sitting up" straight at meals, "jogging" to the kitchen for a snack during TV commercials, and "pushing up" from the recliner to shuffle off to bed!

Somewhere between the people who practically worship their bodies and those who let themselves deteriorate is the balance our Creator wants us to have. Discover that balance right now in 1 Corinthians 6:19-20; 9:24-27; and 1 Timothy 4:8.

▲ TAKE A STEP

People who aren't Christians often put too much emphasis on the physical part of life, but Christians sometimes don't emphasize it enough.

Christians often let "spiritual" activities crowd out regular exercise, proper eating habits, and weight control. But both aspects are important, because our bodies are important. The Bible asks this about our bodies:

Do you not know that your body is a temple of the Holy Spirit? (1 Corinthians 6:20).

How well did you score? With loving concern, discuss how each member of your family could work to become a healthier person. If you scored a perfect 7, ask yourself: What spiritual exercise do I need to emphasize more?

A well-tuned body will last a lifetime

Why is God interested in my physical health?

Health is important because my body is God's temple.

PARENT
How long has it been since you had a physical examination? Your health is one of your family's most valuable assets. Do the right thing and schedule an appointment today.

I pay a high price when I let bitterness build

Q

What does forgiveness have to do with my health?

A

Health can improve when I forgive those who have hurt me, instead of growing bitter.

PARENT
If your family isn't exercising regularly, consider walking together. Use the time to talk. You'll find it's physically and emotionally refreshing!

Your teeth are as sharp as spears, Todd!" the dental hygienist said. "Unless you start relaxing and stop grinding your teeth in your sleep, we'll have to fit you with a mouthpiece to keep you from damaging them."

Todd knew she was right—he hadn't been sleeping well. His aching jaws and constant yawning testified to that. What in the world could be causing him such stress?

"That Mr. Clontz—he's the reason!" Todd thought. He remembered all the hours he'd spent working on extra credit assignments in geometry—until Mr. Clontz had changed his mind and wouldn't accept them.

Todd knew that he should forgive and forget. But every time he saw Mr. Clontz, he relived that awful scene—and got angry all over again.

The hygienist's voice brought him back to reality. "Relax, Todd," she said. "Whatever it is, you'd better set it right or you'll never eat steak again. You won't be able to chew it!"

◆ TAKE A LOOK
James 5:16; Colossians 3:13; Proverbs 28:13

You may find this surprising, but people who study human behavior have found that our ability—or inability—to forgive those who have hurt us has a lot to do with our health, emotionally and physically. So does our ability to admit our own mistakes to others and ask their forgiveness. We actually feel better when we have a forgiving attitude.

The Bible clearly teaches us to *forgive* those who sin against us, and to *confess* our own wrongdoings. Have different family members look up James 5:16; Colossians 3:13; Proverbs 28:13; Matthew 6:14. After reading each verse aloud, decide together what the verse is telling you to do.

▲ TAKE A STEP

If you fail to resolve a conflict you're experiencing with someone, it can affect your health. And that's a high price to pay. Jesus taught,

"If you hold anything against anyone, forgive him, so that your Father in heaven may forgive you your sins" (Mark 11:25).

Todd experienced physical problems because of his unforgiving attitude. Is there someone in your life that you do not want to forgive? How do you feel about what that person did? Are you bitter? On the basis of the Scriptures you read, what would be the healthiest thing to do?

Karen and Josh stood at the bus stop waiting. While Karen fidgeted, arms folded, Josh leaned against a tree and whistled. He didn't seem to have a care in the world.

"Josh! Will you ever act normal?" Karen exploded.

"Since when is whistling against the law?" Josh asked with surprise.

Karen turned away, deep in thought. Her folks had recently been divorced, and each day since then seemed gloomier than the one before. But what really irked her was that Josh was in the same situation, yet it didn't seem to bother him.

Suddenly tears came to her eyes. "Josh, it's not your fault," she admitted. "I just feel like nobody loves me anymore. You keep telling me God loves me. But if He does, why do I feel so confused?"

◆ TAKE A LOOK / Psalm 103:1-5

Karen and Josh both reacted physically, emotionally, and spiritually to their circumstances. But while Karen felt deeply hurt and abandoned, Josh could see through his circumstances to find God at work in his life. They were at two different stages of spiritual health.

You're spiritually healthy if you can see God at work in your life in spite of difficult circumstances and imperfect relationships. Spiritual health involves praising God, obeying Him, and believing His promises day by day and moment by moment.

As you read Psalm 103:1-5, look for two things you can do to insure your spiritual health.

▲ TAKE A STEP

Praise the LORD, O my soul; all my inmost being, praise his holy name. . . . Forget not all his benefits (Psalm 103:1-2).

The first step to spiritual health is to have a personal relationship with God through His Son, Jesus. But ongoing spiritual health requires daily "exercises"—reading God's Word, talking things over with Him in prayer, being involved with other Christians. Then, when problems come, keep your perspective by *remembering* how God has worked in your life in the past, and by *praising* Him for His love and care for you.

"Work out" as a family now by sharing one thing God has done for you in the past and one thing you praise Him for right this minute. You may be surprised at how much better everyone will feel!

Take time to be holy . . . wholly!

Q

How can I stay spiritually healthy?

A

Health in my spirit grows when I praise God and let Him work in my life.

HAPPINESS

H *appiness is . . .*
. . . holding hands with Mom in the car
. . . skating without falling down (too often)
. . . knowing the end of the school year is very close
. . . finishing a massive spring-cleaning project
. . . getting an A on the project you slaved over
. . . discovering a five-dollar bill you'd forgotten about
. . . wrestling with Dad on the floor
. . . finding a Bible verse that really helps
. . . knowing God loves you
. . . sharing that love with somebody else.
Can you think of three more things that make you happy?

◆ LOOKING AT HAPPINESS

Happiness makes you feel good! But true happiness is also more than a feeling. It's a **joyful, contented attitude toward life** that results from a growing relationship with God. Think of it this way: Happiness is not a destination, it's a way of getting to a destination; it's not an end in itself, it is the by-product of working and playing, loving and living God's way. God's Word encourages us to be happy.

"I'm glad school's out. I'm much happier in my natural habitat."

● KEY VERSE ON HAPPINESS

Be happy, young man, while you are young, and let your heart give you joy in the days of your youth (Ecclesiastes 11:9).

▲ LOOKING AHEAD

This week we'll learn the biblical way to see that verse come true in our lives.

Look up Ecclesiastes 11:9 and read the rest of that verse. What is God going to judge each of us for? Think about some things that make *you* happy. What do you think God would say about them?

*J*erry called me at the office today," Mr. Traylor sighed as he walked into the kitchen. "He quit his job."

"Again?" his wife exclaimed. "Your brother has gone through so many jobs I've lost track."

"You said it." He sat down at the table. "Jerry said he wasn't making enough money. He's drowning in debts."

"Maybe he could sell that sports car he just bought."

"He'd rather die first. How else could he impress the girls? I don't know, honey, it's so sad. Jerry is running around trying to find satisfaction in life. He refuses to listen when I talk to him about the Lord. All he wants is more money, more success, more fun. And the harder he looks for them, the further away they get."

Mrs. Traylor sat down with him. "It's strange—we barely have enough to pay our bills, we make do with what we have. And yet we have such joy in our lives."

"You're right. I guess it's true what they say: 'Happiness comes not from having much to live on, but having much to live for.' " They looked at each other and smiled.

◆ **TAKE A LOOK / Luke 12:19-21; 16:24-25; Job 20:4-5**

The search for happiness is one of the main causes of unhappiness. The world seeks happiness through money, power, and sex. The attitude many people have is . . .

I'll say to myself, "You have plenty of good things laid up for many years. Take life easy; eat, drink and be merry" (Luke 12:19).

Read Luke 12:20-21 to find what will happen to people like that. The world's happiness will result in God's judgment. Read the verses below, and write in the blanks how they describe the world's happiness:

This verse says . . .	the world's happiness is:
Job 20:4-5	_____
Ecclesiastes 2:1-2	_____
Matthew 6:19	_____
Luke 16:24-25	_____

▲ **TAKE A STEP**

Read Matthew 6:19-21 thoughtfully. Now make a list of the things you treasure most—your bike, a coin collection, your salvation, etc. If your "treasures" could be destroyed or stolen, cross them off. If they're eternally yours, circle them. How many of each did you have?

I look around, but happiness can't be found

Why is it so hard for some people to be happy?

A

Happiness cannot be found where many people are looking for it.

PARENT
As your family watches TV this week, point out and talk about examples you see of worldly "happiness" (you'll find many) and of true, godly happiness (you'll find very few).

Happiness is to know the Savior!

Q

How can I find true happiness?

A

Happiness that lasts forever comes when I trust Christ for salvation and begin to grow in Him.

PARENT
Bring more joy to everyday life. Be spontaneous, laugh frequently, don't take yourself too seriously. Above all, remind your family often of the joy of knowing God.

Happiness is to know the Savior,
Living a life within His favor,
Having a change in my behavior;
Happiness is the Lord!

Happiness is a new creation,
Jesus and me in close relation,
Having a part in His salvation;
Happiness is the Lord!

Happiness is to be forgiven,
Living a life that's worth the livin',
Taking a trip that leads to heaven;
Happiness is the Lord!
Happiness is the Lord!*

◆ **TAKE A LOOK**
Psalm 1:1-2; 51:8, 12; 128:1-2; John 13:15, 17
True happiness is not just a feeling. It's a settled joy and contentment that comes from having an eternal relationship with God. The Bible often calls those who know this kind of happiness "blessed." As Solomon wrote,
Blessed is he who trusts in the Lord
(Proverbs 16:20).
The blessings of being God's child will never end. Read Psalm 1:1-2; 51:8, 12; 128:1-2; and John 13:15, 17 and you'll learn that you can experience true happiness by spending time in God's Word, obeying, following Christ's example, and confessing sin.

▲ **TAKE A STEP**
True happiness comes only when we see Jesus for who He is—our Savior and Lord. Have you seen Jesus . . . have you personally accepted His death on the cross for you? Until you do, you will never experience true happiness—no matter where you look for it.
After Jesus rose from the dead, he visited His disciples where they were hiding. He showed them His hands and side, where He had been wounded. John 20:20 says they were "overjoyed" when they saw their risen Lord.
If you have "John 20:20 Vision" too, close in a prayer of thanks for the true happiness that is yours in Him. Then, if you know the tune, sing together the song at the top of the page.

*"Happiness Is the Lord" by Ira Stanphill, copyright 1968 by Singspiration Music. Used by permission of Benson Music Group.

Mr. Comstock poked his head into his son's room. Travis was sprawled out on his bed, staring into space.

"Hey, Travis, it's so quiet in here I thought I'd better check up on you!" his dad said. "What are you up to?"

"Aw, nothing, Dad." Travis rolled over and propped his head up with his hand. "I'm just kind of . . . down."

"Want to talk?" Mr. Comstock asked as he leaned against Travis's desk.

"I don't know why I'm feeling this way. I mean, I went on that junior high retreat last weekend and had a terrific time."

"That's right. I've never seen you so excited."

"I was getting up earlier, having great quiet times. I really felt close to God. Then yesterday I flunked that math test, and today I lost my English book. And now I have to work on a science project, and it's the last thing I want to do. What happened, Dad? Things were going so great. How come we can't just always be happy?"

◆ TAKE A LOOK / 1 Peter 1:3-9

Yesterday we learned that true happiness comes from knowing God personally. But if you're a human being (you are, aren't you?), you'll still experience good times and bad—even if you're a Christian.

Solomon recognized this fact of life. He wrote: *When times are good, be happy; but when times are bad, consider: God has made the one as well as the other (Ecclesiastes 7:14).*

Our sovereign God is in control of the good times and the bad ones as well. But why doesn't He let us be happy all the time? Find out how the apostle Peter answered that question by reading 1 Peter 1:3-9.

▲ TAKE A STEP

True happiness is a settled conviction that comes from knowing God. Circumstances can make us happy or sad. But the deep-rooted joy of salvation can never be taken away.

In his letter Peter reminds us of this truth. He says we may have times of grief and trouble, but God is using those tough times to strengthen our faith. So we can be joyful in spite of them.

Write out Philippians 4:4 on a large sheet of paper. Let the family members decorate it. Then hang it in a prominent place as a "Readable Reminder to Rejoice Repeatedly"!

If this is happiness, why do I feel so sad?

Q

Why can't I always be happy?

A

Happiness may come and go, but the joy of the Lord is forever.

PARENT
If you or someone you know has occasional problems with depression, you may want to read HAPPINESS IS A CHOICE by Meier and Minirth (Baker Book House).

God's blessings are catching —pass them on!

"Oh-oh," Tammy thought as she walked to her next class. "Here comes Barbara. Guess I'll have to talk to her." Barbara moped over and Tammy greeted her, "How are you doing, Barbara?"

"Not good," Barbara whined. "I woke up with a crick in my neck and this big zit on my nose. I stayed up late studying for a geometry test, and I still don't know that stuff."

"Well, better go. See you later." Tammy was glad to move on. Then she spotted Sandy. "Hi, Sandy. What's up?"

"The sun is up! Isn't it a gorgeous day? How are you doing, Tammy?" Sandy bubbled.

"Great now. Just being around you cheers me up! Sandy, how come you're always so 'up'?"

" 'This is the day that the Lord has made; I will rejoice and be glad in it!' " Sandy laughed. "There's just so much in life to be happy about that I don't have time to be sad!"

◆TAKE A LOOK / Jeremiah 15:16; Acts 8:4-8; 14:17

Some people, like Sandy, bring happiness wherever they go. Others, like Barbara, bring happiness whenever they leave! Sandy has learned the secret to joyful living. She has a growing relationship with her Savior, and she knows the true happiness that it brings. But she also faces each day with the attitude that, whatever happens, God is in control. God brings many blessings to our lives. Sometimes we ignore them or take them for granted. But He wants us to enjoy them.

Match each verse below with the proper description.

According to this verse . . .	I can be blessed by:
1. Jeremiah 15:16	a. rain, food, seasons
2. Acts 8:4-8	b. suffering for Christ
3. Acts 14:17	c. reading the Bible
4. 2 Corinthians 8:2	d. giving to others
5. 1 Peter 4:13	e. seeing God at work

▲ TAKE A STEP

Think about this verse for a few moments: *The ransomed of the Lord . . . will enter Zion with singing; everlasting joy will crown their heads. Gladness and joy will overtake them, and sorrow and sighing will flee away* (Isaiah 51:11).

Eternal happiness awaits you as God's child! How will that truth affect the way you live—will you be a "Blue Barbara" or a "Sunny Sandy"?

Q

What other things can make me truly happy?

A

Happiness comes when I appreciate the many blessings God gives me.

ANSWERS
1-c; 2-e; 3-a; 4-d; 5-b

HYMNS

O for a thousand tongues to sing my great Redeemer's praise,
    The glories of my God and King, the triumphs of His grace!
Jesus! the name that charms our fears, that bids our sorrows cease;
    'Tis music in the sinner's ears. 'Tis life and health and peace.
He breaks the power of canceled sin, He sets the prisoner free;
    His blood can make the foulest clean; His blood availed for me.

Hear Him, ye deaf; His praise, ye dumb, your loosened tongues employ;
    Ye blind, behold your Savior come; and leap, ye lame, for joy.
My gracious Master and my God, assist me to proclaim,
    To spread through all the earth abroad, the honors of Thy name.
Glory to God, and praise, and love be ever, ever given,
    By saints below and saints above, the Church in earth and heaven.

◆ LOOKING AT HYMNS

Singing hymns is an important part of a worship service. You may have favorite hymns you like to sing with great gusto. On the other hand, you may find some with such difficult melodies or with so many slow, plodding verses that you dread hearing those page numbers announced. But did you ever stop to think that *your* opinion about the hymns you sing is not nearly as important as *God's*?

Music is important to God—especially the music we use to worship Him. He is so interested in music that He included a "hymnbook" right in the middle of the Bible. He wants us to . . .

● KEY VERSE ON HYMNS

Speak to one another with psalms, hymns and spiritual songs. Sing and make music in your heart to the Lord (Ephesians 5:19).

▲ LOOKING AHEAD

This week we'll look at several well-known hymns— and the stories behind them— to see what led their composers to write **songs about our life as God's children**.

How do you think Charles Wesley felt when he wrote the words above? What message was he trying to get across?

Even when I hurt, hymns can offer praise

Q

Why do people write hymns?

A

Hymns may result from happiness or tragedy, but their main purpose is to help me praise God.

PARENT
If you don't have a family hymnbook, you may want to purchase one from a Christian bookstore or from your church.

While studying to become a preacher, George Matheson lost his eyesight. His fiancée returned his ring with a note that she could not go through life married to a blind man. He never married. Years later, at the wedding of a sister, Matheson was overwhelmed by memories of that broken relationship. In his despair, he composed a hymn praising God's love—always reliable, never failing.

• In the Chicago fire of 1873, H.G. Spafford lost nearly everything he owned. A few months later his wife and four daughters boarded a ship for France, where he was to join them later. During that voyage, the ship sank and the Spaffords' four daughters were lost. As soon as he could, Spafford set sail for Europe. As his ship neared the place where his daughters had died, he found it hard to rest. There in the mid-Atlantic he wrote a hymn praising God for the peace He gives even in tragedy.

◆ **TAKE A LOOK / Psalm 149:1-5**
God's people have always sung. Early believers sang from the Psalms, the Old Testament hymnbook. In the centuries since, songs of praise and worship have been a meaningful part of worship.

Many hymns we sing today were written by ordinary people to praise their extraordinary God. Like George Matheson and H. G. Spafford, many hymn writers wrote in pain or despair to praise God, who gave them strength to endure. Some believers, such as Francis of Assisi, wrote to praise God for creation and for the salvation He has provided in Jesus Christ. A few, like Isaac Watts, began writing as children. Others, like Fanny Crosby, didn't begin until mid-life.

Whatever the circumstances, people write hymns for one main reason. You'll discover it by reading Psalm 149:1-5.

▲ **TAKE A STEP**
Difficult or tragic events may inspire hymn writers, but circumstances are not their real reason for writing. Their purpose for composing hymns of praise is to . . .

Sing to the LORD a new song, his praise in the assembly of the saints (Psalm 149:1).

H. G. Spafford and George Matheson, the two men you read about today, wrote hymns titled "O Love That Wilt Not Let Me Go," and "It Is Well With My Soul." Which person do you think wrote which hymn? Find a hymnbook, look them up, and sing them together.

Holy, holy, holy, Lord God Almighty!
　　Early in the morning our song shall rise to Thee;
　Holy, holy, holy, merciful and mighty!
　　God in Three Persons, blessed Trinity!

　Holy, holy, holy! All the saints adore Thee,
　　Casting down their golden crowns around the
　　　glassy sea;
　Cherubim and seraphim falling down before Thee,
　Which wert, and art, and evermore shalt be.

　Holy, holy, holy! Though the darkness hide Thee,
　　Though the eye of sinful man Thy glory may
　　　not see,
　Only Thou art holy; there is none beside Thee,
　Perfect in power, in love, and purity.

◆ **TAKE A LOOK / Isaiah 6:1-3; Revelation 4:8-11**
　　That hymn is based on the words of the angels
who surround God's throne. Catch a glimpse of
that heavenly scene as you read Isaiah 6:1-3 and
Revelation 4:8-11.

▲ **TAKE A STEP**
　　Holy, holy, holy is the LORD *Almighty; The
whole earth is full of his glory (Isaiah 6:3).*
　　One definition of *worship* is "being aware of
who God is and declaring His worth." The created
beings who surround God's throne do this day and
night—without ever stopping!
　　The hymn above—by Reginald Heber (1783–
1826)—helps Christians declare God's "worth" to
Him and to each other. Christians know that God
is one God. And yet He reveals Himself to us in
three ways, as three Persons—God the Father, God
the Son (Jesus), and God the Spirit. The word *holy* is
repeated three times to remind us of God's three
Persons.
　　To emphasize the teaching of the Trinity, the
writer of this hymn uses a "trinity of words" in
each verse to say something about God. In stanza
one, he mentions three attributes of God: He is
holy, merciful, and mighty.
　　Stanza two closes with three words that declare
that God is eternal: He was ("wert"), and is ("art"),
and "evermore shalt be."
　　Stanza three describes three of God's perfect
qualities. After you've found them in the words of
the hymn, close your family time by singing this
majestic praise song.

**Sing a
song,
hum a
hymn,
give God
the glory!**

Q

*How do
hymns
help me
worship?*

A

*Hymns
encourage
me to wor-
ship God
by describ-
ing Him
and His
works.*

PARENT
*This week play
some recordings
of hymns during
meals or quiet
family times.
(Remember,
most public
libraries have
tapes and
CDs you can
check out.)*

Watch what you sing and how you sing it

Q

Is one style of Christian music better than another?

A

All forms of Christian music should honor God in what they say and how they say it.

I '*ll fly away, O glory, I'll fly away. One glad day when Jesus comes again, I'll fly away.*"

Mrs. Burns cringed as the men's quartet—accompanied by piano, guitar, and banjo—sang this American folk hymn. "How can anybody think that kind of music belongs in church?" she thought to herself. "It sounds like something from 'Hee Haw.' " She glanced at the bulletin and breathed a sigh of relief. Quietly she turned to the next hymn, "The Church's One Foundation."

Beside her sat Mr. Burns, who had grown up in the rural South and was thoroughly enjoying this unaccustomed treat. "It's just like when I was a kid," he thought. "I'd almost forgotten what real singing was like. Makes that organ music sound dull in comparison. I sure hope these guys sing again soon." And his feet began to tap in time to the music.

◆ **TAKE A LOOK / Ephesians 5:19-20**

By studying ancient instruments, we know that the sounds of music have definitely changed. Even the music of Jesus' time might sound strange to us today. Nowadays music is written in a wide range of styles: classical, country, contemporary, and more.

With each person having personal likes and dislikes, how can we know if one style of Christian music is better than another? Let's try to answer that question by looking at the music of the Bible.

As we've already learned, the book of Psalms is the Bible's hymnbook. The fact that it records only the words, not the actual music, teaches us three facts: (1) The words of the song are very important; (2) we have freedom to use our talents to create music in different styles; (3) whatever the style, everything we sing should have one purpose: to please God.

You'll see how important that purpose is as you discover to whom we sing our hymns in Ephesians 5:19-20.

▲ **TAKE A STEP**

Our purpose in singing should not be to please ourselves alone. We should desire above all to please God, to . . .

Sing and make music in your heart to the Lord (Ephesians 5:19).

Why do you think there are different styles of worship music? What is your favorite style of music? Do you enjoy it only because it brings you pleasure, or do you think it brings God pleasure too?

*T*aking your cues from the brief descriptions below, can you match the three authors with the famous hymns they wrote?

A. Amazing Grace

B. A Mighty Fortress Is Our God

C. All Creatures of Our God and King

1. Francis of Assisi, the patron saint of animals, lived a simple life, close to nature.

2. As a young man, John Newton lived an immoral life and even served as a seaman on slave ships. After his conversion at age 39, he continued to marvel at God's mercy in saving someone as wicked as he had been.

3. The great reformer, Martin Luther, was keenly aware of Satan's attacks on Christians. His most famous hymn reminds us that God has won the victory and will never fail.

◆ **TAKE A LOOK / Psalm 3**

Understanding the stories behind the hymns helps us grasp the deep feelings of faith, worship, and praise the writers were trying to express.

The psalms of David provide a good example. By comparing the events of David's life with the hymns he wrote, we can better understand his feelings and see his faith at work in both happy and tragic times. One such tragic time in David's life was when his own son Absalom led a rebellion. King David was forced to flee Jerusalem with his supporters. Absalom actually took over David's house.

These events were a low point in David's life. As you read Psalm 3, written as David fled, try to imagine his feelings. What does this psalm tell you about David's faith?

▲ **TAKE A STEP**

When David's own son turned traitor, the kingdom was in a state of confusion. David fled for his life. Yet his confidence in God was firm. Though he didn't know when or where enemy troops might attack him, he was able to say,

I lie down and sleep; I wake again, because the LORD *sustains me (Psalm 3:5).*

Like David, you may have been through some tough times. You may even be in one right now. Take a moment to let each family member share a tough time he or she is experiencing. Do you have a favorite hymn that reminds you of God's strength? Why not write your own!

What He's done for others, He'll do for me

How does knowing the story behind a hymn help me better understand it?

A

Hymns remind me that, as God has strengthened others, He will help me through tough times too.

JUDGMENT

Kenny shuddered as he walked into the courtroom. He had never been so scared. But then, he'd never been on trial before.

He was wearing a brand-new suit. Every hair was in place. He stood up straight, just like his father. As he stepped into the room, he saw his parents and gave a little nod. They looked scared too.

Then he felt the stares. Why was everyone looking at him so strangely? He wasn't a criminal—was he? His lawyer, Mr. Simpson, greeted him with a kindly smile. "Did you sleep at all last night?" he asked as he put a hand on Kenny's shoulder and steered him toward a chair. "A little," Kenny replied in a voice pitched high from tension.

Almost as soon as they were seated, the bailiff called out, "All rise." A black-robed judge entered the room. "Superior Court is now in session. The Honorable Judge Walter Gregg presiding."

◆ LOOKING AT JUDGMENT

Visiting a courtroom is an impressive experience. Judges, juries, and courts are set up by governments to make judgments—**fair decisions regarding guilt or innocence in personal conflicts or crimes.** Judgment is not based on a judge's personal opinion; it is based on the law.

Though it may not be a very comforting subject, the Bible clearly says everyone will face some kind of judgment by God:

● KEY VERSE ON JUDGMENT

He comes to judge the earth. He will judge the world in righteousness and the peoples in his truth (Psalm 96:13).

*"Judged and found lacking,
but not enough."*

▲ LOOKING AHEAD

This week we'll get a glimpse of the sheer awesomeness of God's judgment by comparing it to Kenny's trial experience.

God's children need not fear His wrath. Read 1 John 4:16-18; John 5:24; and Romans 8:1 to see how people can have real confidence in facing God's judgment.

*T*he defendant, Kenneth Watkins, is charged with one count of vehicular homicide, two counts of theft by taking, and one count of driving under the influence of alcohol . . . "

As the words droned on, Kenny thought back to the night he got in trouble. Steve, Tommy, and he had been looking for some fun. Who could have guessed they'd wreck the car they stole . . . and Steve would get killed?

They had done some other crazy things in the past, but nothing bad had happened to them. Like throwing water balloons off the bridge at cars below. Or shoplifting magazines at the drugstore. Kenny had always gotten only a lecture from his father.

"How does the defendant plead?" the judge demanded. Kenny's lawyer stood up. "Guilty, Your Honor."

Nobody was laughing now.

◆ **TAKE A LOOK / Romans 5:8-9; Acts 17:30-31**
While Kenny was in criminal court, another judge was conducting a civil trial to settle a lawsuit between two businessmen. A third judge was holding a hearing about a disputed will. Many people were in court that day, but not everyone was having the same kind of trial.

In a similar way, the Bible teaches that everyone will come before God for judgment, but not everyone will face the same kind of judgment. Those who have accepted Jesus Christ's payment for their sin have already been declared "not guilty."

They do not have to fear God's punishment. Instead, they will be judged on the basis of what they have done as believers so they can be given rewards. But people who have never repented are guilty and must face God's anger. They will be sentenced to pay the price for their sins.

The Bible describes the first kind of judgment (for believers) in Romans 5:8-9 and 2 Corinthians 5:10, and the second (for unbelievers) in Acts 17:30-31 and Revelation 20:11-15.

▲ **TAKE A STEP**
It is a dreadful thing to fall into the hands of the living God (Hebrews 10:31).

Kenny's life of rebellion and sin finally caught up with him. Yet, his fear is nothing compared to the fear unbelievers will feel when they stand before God. But God has provided an escape plan from that judgment. What is it? (Read John 3:17-18 and Romans 10:9-13.)

Judgment is for one and all, great and small

Q

Who will be judged?

A

Judgment will come to all people, but it's different for believers than for unbelievers.

He is the Judge because He is God

Q

Who is the judge?

A

Judgment will be made by God Himself, our Creator and Father, through His Son Jesus.

As he faced the judge, Kenny's legs were shaking so badly he could hardly stand. He wondered if the judge ever smiled. "Son, do you realize the seriousness of the charges against you?" asked the man in the black robe.

"Yes, Your Honor." Kenny tried to look up, but he couldn't. He wished his father was the one sitting behind the huge desk.

Somehow, Kenny knew his dad loved him no matter what. But it was hard to imagine this stern judge showing any compassion. "The court does not take lightly the laws of this state. And neither should you. Because of your actions, a young man has lost his life. Do you have anything to say for yourself?"

"I realize what I did was wrong, Your Honor," Kenny replied, his mouth dry. "We didn't think anybody would get hurt."

"You should have thought about that," the judge intoned, "before you broke the law."

◆ TAKE A LOOK
Psalm 96:13; Romans 2:16; 2 Timothy 4:1

Judges make and carry out decisions affecting the lives of many. But judges are people too. They do the same things ordinary folks do—until they put on their official robes. Then they have all the authority of the law behind them.

Human judges are given authority to judge others when they are elected or appointed. But God's authority to judge comes because of who He is—the Creator, the Lord of the universe.

Psalm 96:13, Romans 2:16, and 2 Timothy 4:1 explain that God will judge through His Son, Jesus Christ.

▲ TAKE A STEP

Since Adam and Eve's sin, every human being deserves God's punishment. But God has held back His judgment. In His love and mercy, His compassion and patience, He has given mankind time to repent. Though He has allowed wickedness to continue for a time, one day God will judge the earth. God's patience with sinful humanity will end, and all the wicked people from the beginning of time will appear before Him. At that time,

God will judge men's secrets through Jesus Christ (Romans 2:16).

When Kenny looked at the judge, why did he wish his father was the judge? How do you feel knowing that God, the ultimate Judge, is your heavenly Father?

Kenny glanced around the courtroom. He saw his parents sitting in the first row, worried but trying not to show it. Sadly he thought back to that dreadful night 10 months ago when they had come to the police station to post his bond and get him out of jail. White-faced and tense, his father had signed the bail form. Tears continually welled up in his mother's eyes. When they all got in the car, she cried openly. And it seemed to Kenny that she didn't stop crying until after Steve's funeral.

Many times during the next few months, Kenny noticed his mother's red-rimmed eyes. As the trial drew nearer, he saw his dad lose interest in all his favorite hobbies.

Now Kenny noticed Steve's parents sitting at the back of the courtroom. Once he had been as welcome in their home as their own son. Today he could hardly bear to look into their eyes.

"They should have had this trial the very next week and gotten it over with," Kenny thought. "The waiting's hard on everyone."

◆ TAKE A LOOK / John 5:22-30; 2 Peter 3:3-9

Our courts try to protect the rights of all citizens, even those accused of a crime. To allow both the prosecutor (who charges someone with a crime and attempts to prove it) and the defense attorney (who defends a person against those charges) to have time to prepare their cases, it's usually a long time from a person's arrest to the trial.

God too has allowed time to pass between the offense and the time of judgment. He told Adam and Eve that the punishment for sin would be death. And yet even after the "crime" was committed, the punishment they deserved didn't come immediately. In His mercy God gave them time to repent. Many years have passed since that first offense and God still has not judged the earth. But John 5:22-30 assures us that Judgment Day will come. Why has God waited so long? Find out by reading 2 Peter 3:3-9.

▲ TAKE A STEP

The Lord is not slow in keeping his promise, as some understand slowness. He is patient with you, not wanting anyone to perish, but everyone to come to repentance (2 Peter 3:9).

Through Jesus Christ, God has given mankind the opportunity to repent and escape His wrath. And He has given the time to turn to Him in faith. But that time is growing shorter. Are you ready for Judgment Day?

Judgment Day is coming . . . but when?

Q

When will judgment occur?

A

Judgment will come in God's time; meanwhile He has mercifully given us time to repent.

It's not too late to change your fate

A

Judgment results in eternal punishment for those who don't believe in Jesus.

Will the defendant rise and stand before the judge!" the bailiff bellowed, pointing to where Kenny was to stand.

The judge sternly looked at Kenny in silence. "Young man, this time you're getting more than a lecture. The laws of this state are strict when it comes to the crimes you have committed. You must face the consequences of your actions." The room was deathly quiet, except for the sound of someone softly sobbing—Kenny's mother.

"According to the law," the judge continued, "I have no choice but to sentence you to five years in prison. Case closed."

Five years! Immediately Kenny realized that, about the time his classmates would be graduating from college, he would be getting out of prison. Five years! His heart sank and tears welled up in his eyes. It was too late to do anything different now.

◆ TAKE A LOOK / Matthew 13:24-30, 36-43

We make decisions about our future every day. In fact, we take for granted the fact that we can change our situation if we want. But as Kenny discovered, not everyone has that freedom. There are times in life when we must live with the consequences of the decisions we have made. When the judge sentenced him, Kenny realized he couldn't change a thing. He couldn't undo his decision to steal the beer and the car. And so he had to spend five years in prison.

Every day, all around the world, people reject Jesus as their Savior. They are making a decision that will affect their future not only on earth, but for all eternity as well. Those who do not receive Jesus as Savior will one day stand before "the judge of all the earth" and will hear Him pronounce them guilty.

In Matthew 13:24-30,36-43, Jesus told a parable that describes the eternal consequences of this life-and-death choice.

▲ TAKE A STEP

"They will go away to eternal punishment, but the righteous to eternal life" (Matthew 25:46).

Eternal punishment in hell—separation from God and all that is good. Eternal life in heaven—fellowship forever with our loving God. The choice is yours. When Judgment Day comes, the opportunity to make the right choice will be gone. If you've already made that choice, who could you encourage to do the same today?

HELPING

*T*he little boy's arms ached as he edged his way along the crowded sidewalk carrying the heavy bag of groceries.

Suddenly, what he had been dreading actually happened—someone jostled him . . . the bag shifted . . . the paper ripped . . . and groceries tumbled onto the sidewalk, rolling everywhere!

The boy scrambled to pick up the potatoes, apples, and canned goods. But it seemed an impossible job. "How will I ever get all this home?" he thought. "I can't carry it all by myself."

As he crouched there, protecting the pile of groceries and wondering what to do next, a man stopped, smiled, and said these wonderful words: "Looks like you could use some help, son."

Quickly the man and the boy gathered all the groceries into their arms and headed toward the boy's apartment. As they walked, the boy gazed at the smiling man beside him. When they were almost there, he blurted out the question on his mind: "Hey, mister, are you Jesus?"

"No," the man chuckled, "but I know Him!"

◆ LOOKING AT HELPING

Did the boy really think the man who helped him might be Jesus? Perhaps he did. Maybe all the boy knew about Jesus was that He helped people in trouble. Maybe he didn't know that Jesus had returned to heaven long ago. But what the boy actually saw was that when Christians are helpful toward others they make Christ real.

Helping means **responding to others' needs in practical ways.** Every Christian has been given this instruction:

● KEY VERSE ON HELPING
Encourage the timid, help the weak, be patient with everyone (1 Thessalonians 5:14).

▲ LOOKING AHEAD
God helps His children in many ways. Do you need proof? First read Psalm 124:8; 46:1; 86:17; and 118:13. Then think together of at least four ways you know the Lord has helped *you.*

"I don't have to help my Mom with the housework. She knows how."

The God who never changes also never fails

K *now this hymn? Then sing it together—loudly!*
"O God, our help in ages past, our hope for years
to come,
Our shelter from the stormy blast, and our eternal
home!
Before the hills in order stood, or earth received her
frame,
From everlasting Thou art God, to endless years
the same.
A thousand ages in Thy sight, are like an evening
gone;
Short as the watch that ends the night, before
the rising sun.
O God, our help in ages past, our hope for years
to come,
Be Thou our guide while life shall last, and our
eternal home."

Q

How does God help me?

A

Help in times of trouble comes from our unfailing God.

PARENT
Discuss with your older child how humanity today has put its "faith" in technology and science, leaving God out of the picture. Why is this an unwise thing to do?

◆ TAKE A LOOK / Psalms 18; 28; 33; 60; 124

God helps His people. That's a truth the Old Testament poets and prophets often repeated in their writings. Living at the mercy of natural disasters, famines, and diseases, God's people understood well that the One who made all things also controls them, and that the One who gave kings their power could also remove it. When their nation was attacked by stronger enemies, they turned to God as their only sure defense. Yes, God alone was their help in time of trouble. And you know what? He still is today!

You'll see how knowing that God was on their side brought strength and confidence to His people as you read Psalms 18:29; 28:2, 7-9; 33:20-22; 60:11-12; 124:1-7.

▲ TAKE A STEP

Sometimes it seems people today don't really need God's help. Diseases such as smallpox no longer kill thousands. New technologies keep many safe from floods and storms. Incredible inventions make everyday chores easier. Most of us have enough food to eat. Instant communications have made it seem as if world leaders are in control of earth's destiny—not God.

But God has not changed. He still controls this world. The human mind and man-made machines will ultimately fail, but God will not. Work on memorizing this verse, so that no matter what happens you can say:

Our help is in the name of the LORD, the Maker
of heaven and earth (Psalm 124:8).

*N*ow that he'd gotten the washing machine running again, the repairman sat down at Mrs. Watkins's kitchen table to write out the bill. She noticed him glancing at the Scripture plaque on the wall. "That sure is tough to do sometimes, isn't it?" he sighed.

"Give thanks in all circumstances," she read softly. "Yes, it is. But if we believe God is in control, then we can do it."

"Sure is hard, though, when everything is going bad." His eyes glistened with unshed tears.

Mrs. Watkins knew nothing about this repairman; she'd picked his name from the yellow pages. But as she asked a few questions, she learned that his wife of 32 years was critically ill. They had no children and had never attended church regularly. In this crisis, there was nowhere for him to turn for help. Or was there?

◆ TAKE A LOOK
Acts 11:27-30; 16:9-10; 20:34-35
That very afternoon Mrs. Watkins sent home-made soup home with the repairman. During the next few weeks, she and several of her friends helped his wife during her convalescence.

Genuine friendships blossomed among the women, so no one was surprised when the couple began attending church. And everyone rejoiced when, a few months later, they both put their trust in Jesus Christ as their Savior.

We often cross paths with people who have physical, emotional, and spiritual needs. We can share God's love for them by reaching out in love, accepting them as they are, and helping to meet their needs. Read Acts 11:27-30; 16:9-10; and 20:34-35, and try to figure out three kinds of people God wants us to help.

▲ TAKE A STEP
The early believers set a good example for helping others. They provided for *Christians* in need, sent the gospel to *unbelievers* like the Macedonians who had never heard about Jesus, and reached out in love to those who were *weak*. Their helpfulness made God's love come alive for many others. And they did it all because they believed this truth taught by Jesus:

"It is more blessed to give than to receive" (Acts 20:35).

Share an occasion when you were blessed because you gave—of your time, money, or talents. Then thank God in prayer together for those who have helped you.

Take my hand and I'll pick you up

Q
Whom should I help?

A
Helping means reaching out with God's love to all who are in need.

*Do some
people
have a
special gift
for helping
others?*

A

*Helping is
a special
gift of the
Spirit,
but all
Christians
are to help
others.*

PARENT
*Participating in
special group
projects is a
good way to
make a little
help go a long
way. What
church or
community
volunteer
projects could
you and your
family serve?*

Hey, Grandpa, it's too cold for you to go outside."
Charlie darted out the front door, picked up the
paper, and was back in a flash. "Do you need me to
run upstairs and get your afghan?"

Grandpa smiled. "No, son, these old joints will
loosen up soon and I'll be all right. You have a good
day now."

Charlie breezed through the back door and noticed
his mother sitting at the table. Rubbing her back, he
said, "You look awfully tired, Mom. Were you up with
Bethany again last night?"

"Um-hmm," she mumbled. "Her coughing keeps
her awake. Another night like last night and I'll be dead
on my feet when your dad gets home this weekend."

"Hey, Mom, I don't have practice after school, so
I'll come straight home. I could look after Bethany for a
couple of hours while you take a nap before dinner.
How's that for a deal?"

Mrs. Burns grinned. "I'll take it!" she said with relief.

◆ **TAKE A LOOK / 1 Corinthians 12:27-31**
What would you do if you had a grandfather
stiffened by arthritis and a mom worn out from
nursing a sick baby? Would you help? Would you
notice?

God gives all Christians spiritual gifts—special
talents and abilities to enable them to serve others.
The ability to help others is one of those special
gifts. You'll find it listed with several others in
1 Corinthians 12:27-31.

▲ **TAKE A STEP**
Those who have the gift of helping have the
desire and ability to work behind the scenes,
enabling others to use their gifts more effectively.
This gift is also found in people who, like Charlie,
are constantly sensitive to the needs of others. In
most cases they reach out to help without being
asked.

Every Christian should be sensitive to the needs
of others. We ought to follow Christ's example:
*When he saw the crowds, he had compassion on
them, because they were harassed and helpless,
like sheep without a shepherd (Matthew 9:36).*

Can you identify with that feeling? If not, ask
God to give you greater compassion for others. But
don't stop with a feeling. Do you know a "harassed
and helpless" person? What is causing the problems in that person's life? How can you help him
or her today?

*L*ittle Chloe stood watching from as far away as possible. She had heard people talking about these men the whole time she and her father had been in Jerusalem. Were they really drunkards? Or was God with them?

Now the men were heading for the temple. They seemed to be staring at that crippled beggar.

"Now I'll be able to see whether they are good or bad," she thought. "If they hurt him, I'll know they are bad. But if they give him money, then maybe they **are** from God."

Chloe watched silently. The men walked over to the beggar.

"They must be bad men! They have no money in their hands at all. They're teasing the poor man!" She inched closer to hear what they said. "Silver or gold I do not have, but what I have I give you. In the name of Jesus Christ of Nazareth, walk" (Acts 3:6).

The man jumped up and walked! Chloe realized that they had given him far more than money could buy.

◆ **TAKE A LOOK / Acts 9:11-17, 26-28; 18:1-3**
When people are asked to help, often the first thing they wonder is, "How much money do you want?" Peter and John knew the crippled man needed more than money. While giving money can help in some situations, sometimes there's a better solution. God wants us to give *whatever* is needed.

Many people helped the apostle Paul in his missionary work; some in fact did give money. Listed below are the names of some of Paul's helpers. As you look up the verses, jot down how you think each one helped Paul.

Person:	Passage:	How they helped:
Ananias	Acts 9:11-17	_____
Barnabas	Acts 9:26-28	_____
Priscilla & Aquila	Acts 18:1-3	_____
Epaphras	Colossians 1:7-8	_____
Aristarchus, Mark, & Justus	Colossians 4:10-11	_____
Luke	Colossians 4:14	_____

▲ **TAKE A STEP**
Let us encourage one another (Hebrews 10:25).

Paul's friends accepted him, comforted him, showed him hospitality, and stuck with him through thick and thin. Think together of some more ways to help others. Then pick one to be your "People Pepper-Upper" today!

Money's not the solution for every destitution

Q

Does helping others always involve giving money?

A

Helping means giving others encouragement, acceptance, and comfort— not just money.

DATING

*A*t first Kent was excited about the idea of asking a date to Frank's party. Several names—all attached to cute faces—quickly came to mind, but he decided to ask Melody Malone, the petite, dark-haired girl who played the flute in the school band.

On Monday he almost asked Melody in the library, but chickened out. "Aw, she wouldn't want to go with me," he thought.

On Tuesday Kent sat by Melody and her friends in the cafeteria. "I can't ask her in front of all these people," he thought. "She might say no and I'd look like an idiot."

But by Wednesday night he knew he had to do something or miss the party. With sweaty palms, he dialed Melody's number. "Uh, Melody?" he stammered, "I know you've probably got something else to do, but would you go with me to Frank's party Friday night?"

◆ LOOKING AT DATING

In Bible times young men and women didn't date. With few exceptions, their fathers arranged their marriages, and that was that, like it or not. So the Bible doesn't discuss dating as such.

Instead, it talks about developing proper relationships. And since dating involves **spending time informally with members of the opposite sex**, Paul's advice to Timothy in the New Testament provides this appropriate starting point:

● KEY VERSE ON DATING

Treat younger men as brothers, older women as mothers, and younger women as sisters, with absolute purity (1 Timothy 5:1-2).

▲ LOOKING AHEAD

Dating may not have existed in Bible times, but true love has never changed. Read a young woman's description of her beloved in Song of Solomon 2:3-9, and the man's description of her in 6:4-9. Then ask Mom and Dad to tell you about their first date together!

"I can't believe she married the prince after only one date."

*F*or Lucia, finding a husband was no problem at all. When she was born, her parents arranged for her to marry a neighbor's son.

So Lucia had known for her entire life that she would marry Stefan when she turned 18. Her main goal till then was to prepare herself to be a good wife and mother. After all, that was the way it was done in her country. Lucia never questioned this arrangement until a relative from America visited the "homeland" with her family. Her cousin talked about the boys she'd dated, about "going steady," about "falling in love." This completely confused Lucia. People just didn't do those things!

Lucia pored through her Bible, looking for verses that talked about this dating business. Surely if that was the way to find a husband, God would say so in His Word! She read and read . . . and what do you think she found?

◆ TAKE A LOOK
Genesis 24:1-4, 10-21, 57-59, 62-66

Tim Stafford writes: "God invented sex, but dating is an American creation. And a stranger custom cannot be found among primitive tribes anywhere."

In a way he's right. People of other times and places have followed a variety of customs for bringing boys and girls together. Strict Spanish fathers don't allow their daughters to see or speak with a boy unless her private chaperone is along. Many tribal fathers allow their daughters to marry only after the prospective groom has paid for her with livestock or other goods! But in the United States meeting and arranging lifetime partnerships has been left up to the young people themselves.

The story of Isaac and Rebekah in Genesis 24:1-4, 10-21, 57-59, 62-66 will give you an idea of the marriage customs during Bible times.

▲ TAKE A STEP
So she became his wife, and he loved her (Genesis 24:67).

Lucia couldn't find anything resembling her cousin's custom in the Bible. But she did read about couples who learned to love deeply after they were married.

Divide into two teams for a family debate. One side will argue for arranged marriages, and the other for dating. Have each team list the pros for their position and the cons of the other. Take turns presenting your cases.

The camels are coming! The camels are coming!

Q
What does God think about dating?

A
Dating is important to God because He cares about all my relationships.

PARENT
Tim Stafford's question-and-answer book on sex, *A LOVE STORY* (Zondervan), would be helpful reading for your teenager.

God gives the best if you leave the choice to Him

Q

How can I have enjoyable dates?

A

Dating is enjoyable and fulfilling when I put my date first, before my own interests.

My, you're home early," Mrs. Bradley remarked as 16-year-old Ernie hustled through the den pulling at his tie and shucking off his coat. "I didn't expect you until midnight. Hey, be careful of your boutonniere."

"Who cares about a dumb flower?" Ernie spat out. "And who cares about stupid silly girls either? It'll be a long time before I spend money on another one!"

"Whatever happened?" his mother asked mildly, hoping to calm the storm. She knew Ernie had saved to buy tickets for the homecoming festivities, a flower for Sherrie, dinner, and gas for the car. Something must have gone terribly wrong.

Ernie angrily explained: "When we got to the restaurant, the girls wouldn't order dinner. They ordered the salad bar and then they took maybe three bites—Joe and I paid seven dollars each for three bites of lettuce! After we got to the school, they went to the rest room about five times. And they couldn't carry a conversation on a pizza plate. Mom, dating is just a waste of time and money. I'd rather go fishing."

◆ TAKE A LOOK / Philippians 2:3-4

Not everyone finds dating to be an enjoyable experience. Like Ernie, some young people come home from their dates feeling let down—even totally frustrated—wondering why the evening didn't meet their expectations. Perhaps they'd find greater enjoyment in dating if they looked at it with God's purposes in view.

Some of the most common reasons for dating today include: to gain status in a group, to build self-esteem, to engage in sex, or just to have fun. Philippians 2:3-4 explains why dating for those reasons only brings frustration.

▲ TAKE A STEP

Dating for self-centered, self-serving reasons is doomed to failure. God intends that our relationships with others be centered in Him and in them, not in ourselves. We should always put others first, even in the dating relationship:

Each of you should look not only to your own interests, but also to the interests of others (Philippians 2:4).

How did Ernie and his date fail to look to the interests of others?

Let the girls in the family suggest some ways that Ernie and Joe could put their dates first. Then the fellows can think of some ideas for Sherrie and her friend.

R andy angrily punched Paige's phone number. Without even greeting her, he demanded, "Why were you talking to Ethan today?"

"Good grief," Paige answered mildly. "He's in my biology lab. We're working on a project. Do you think just because I'm going out with you that I'm not going to speak to another guy?"

"No, but I don't expect you to let him walk you to class. You're wearing my bracelet and that ought to mean something," Randy fumed. "Stay away from him!"

That got Paige riled. "You've got some kind of nerve, Randy Reynolds! I don't belong to you and I'm not going to cut myself off from the rest of the world just because I'm wearing your I.D. bracelet. I like wearing your bracelet because I like you, but I guess it's time to give it back before it turns into a pair of handcuffs!"

◆ TAKE A LOOK / 2 Timothy 2:22

What Randy and Paige may not have realized is that any relationship not built on God's guidelines can quickly seem like a prison.

Yesterday we discovered that people date for different reasons. Some date to gain popularity or status; others need to build their own self-esteem; some simply want a sexual partner. But God has a better idea.

We noted earlier that the Bible doesn't mention the word dating. But God does have a lot to say about relationships. Read 2 Timothy 2:2 for a God-pleasing guideline for your next (or your first!) date.

▲ TAKE A STEP

Flee the evil desires of youth, and pursue righteousness, faith, love and peace, along with those who call on the Lord out of a pure heart (2 Timothy 2:22).

This verse offers godly guidance for all the relationships of life—but especially dating. Let's examine it by discussing these questions:

1. What are three evil desires you should flee?
2. Who must be first in your life to enable you to pursue "righteousness, faith, love and peace"?
3. What one quality should all your companions have?
4. What do you think having a "pure heart" means?
5. What advice would you give Randy and Paige now?

God has a better idea for dating

Q
How can I please God in my dating relationships?

A
Dating pleases God when I pursue righteousness, faith, love, and peace in every date.

PARENT
An easy-to-read book for teens on dating is UPDATE by Fred Hartley (Fleming H. Revell Publishers).

I'm following my "Maker's instructions"

"**C**ome on, Karen. A few kisses never hurt anybody!" "Look, Greg," Karen replied softly, "I like being with you, but I am not going to get physically involved. That's the standard I've set, and I'm not going to break it—for you or anybody else."

"I'm not trying to get 'physically involved,' as you put it," Greg replied sarcastically. "You're being too dramatic. What do you think'll happen? Maybe you need to learn the facts of life—you can't get pregnant from a few kisses."

"Greg, it's hard to stop with just a few kisses. The feelings men and women have for each other—they're powerful. I know God designed those feelings, but He also gave us instructions for expressing them. You may not believe that; a lot of people don't. But I think things work better when you follow the 'Maker's instructions.'"

Q

Why is premarital sex wrong?

A

God intends that sex be reserved for marriage.

◆TAKE A LOOK
1 Thessalonians 4:3-8; 1 Corinthians 6:18–7:5

Karen and Greg's disagreement over a few kisses revealed some basic differences in their views of sex—the intimate physical relationships between men and women. Greg seemed to think that sex outside of marriage is okay if nobody "gets hurt" (in other words, pregnant). That's a common view in today's world. Karen, on the other hand, agreed with God's view that sex before marriage is wrong.

Tim Stafford (whom we've already quoted this week) says this about God's view of sex: "Sex is dynamite. You don't play with dynamite, you use it very carefully—and in just the right spot. The right spot for sex is marriage. There, two people who have committed themselves to each other can give their bodies to each other. . . . They can be secure about it, knowing that their commitment is forever."

Proverbs 6:32, 1 Thessalonians 4:3-8, and 1 Corinthians 6:18–7:5 present God's view of sex. (By the way, the Bible uses two words to describe sex outside of marriage: fornication and adultery.)

▲ TAKE A STEP
Each man should have his own wife, and each woman her own husband (1 Corinthians 7:2).

Are you willing to reserve the sexual relationship until marriage? You'll find it's worth the wait. Think together of some rules for dating to help you achieve that godly goal.

REPENTANCE

D"*ad, I said I was sorry. What more do you want me to do?"* Dean said defiantly. Mr. Cranshaw looked sternly at his twelve-year-old son. Dean had indeed said he was sorry, but his tone of voice and facial expression indicated he wasn't really concerned about what he had done. He was only sorry he'd gotten caught.

"I think you need to answer one more question," Mr. Cranshaw said. "You took your brother's dirt bike without asking. Would you do it again if you knew you wouldn't get caught?"

"Sure I would!" Dean said belligerently. "If the sorry thing hadn't blown up, nobody would know and I wouldn't be in trouble."

"Um-hmm," Mr. Cranshaw mused. "Am I hearing you say that you think an action is bad only if you get caught?"

"I don't know," Dean grumbled, lowering his head.

"I think you do know," his father replied. "Let's call what you did by its name—sin. I think you need to repent, to agree with God that you have sinned and then turn yourself around. Am I right?"

Tears welled in Dean's eyes. "Y-y-yes," he stammered. "It was wrong and I really am sorry." His dad gave him a big hug.

◆ LOOKING AT REPENTANCE

Some may think repentance is simply being sorry for the wrong they have done. Others may think it is promising to do good. But as Dean realized, repentance is **agreeing with God about our sin and then changing our behavior.** As Jesus Himself said . . .

● KEY VERSE ON REPENTANCE

"I have not come to call the righteous, but sinners to repentance" (Luke 5:32).

▲ LOOKING AHEAD

Repentance is a decision to turn away from every thought, word, deed, and habit that God says is wrong.

According to 2 Corinthians 7:9-11, what does true repentance involve? Think about the difference between "godly" and "worldly" sorrow. Do you think Dean experienced both?

"I think it's a bad sign, son, when you end your confession with 'to be continued.' "

If you break one, you break them all

The Ten Commandments form the core of God's law. Do you know them well enough to number them in order? (See Exodus 20:1-17 if you need help.)

You shall not steal.
Honor your father and mother.
You shall have no other gods before Me.
You shall not covet (desire with great envy).
You shall not murder.
You shall not misuse the name of the Lord your God.
You shall not give false testimony (lie).
You shall not commit adultery.
Remember the Sabbath day by keeping it holy.
You shall not make for yourself an idol (put anything ahead of God Himself).

◆ **TAKE A LOOK / Psalm 14:1-3; Romans 3:10-12, 23**

The Ten Commandments summarize what God requires of all people. Failing to meet these standards is what the Bible calls sin.

Sin may not be a popular subject, but it is a universal fact. You'll find sin described in the newspapers, depicted on TV, and even practiced in your neighborhood. In fact, everyone experiences it personally every day!

Sin has many consequences. It separates us from other people. It causes much of the world's misery. But its most dreadful result is that it separates people from God—eternally.

Read how the Bible describes sin in Psalm 14:1-3 and Romans 3:10-12, 23.

Q

Why do I need to repent?

A

Repentance is required of everyone, because we all have sinned.

▲ **TAKE A STEP**

Salvation means deliverance from sin and its penalty. By His life, death, and resurrection, Jesus Christ paid for sin. Repentance—agreeing with God about your sin and turning from it—is the first step of salvation. As Paul wrote:

I have declared to both Jews and Greeks that they must turn to God in repentance and have faith in our Lord Jesus (Acts 20:21).

Some people have a hard time believing they have sinned, especially when they've lived "good" lives and haven't done anything nearly as bad as the criminals they read about daily.

But from God's viewpoint, everyone has sinned; no one can obey Him perfectly.

Reread the Ten Commandments listed above. Have you obeyed each one perfectly . . . or do you need to agree with God about your sin?

I have decided to follow Jesus," Peggy sang in Sunday school. She believed God made the world, but she didn't know much more about Him. Until she met Joyce.

Joyce had recently moved in next door and was in four of Peggy's classes. As their friendship grew, they talked about everything—boys, clothes, parents, and God.

Joyce told Peggy that God's Son Jesus had died to pay for humanity's sin. When Joyce mentioned repentance, Peggy's curiosity grew. She felt she should do something about it, but she wasn't sure what. So here she was—in Sunday school for the first time.

"No turning back, no turning back!" As Peggy continued to sing, those talks with Joyce became clearer. "That's what Joyce meant," Peggy thought, her eyes wide. "If everyone's a sinner, then that includes me. Jesus' death paid for everybody's sin, but each person has to repent and believe individually. So I'm the one who has to decide."

◆ **TAKE A LOOK / Acts 2:36-41; Romans 10:9-13**

Some people think that being born in a Christian family or going to church as a child makes them Christians. But as Joyce realized, it's a decision each person must make individually. And it begins with repentance.

Repentance doesn't mean that you must become a better person before Christ comes into your life. It does mean you see yourself as a sinner and want to turn away from anything that displeases God. When you become a believer, His Spirit within you will enable you to live in a way that pleases Him.

Read Acts 2:36-41 and Romans 10:9-13 to find out more.

▲ **TAKE A STEP**

Have you repented and given Jesus control of your life? If you aren't sure, pray this prayer now:

"Lord Jesus, I admit that I am a sinner. I have sinned in my thoughts, words, and actions. I am sorry for my sins and I turn from them in repentance. I believe that You died for me, paying the penalty for my sin, and that You rose again. Come into my life as my Savior and Lord. Cleanse me and take control of me. I want to serve You and love You all my life. Amen."

If you prayed this prayer and meant it, thank Christ that He has come into your life as He said He would. And be sure to tell another Christian what you've done!

Repentance is a big word— and a big decision

Q

How do I repent?

A

Repentance involves agreeing with God about my sin and turning from it.

PARENT
The process of repentance also involves restitution when necessary. Teach your child that when his sin affects the property or reputations of others, he must do what he can to make it right.

You're in the family of faith forever!

T hat morning in Sunday school, Peggy asked Jesus Christ to be her Savior. But now, almost a month later, she still had the same sassy attitude toward her mom.

"I don't understand it," she muttered to Joyce as they waited for the bus. "I know I'm not honoring my mom when I yell at her. And that's sin. Am I really a Christian?"

"Sure you are, but you're a baby Christian, and it takes time to grow up." Joyce smiled at her friend. "Each day make it your goal to obey God in everything—even in the way you talk to your mom. Then, when you know you've sinned, confess it and turn from it. And if you've hurt anyone, try to make it right."

"You mean like when you apologized to your mom for talking on the phone after 10:00? I thought that was kinda silly since she didn't already know about it." Peggy paused. "But, I guess you and God knew, right? I think I'd better talk to my mom."

Will I have to repent more than once?

Repentance on a daily basis keeps my fellowship with God fresh.

◆ TAKE A LOOK / John 13:1-10

Suppose, like Peggy, you've been rude to *your* parents. There may be tension in the air, upset feelings, bad attitudes; but have you stopped being their child? Of course not! The *relationship* hasn't changed, but the *fellowship* has been hurt. Your membership in a family depends on your *birth*; your fellowship with other family members depends on *behavior*. When you apologize, your family will forgive you, and your fellowship with them is made right again.

It's that way in God's family too. When believers sin, they don't stop being His children; but their fellowship with God is broken until they confess and repent of that sin. Because we're human, we need to practice that kind of repentance every day.

Jesus illustrated this truth when He washed the disciples' feet. After you read John 13:1-10, tell how it illustrates the truth that salvation is a one-time event, but being cleansed from sin is an everyday need.

▲ TAKE A STEP

If we confess our sins, he is faithful and just and will forgive us our sins and purify us from all unrighteousness (1 John 1:9).

Today and tomorrow, spend time together memorizing that verse. Then practice it each and every day to keep your fellowship with God fresh and fulfilling!

Peggy and Joyce had become good friends, but their moms saw each other only occasionally—like tonight at the PTA.

"You know," Mrs. Adkins said to Mrs. Rollins, Joyce's mother, "I just can't tell you how glad I am that Joyce became Peggy's friend. She's such a good influence. Before we moved here, Peggy was running around with the wrong crowd. I was afraid she was headed for trouble. But since she met Joyce, she's a different girl."

Mrs. Rollins smiled at her neighbor. "You're right," she replied, "Peggy is a different girl from the one we first met. But it's not because of Joyce. It's because of Jesus."

Mrs. Adkins looked puzzled. "That's what Peggy says too. She's tried to explain about Jesus coming to live inside her, but I don't really understand. Anyway, whatever it is, I'm living with a wonderfully different daughter!"

◆ TAKE A LOOK / 1 Peter 2:11-17

When Peggy repented and turned her life over to the Lord, her commitment to Him was total. She wanted to grow as His child. And grow she did!

She attended church regularly with Joyce and studied the Bible on her own. She marked the passages with commands or instructions. But Peggy did more than underline the words. By the power of the Holy Spirit she obeyed what she read. And little by little, her life began to change. She was becoming more like Jesus every day.

As a loving Father, God expects His children to grow more Christlike in their character and behavior. As we do, the change will be obvious.

In 1 Peter 2:11-17, the apostle Peter describes both the results repentance can have on us and its effect on those around us.

▲ TAKE A STEP

Peter echoes the words of Jesus, who told His followers:

"You are the light of the world. . . . Let your light shine before men, that they may see your good deeds and praise your Father in heaven" (Matthew 5:14-16).

Think about your own life this past week. When people looked at you, what did they see? Could you honestly say they saw Jesus at work in your life?

Others will know when they see you "glow"

What will happen to me when I repent?

Repentance brings changes in my life that others can see.

PARENT
Is there a habit you need to end? A wrong done to a neighbor, co-worker, or family member you need to confess? Ask your family for prayer as you correct the situation in God's strength.

EASTER

● ● ● ● ● ● ● ● ● ● ● ● ● ● ●

From the Jerusalem Clarion, 18 Nisan, 33 A.D:
Body of Executed Traitor Missing from Tomb!

JERUSALEM—The body of Jesus of Nazareth is missing from the tomb where it was placed shortly after his crucifixion last week.

Because this self-proclaimed Messiah had repeatedly claimed he would come back to life, Roman and Jewish authorities had sealed the tomb and positioned a Roman guard unit there.

Their fears seem to have come true, however, as unconfirmed reports indicate Jesus' followers somehow stole the body.

Wanted for questioning are: Peter, alias Cephas; James and John Bar-Zebedee; and the dead man's mother, Mary of Nazareth. The high priest offers a reward for information regarding their whereabouts.

◆ LOOKING AT EASTER

First-century Jerusalem didn't have live TV coverage.

But can you imagine how today's news correspondents might cover the story at the empty tomb?

Today, almost 2,000 years later, some people still doubt that Christ's resurrection actually happened. Instead of examining the evidence, they accept theories that try to explain it away. As Christians, we need to understand why Jesus' resurrection is so important. The apostle Paul tells us why in this verse:

● KEY VERSE ON EASTER

If Christ has not been raised, our preaching is useless and so is your faith (1 Corinthians 15:14).

▲ LOOKING AHEAD

The central belief of the Christian faith is that Jesus rose from the dead. That's a historical fact, not a fanciful myth. We'll take a hard look at the evidence this week.

Matthew's report of today's headline story differs from the one above. After you read Matthew 28:11-15, write a version of the facts titled "The Chief Priests' Conspiracy."

"Yes, son, Easter is a religious holiday, but 'Where is Easter Island?' isn't an unconstitutional question."

*I*t can't be," the high priest whispered. "It's not possible!"

"Look," the soldier replied in a surly tone, "we never left that tomb for one moment. Besides, we knew if anybody tried anything, it would be at dawn. We were ready for them.

"But suddenly the ground shook, and we saw this . . . this . . . I don't know what. He appeared right in front of our eyes and rolled the stone away like it was nothing!

"Scared me so bad I fainted dead away. So did my mates. But I'll vouch for this: This Jesus' lily-livered followers didn't do it. It was something supernatural."

"Well, don't worry," Caiaphas said. "We'll handle it from here. You back us up when we say Jesus' followers stole the body, and we'll clear you with the governor. But don't ever mention an angel. Next thing we know, the people will be believing that this Jesus is actually alive."

◆ TAKE A LOOK / Matthew 28:1-15

The soldiers were threatened by it. The Jewish leaders were powerless to change it. Jesus' followers were thrilled by it. And everybody in Jerusalem knew it: Jesus' tomb was empty!

But is it possible that the disciples stole His body and then made up a rumor about the Resurrection? That's what the Jewish leaders claimed, as you'll discover by reading Matthew 28:1-15.

▲ TAKE A STEP

The theory that the disciples stole Jesus' body is full of holes. In the first place, they couldn't possibly get past the guards, who would have paid with their lives if they had fallen asleep on duty. Secondly, at this point the disciples were cowardly fishermen, not fearsome fighters. In fact, they went into hiding after the crucifixion.

But the best evidence is what took place in the disciples' lives. Only a risen, living Jesus could transform them from cowards in hiding to courageous Christians. Despite extreme persecution, not one ever denied that Jesus was risen. In fact:

With great power the apostles continued to testify to the resurrection of the Lord Jesus, and much grace was upon them all (Acts 4:33).

Because they knew the truth of the Resurrection, the disciples changed their world. And Jesus is alive today! What are you doing to change your world?

The mystery of the missing Messiah

Q

Could the disciples have moved Jesus' body?

A

Easter is celebrated because Jesus left His tomb supernaturally, not because His disciples carried Him out.

No doubt about it—the women were right!

"What are you doing to stop this wild rumor?" Caiaphas demanded furiously. "We're losing control of the people, and it's all because of some silly women! They probably got lost and went to the wrong tomb—an empty one. Then they started this wild story that Jesus is risen. Women!" He spat out the word. "Why don't their husbands keep them at home!"

The younger priest was shaken by the high priest's outburst. "Sir," he tried to explain, "these aren't ignorant country women. One is even the wife of Herod's manager. They've been traveling with Jesus, spending their own money to look after his needs. You saw them yourself at the Crucifixion. They stayed till the end. Surely they went to the tomb. When you put their story with what the guards said, don't you think it might be possible that—"

"Of course not, you fool! Dead men don't come back to life. Now get out!"

◆ **TAKE A LOOK / Luke 8:1-3; 23:55-56; 24:1-12; Matthew 27:55-61**

The Bible doesn't tell us what the high priest said about the women. But critics have claimed that the women were so upset by grief that they lost their way and went to the wrong tomb. There, the story goes, a gardener tried to point them to another tomb. Supposedly, the women were terrified, thinking him an angel, and jumped to the wrong conclusion.

But that theory doesn't fit the facts. The women had loved and served Jesus. They stayed with Him to the end and even watched the burial. In many ways their loyalty and courage exceeded that of the disciples'.

Find out who these women were and how far their faithfulness to Jesus led them by reading Luke 8:1-3; 23:55-56; 24:1-12; and Matthew 27:55-61.

▲ **TAKE A STEP**

Matthew and Luke carefully tell us that . . .
The women who had come with Jesus from Galilee followed Joseph and saw the tomb and how his body was laid in it (Luke 23:55).

Could all these women forget where Jesus was buried? If that were true, the priests could have pointed out the "right" tomb, and even produced the body of Jesus. They did none of those things.

There's only one solution to this "mystery." Did you find it in Luke 24:6-8? Why do you suppose so many people won't accept that solution?

Q

Did the women go to the wrong tomb?

A

Easter is celebrated because Jesus Christ really rose from the grave.

*S*ince becoming roommates, Craig and Anthony had talked a lot about Jesus. Now they were winding up another discussion. "Think about this," Craig concluded. "The resurrection of Jesus Christ is either a vicious hoax, or it is a fantastic fact of history."

Anthony smiled sarcastically. "You prove scientifically that Jesus Christ rose from the dead and I'll believe it."

"Well, under those circumstances you'll die without believing."

"Aren't you even going to try to prove it?" Anthony demanded.

"No," Craig replied. "The Resurrection is a fact of history. No historical fact can ever be repeated, so it can't be verified scientifically. So if that's what it takes for you to believe, it won't happen. You'll die without Jesus as your Lord and will spend eternity apart from Him."

Anthony sat in silence. "Uh, Craig, remember what you said the other day about becoming a Christian? Could you go over that again?"

◆ TAKE A LOOK / Luke 1:1-4; Acts 1:1-3

Like Anthony, many people feel they can't accept something unless it can be proved scientifically. But there are many things the scientific method cannot investigate, because it involves controlled experiments. For instance, the scientific method doesn't help at all with historical events, because they happen once and can't be repeated.

Historians look for different evidence: letters, diaries, or books telling about an event; favorable eyewitness reports in those documents; reports from hostile witnesses; and things that happen as the result of an event.

Luke, a physician, wrote two such historical documents. The book of Luke is his account of Jesus' life. Acts is a history of what happened after His resurrection. After you read Luke 1:1-4 and Acts 1:1-3, tell why you think Luke was a careful historian.

▲ TAKE A STEP

Luke wrote:
I myself have carefully investigated everything from the beginning (Luke 1:3).

Christ's resurrection stands up to historical investigation. That's why it is the foundation of our Christian faith. Now, how would you answer Anthony's last question?

You can't view history under a microscope

Can the Resurrection be proved scientifically?

Easter celebrates a historical fact supported by eyewitness accounts.

PARENT
Children are constantly exposed to "scientific" theories that contradict Scripture. Have you taught your child to trust the Bible and question the theories? Books on science and the Bible in your church library or Christian bookstore can help.

Two thousand years of nonstop results

Q

How has the Resurrection changed history?

A

Easter reminds us that because of Christ's resurrection, the world has never been the same.

It's unthinkable!" the high priest exclaimed to his companion. "I can understand how the masses—ignorant and uneducated as they are—would look to those apostles as miracle workers. But Saul? Gamaliel's star pupil? I can't believe it!"

"So true," the other priest agreed. "But he's not the first, you know. Nicodemus and Joseph of Arimathea were following the Galilean even before he was executed."

"And now look—three years later, Jerusalem is full of converts to Jesus," the high priest said crossly. "And more joining every day! Even my own daughter."

"Some of them still come to synagogue on the Sabbath, but they always meet to worship on the first day of the week too—Jews and Gentiles together. They claim it's a way of celebrating Jesus' resurrection." He shook his head sadly. "Gamaliel must be beside himself with grief over Paul."

◆ **TAKE A LOOK / Acts 5:27-39**

As leaders of the Jewish nation, the high priests had a big problem: Jews by the hundreds were deserting the "faith of their fathers." They formed the core group of the Christian church, whose very existence is one of the best evidences that the resurrection of Jesus really happened. Read Acts 5:27-39. Was Gamaliel correct?

▲ **TAKE A STEP**

"If it is from God, you will not be able to stop these men; you will only find yourselves fighting against God" (Acts 5:39).

The church grew and spread throughout the known world in spite of tremendous persecution. Nothing could stop it. Not only that, but Jewish believers quickly gave up worshiping on Saturdays and began meeting on the first day, Sunday.

There is no other explanation for this except the truth: They wanted to celebrate their Savior's resurrection once a week.

Even more dramatic evidence for the Resurrection is the changed lives of those who knew Jesus. The early Christians were tortured, beaten, and executed to prevent the spread of their teaching. Yet they willingly gave up their lives.

Facts like these prove the Resurrection. And so do the experiences of the millions of people who have come to know Jesus as Lord down through the centuries. Is your life serving as "proof" of the living Lord? How could you share your evidence today?

LOYALTY

*T*hey *stand before the judge—young and old, tall and short, dark-skinned and light. Many have tears in their eyes; all are filled with joy. They come from dozens of countries, speaking a variety of languages, though all of them have learned some English.*

Then the long-awaited moment arrives. Together they raise their right hands and recite the oath of allegiance.

These people are new citizens of the United States of America. From this moment on, they have the same rights and obligations as a native-born citizen. They must obey the laws of their new country, pay its taxes, and support its government. In a word, they must be loyal.

◆ LOOKING AT LOYALTY

Some people experience loyalty when Fido meets them at the bus stop day after day. Others think loyalty is sticking by someone in dangerous circumstances. Some families define loyalty as blood ties. But there's more to loyalty.

The word *loyalty* comes from the Latin word for *law*. It refers to being faithful to keep legal obligations. More broadly it means **a total commitment to a person or cause in good times and bad.** God Himself is our model for loyalty. He is steadfast, trustworthy, and faithful. He keeps His promises.

● KEY VERSE ON LOYALTY

Know therefore that the LORD your God is God; he is the faithful God, keeping his covenant of love to a thousand generations of those who love him and keep his commands (Deuteronomy 7:9).

▲ LOOKING AHEAD

John 19:16-18, 25-30, 38-42 tell about three men who risked their lives by remaining loyal to Jesus when things looked bad. How do you think the apostle John ("the disciple Jesus loved"), Joseph of Arimathea, and Nicodemus showed loyalty? What would you do if your family members were in tough circumstances?

"Goodbye, Dad. I'm defecting to the West."

The glue that keeps us sticking together

Q

Is loyalty more than a feeling?

A

Loyalty is an obligation I have to others regardless of how I feel.

PARENT
Perhaps you know of someone who will be taking the citizenship oath soon. Plan to help them celebrate that special milestone with a small gift or a meal.

When someone becomes an American citizen, he or she takes this oath. (What does it tell you about loyalty?)

"I hereby declare on oath that I absolutely and entirely renounce and abjure all allegiance and fidelity to any foreign prince, potentate, state, or sovereignty of whom or which I have heretofore been a subject or citizen; that I will support and defend the Constitution and laws of the United States of America against all enemies, foreign and domestic; that I will bear true faith and allegiance to the same; that I will bear arms on behalf of the United States when required by the law; that I will perform work of national importance under civilian direction when required by the law; and that I take this obligation freely without any mental reservation or purpose of evasion; so help me God."

◆ TAKE A LOOK
Numbers 30:2; Deuteronomy 23:21

That oath is a verbal agreement pledging loyalty to a nation. People take many other oaths. The marriage vow, the Armed Forces oath, the oath of office for elected officials, oaths taken in courtrooms—they all bind two people (or groups) together in legal agreements requiring loyalty on both sides. Special ceremonies often mark these agreements, reminding the participants that what they are doing is important and legally binding. In many cases, oaths and vows have the force of law behind them.

God shows how important loyalty is when He speaks of oaths and vows in Numbers 30:2 and Deuteronomy 23:21. You'll see how strongly God wants us to be loyal to one another by reading Malachi 2:10,13-16, which focuses on the marriage vow.

▲ TAKE A STEP

God's words about loyalty in marriage can be applied to all our relationships in which loyalty is important:

Guard yourself in your spirit, and do not break faith (Malachi 2:16).

How loyal are you to your family members and friends? Loyalty expresses itself in what you say and how you act toward them. Using the oath of citizenship above as a model, make up your own oath of family loyalty. Then plan a ceremony for later this week in which you'll "pledge allegiance" to one another.

Tom Sawyer and Huckleberry Finn had seen Injun Joe murder a man. They were terrified that if they told he would come after them. "Now, look-a-here, Tom, let's swear to keep mum."

"I'm agreed. It's the best thing. Would you just hold hands and swear that we—"

"Oh, no. That's good enough for little rubbishy common things, but there orter be writing 'bout a big thing like this. And blood."

Tom's whole being applauded this idea. So he unwound the thread from one of his needles, and each boy pricked the ball of his thumb and squeezed out a drop of blood. In time, after many squeezes, Tom managed to sign his initials, using the ball of his little finger for a pen. Then he showed Huck how to make an H and an F, and the oath was complete. "Tom," whispered Huckleberry, "does this keep us from ever telling—always?"

"Of course it does. It don't make any difference what happens, we got to keep mum. We'd drop down dead—don't you know?"

"Yes, I reckon that's so."*

◆ TAKE A LOOK / Hebrews 9:1, 11-28

To show their loyalty, Tom and Huck became "blood brothers." That kind of covenant is one of the oldest and most solemn kinds of vows people can ever make to one another.

God made up the idea of a blood covenant. He made a blood covenant with Abraham when He promised him a new land and offspring to fill it. He made a blood covenant with the Israelites when He told them to spread lamb's blood on their doorposts so the death angel would pass over their homes. And He made a new blood covenant when Jesus shed His blood in payment for our sin.

God's blood covenant is different from human covenants, because He has done all the work. He makes—and keeps—all the promises. You can understand God's covenants better by reading Hebrews 9:1, 11-28.

▲ TAKE A STEP

Christ is the mediator of a new covenant (Hebrews 9:15).

Because God has made a blood covenant with humanity, His loyalty to His children never fails. His Word is good—forever. Together, think of three of God's promises to you. Then thank Him in prayer for keeping them!

God gave His Word, and He'll keep it forever

Q

How has God shown loyalty to us?

A

Loyalty on God's part is based on the covenant He has lovingly made with us.

*Condensed from Chapter 10, THE ADVENTURES OF TOM SAWYER by Mark Twain.

Loyalty begins at home (And aren't you glad!)

Q

To whom should I be loyal?

A

Loyalty should be shown to all the special people in my life—especially my family.

M ay I speak to you?" Mr. Hargis asked sternly as he stepped into the Smiths' kitchen. "It's about your sons."

"Why, of course," Mr. Smith replied pleasantly. "Would you like a cup of coffee?"

"No, thank you," Mr. Hargis answered curtly. "Mr. Smith, your sons have put a BB hole in my sliding glass door. They're going to pay for it. It's clear to me they've got no respect for —"

"Excuse me just a minute, please," Mr. Smith said, stopping Mr. Hargis's accusations in midstream. "My boys may have BB guns, but they also know when and how to use them. Are you sure it wasn't someone else?"

"I've never seen anyone else in the neighborhood with a BB gun. It must have been them. They'll have to replace my door."

"Mr. Hargis, I don't like to disagree, but that doesn't sound like my sons. I promise I'll talk to them about it tonight and get back with you tomorrow. Thank you for coming over."

◆ TAKE A LOOK / Ruth 1:3-18

Loyalty keeps people together. We should be loyal to our fellow workers, our country, our church, our friends, and our family.

Mr. Smith was loyal to his sons. So when Mr. Hargis accused them of vandalism, he planned to investigate carefully before blaming or punishing them.

The Bible is full of stories about people who honored their commitments wholeheartedly, without worrying about what might happen as a result. As we study their lives, we can draw strength and courage from their examples. Meet one such person who was supremely loyal by reading Ruth 1:3-18.

▲ TAKE A STEP

"Where you go I will go, and where you stay I will stay. Your people will be my people and your God my God. Where you die I will die, and there will I be buried" (Ruth 1:16-17).

Ruth's life pictures loyalty in action. Her words have often been used in marriage ceremonies as part of the vows the bride and groom make to each other.

How did Mr. Smith show loyalty to his sons? Why do you think it's important for parents to be loyal to their children . . . children to their parents . . . husbands and wives to each other? Today would be a good day for your "family loyalty oath" ceremony, wouldn't it?

• When Mrs. Rhodes introduced her daughter, her friend commented on how nice Ellen looked. "Yes, well, I'll say this about her," Mrs. Rhodes remarked. "She's not the brightest of our children, but she's pretty."

• Mr. Johnson and his wife were late for dinner with another couple. He apologized angrily: "I hate being late, but my wife is never on time. I'm sorry she held us up."

• "Hey, potato boy!" Rodney teased his overweight friend in the desk across the aisle. "How many scales have you broken lately?"

• "She may be my sister, but she's an air head," Bob said sarcastically to his friends. "Look up the word dumb in the dictionary and you'll find her picture there."

◆ **TAKE A LOOK**
Matthew 18:15-17; Luke 6:37; James 4:11
Each of those stories depicts disloyalty in action. It's easy to hurt the people we love by belittling them with cutting remarks or embarrassing them in front of others.

God wants us to be loyal to others as well as to Him. Because He is steadfast, trustworthy, and faithful, God provides us an example of loyal love. He always tells the truth. He always puts His love into action. And His Word tells us how to treat those who deserve our loyalty.

Read the verses below, and then draw a line to the statement at the right that describes the actions we should take.

This Scripture . . .
1. Matthew 18:15-17
2. Luke 6:37
3. James 4:11
4. Philippians 2:4

says loyalty means:
a. Not being critical or condemning
b. Not slandering or speaking against
c. Protecting others from embarrassment
d. Privately discussing a problem with the person involved

▲ **TAKE A STEP**
Think about the opening stories again. Do they remind you of something disloyal you've done lately? Paul beautifully describes loyal love in 1 Corinthians 13. Let the verse below encourage you to treat your family and friends with loving loyalty at all times:

[Love] always protects, always trusts, always hopes, always perseveres (1 Corinthians 13:7).

If the going gets rough, the loyal hang tough

Q

How can I show loyalty in daily life?

A

Loyalty demands that I treat others with love.

PREACHERS

*Y*ou're frantic! Your church has put you in charge of finding a guest preacher for the upcoming Bible conference. So far the applicants haven't seemed all that great. Maybe if you just looked over the resumes you've received one more time, one would pop out . . .

• Noah. Occupation: boatbuilder. Comments: persistent; gives attention to detail; follows instructions. Experience: preached 120 years. Results: no one listened.

• Moses. Occupation: politician-turned-shepherd. Comments: very humble; may not hold a crowd's attention; has a speech problem.

• Jonah. Occupation: traveler. Comments: doesn't seem really dependable; illustrates his sermons with some strange fish stories.

• John. Occupation: unknown. Comments: dresses in odd, rough clothing; requires an unusual diet. Stresses repentance in his sermons; may turn people off.

◆ THINKING ABOUT PREACHERS

You probably wouldn't have chosen one of these men to speak at a Bible conference. Yet each man was handpicked by God to deliver His message. Each was on God's "all-star team of prophets."

Today we think of a preacher as the leader of a local church. Sometimes he's called a minister, a pastor, an elder, or a priest; but just like the prophets of old, a preacher is **one who proclaims God's Word.** He obeys this command Jesus made to all His followers:

● KEY VERSE ON PREACHERS

"Go into all the world and preach the good news to all creation" (Mark 16:15).

▲ LOOKING AHEAD

God uses people with different personalities and talents to preach His Word. Start learning what preachers do by reading Paul's instructions to the young preacher Timothy in 2 Timothy 4:1-2.

What four things is a preacher to do? How is he to do them?

*A*lthough he received little education, his preaching has touched the hearts and minds of millions of people around the world. Born in 1628, the son of a tinker (a person who mends and makes utensils), he served in the army when he was 16 and 17, then returned home to work with his father. He never thought of serving God in any way, let alone as a preacher.

But God had other plans. At age 19 he married a Christian girl and eventually came to know the Lord himself. When he was 27, he began to preach. Arrested for preaching without a license, he remained in prison for 12 years.

But still he preached—through the power of his pen! This preacher/prisoner wrote a book that has influenced hundreds of other preachers, led many people to know the Lord, and is second only to the Bible as an all-time religious bestseller.

◆ TAKE A LOOK / 2 Timothy 2:15-16, 22-26

Called by Encyclopedia Britannica "the greatest literary genius produced by the Puritan movement," this uneducated preacher from an obscure town in England wrote *The Pilgrim's Progress*. His name is John Bunyan.

Today, most preachers have far more education than John Bunyan did. Many have gone to college or attended a Bible school or studied at a seminary.

But education is not the only qualification a preacher should have. Paul's advice to Timothy in 2 Timothy 2:15-16, 22-26, reveals some qualities God looks for in a preacher. And so should you!

▲ TAKE A STEP

Every preacher's goal should be this: to be a servant approved by God,

A workman who does not need to be ashamed and who correctly handles the word of truth (2 Timothy 2:15).

John Bunyan correctly handled God's Word. He did all he possibly could to get its message to the people. He did nothing that caused anyone to doubt its truth.

Who are some of the faithful preachers whose ministry has blessed your life personally? Think about pastors, missionaries, Bible teachers, and even education directors. Close in prayer, thanking God for them and asking His blessings on them now.

The preacher's power comes from God

What education is a preacher required to have?

Preachers must be able to proclaim God's Word faithfully and accurately.

PARENT
It's your responsibility to insure that your family is taught by a preacher who is true to God's Word, not the teachings of men.

He's not a superman, but he serves a super God!

Q

Are preachers better than other believers?

A

Preachers are people just like us, but their gift is explaining God's Word.

PARENT
From time to time drop a note of encouragement to your own pastor or to guest speakers in your church.

Can you imagine that a great preacher would . . .
. . . often be accused of extravagance?
. . . feel lonely away from his books?
. . . not talk to anyone after a church service?
. . . love to play practical jokes?
. . . think his ministry was a failure?
. . . use so much humor in his sermons that someone would try to kill him for it?
. . . feel inferior and need constant reassurance that his congregation loved him?
. . . think tape recorders were an abomination?

◆TAKE A LOOK / 1 Kings 19:1-13
All of those statements describe men of the past who were recognized as forceful, faithful preachers.

Like us, they were mere human beings. No two of them were alike. Some were fiery and emotional; others were cool and reserved. Some had weak voices that didn't carry far; others had booming voices that could reach thousands without amplification. Some were well educated. Some had little education. In fact, most of them were normal! All had individual strengths and weaknesses God used to reach others.

God delights to use people in spite of their weaknesses. Would you like proof? Read the story of the great Old Testament preacher Elijah in 1 Kings 19:1-13.

▲ TAKE A STEP
Elijah wasn't the first preacher (and he certainly won't be the last) to say, "It's just not worth it, Lord! I'd rather be dead."

Being a preacher is hard work! A preacher never goes off duty. He must deal with lots of overtime, intense concentration, innumerable people with seemingly impossible problems, hectic schedules, and tight finances. Like Elijah, some become discouraged.

Now that you know your preacher isn't a "superman," what can you do to help? There's an answer in this verse:

Remember your leaders, who spoke the word of God to you. Consider the outcome of their way of life and imitate their faith (Hebrews 13:7).

List three ways your family can "remember your leaders" so they will not be easily discouraged. Choose one thing on that list to do this week and get started today.

88 / PREACHERS DAY THREE ❑

*S*ix-year-old Ansley was pouting in the back seat of the car as the family drove home from church.

Her father was puzzled. "Why are you so grumpy today?" he asked. "I thought my favorite little girl loved to go to church."

"I like church all right," Ansley burst out, "but I don't want to go to Sunday school ever again. Not ever."

Mr. and Mrs. Jenkins looked at each other. "Well," her father replied calmly, "I can see that you've got some angry feelings about Sunday school. How come?"

"It's Kevin Hunt. He's so bossy. Today when I was swinging, Kevin came up and made me get off. He said it was his swing because his daddy is the preacher. He said nobody could have a turn unless he said so. Kevin always does things like that—every time we play. And it's no fun."

Then tears welled up in Ansley's eyes. "Is that really true, Daddy? Is Kevin really in charge of the playground?"

◆TAKE A LOOK / 1 Timothy 5:17; Titus 1:5-10

Kevin seemed to think that since his father was the pastor of the church, he was also the boss of the church. So Kevin used his father's position to bully his classmates. But as Mr. and Mrs. Jenkins were quick to explain to Ansley, Kevin had it all wrong. The preacher is not the boss of the church.

Not every preacher is the pastor of a church, but those who are pastors usually have help from a group of people chosen from the congregation. Depending on the kind of church, this group may be called the vestry, the session, the administrative board, the deacons or the elders.

You'll see that no one person is supposed to do all the work alone when you read 1 Timothy 5:17. And reading Titus 1:5-10 will explain the qualifications for those church leaders.

▲ TAKE A STEP

Appoint elders in every town (Titus 1:5).
Elders . . . direct the affairs of the church (1 Timothy 5:17).

See if you can answer these questions about the people who "direct the affairs" of your church: What name are they called collectively? What process does your church use to choose them? What are their duties in your church?

If you're not sure, why not ask your pastor? You'll understand his work better when you know those he counts on for help.

Who's in charge here, anyway?

Q

Does the preacher run the church?

A

Preachers work together with other leaders to make sure the church does its job correctly.

Is the preacher too busy to get anything done?

Q

What is the preacher's main responsibility?

A

Preachers are responsible to study and pray in order to help people understand God's Word.

When Pastor Simms got home late Saturday afternoon, he was exhausted.

"John, you can't keep this up," Mrs. Simms murmured as she rubbed her husband's tired, sore back.

"What else could I do?" he replied. "I had told Mrs. Jenkins I was coming by when Betty Franklin called and told me Ed had been taken to the hospital. I had to go."

"Well, that may be, but did you have to come back and mow the lawn at the church? You didn't even stop for lunch, did you?"

Pastor Simms gulped down a second glass of lemonade. "What would the visitors think if they drove up and could barely see the sidewalk for the weeds? They'd think no one cares."

Mrs. Simms looked long and hard at her husband. "Honey, I'm beginning to think no one does. Not enough people are helping out."

"We'll have to talk about this another time. I've got to finish my sermon. Don't wait up for me."

◆ TAKE A LOOK / Acts 6:1-7

Pastor Simms's small congregation expected a lot from him, and he expected even more of himself. As a result, he was trying to do things a pastor isn't meant to do.

During the days of the early church when Jesus' disciples were preaching the Good News in the city of Jerusalem, they soon discovered that ministering to all the believers was more work than the 12 of them could handle. As you read Acts 6:1-7, you'll see what the problem was, why they needed to solve it, and what happened when they did.

▲ TAKE A STEP

"It would not be right for us to neglect the ministry of the word of God in order to wait on tables" (Acts 6:2).

As preachers of God's Word, the disciples had their priorities right. Studying God's Word, spending time in prayer, and teaching and preaching were their main responsibilities.

Volunteer your time to help your pastor with some of the things that need to be done in your church. He'll appreciate it, and you'll enjoy it! And if you've never invited your pastor and his family to share a meal with you, why not make plans to get to know them better. You'll be glad you did.

SALVATION

*J*ason and Woody had spent the day surfing, catching wave after monstrous wave. Now back at the campground, tired and sunburned, they sat around their campfire wolfing down hot dogs.

"You know, pal," Woody said slowly, "you almost blew it when you took that spill out there today. If the board had hit your head instead of your shoulder, you'd be shark meat. Where do you think you'd be then?"

Jason rubbed the dark bruise on his left shoulder and shivered. Woody was right. That had been a close call. "I don't really know," he murmured. "I guess I'd go to heaven—maybe."

Woody threw more driftwood onto the fire. "I used to think that too," he replied, "until I learned that it takes more to get to heaven that just hoping it'll happen."

Jason's eyes bulged. He'd never heard Woody talk like this before. Not Woody—the best surfer in five counties! Not Woody—who laughed at the largest waves and lived to have a good time. Did Woody really know something about going to heaven?

◆ THINKING ABOUT SALVATION

Like everyone else in the world, Jason was not personally qualified to enter heaven. His sin separated him from God. But Woody knew **God's plan to save people from the penalty of sin**. So he wanted to talk to Jason about Jesus because he knew that . . .

● KEY VERSE ON SALVATION

Salvation is found in no one else, for there is no other name under heaven given to men by which we must be saved (Acts 4:12).

▲ LOOKING AHEAD

Like Jason, some people haven't realized they must make a personal commitment to follow Christ in order to experience His salvation. What word used three times in John 3:16-18 helps you understand that each individual must make a decision?

"His version of sin is different from the press account."

What God said is true— I'm a sinner and so are you

Jason stared into the fire and pulled a blanket over his shoulders. He'd often thought about God. No surfer in his right mind would deny a Creator's handiwork. But somehow it always seemed enough to him to know that God existed and to try being good to other people. But now Woody was saying something entirely different.

Woody interrupted his thoughts. "Jase, sin has put a huge gap between God and people. The Bible says, 'All have sinned and come short of the glory of God.' It also says that 'the wages of sin is death.' That means unless each person gets his sin problem taken care of, he will be separated from God forever. That's why you and I need a Savior."

Woody poked the fire, then went on. "It's like a man out there in the ocean, swallowing water, drowning. His sin is dragging him down, away from God. He can't save himself. He doesn't have any hope unless a lifeguard comes along."

◆ **TAKE A LOOK**
Proverbs 6:16-19; Galatians 5:19-21

It's as simple as that. People need salvation because sin has separated them from God. Since the time of Adam, no one—except Jesus Christ— has lived without sinning. Everyone has failed to meet God's standard of perfection.

King David, who wrote many of the psalms, understood that everyone has sinned. He stated it this way:

No one living is righteous before [God] (Psalm 143:2).

Sin can be defined several ways. It is missing God's standard . . . breaking His laws . . . treating others unjustly. In more than one place, God's Word clearly lists some actions and behaviors that are sin. Read Proverbs 6:16-19, Galatians 5:19-21, and Colossians 3:5-8 to learn that what God says is true: Everyone has sinned.

▲ **TAKE A STEP**

Others may not see our sin. Sometimes we don't even see it ourselves. But nothing is hidden from God.

The first step in finding salvation is to see yourself as a sinner who is totally unfit to be in God's presence. As you close your family time, think of some of the excuses people often make when asked to accept the truth that they are sinners. Others may come to mind when you reread Proverbs 6 and Galatians 5. Add them to your list.

Q

Why do I need salvation?

A

Salvation is necessary for me and every person because everyone has sinned.

*J*ason, you need a lifeguard. And Jesus is that Lifeguard, the Savior. He'll save you—but you've got to be willing to be rescued. You need to realize there's no way you can save yourself." As Woody spoke, he could see the interest in Jason's face.

"I think I understand what you're saying," Jason said slowly. "Everybody I know has done wrong things. But can't I do a lot of good things and make up for sin?"

"That won't work with God," Woody replied. "Sin has to be paid for. Remember, 'The wages of sin is death.' Either you have to die for your own sin, or someone has to die in your place. That's what I meant when I said Jesus rescues us. His death on the cross was enough to pay for our sin. He literally died in our place. And His payment for sin is the only one God accepts."

Jason thought about that for a moment. "But Jesus died so long ago. How can it really matter right now?"

◆ TAKE A LOOK
2 Corinthians 5:21; 1 Peter 2:24; 3:18

Salvation means deliverance from sin. Because all human beings have sinned, we need a Savior—one who brings us that deliverance from sin. This is why . . .

The Father has sent his Son to be the Savior of the world (1 John 4:14).

God's Word makes it clear that Jesus is the Savior, as you'll see by reading 1 Corinthians 15:3; 1 Peter 2:24; 3:18; and 1 John 3:5. Then 2 Corinthians 5:21 will help you understand this truth: On the cross Jesus, who had no sins of His own, took our sins upon Himself.

▲ TAKE A STEP

The accumulated sins of everyone who has ever lived, or will ever live, were laid on Jesus. He paid the penalty for them—completely. God's only Son endured separation from His heavenly Father. Jesus was an innocent Savior dying for guilty sinners.

To try to "earn" salvation by doing good works or by keeping religious laws is an insult to God. If we could buy our salvation, then Christ's death wasn't necessary.

Jesus' death is the only acceptable payment for sin. Ephesians 2:8-9 describes salvation as a gift. Close your family time by discussing what a gift really is. Do you always deserve it? Is it still a gift if you pay for it? Reread those verses and find two words that tell you how to accept God's gift.

The life-giving Lifeguard —He's like no other

Q

How does God provide salvation?

A

Salvation is purchased only by Jesus' death on the cross.

Love is the life preserver God throws to me

Q

Why did God provide salvation?

A

Salvation through Jesus Christ demonstrates God's love for me.

*The Love of God, F. M. Lehman. 1917, Ren. 1945 by Nazarene Publishing House. Used by permission.

The fire was dying now, but in Jason's heart the light was dawning. "I'm beginning to see what God did," he murmured, "but I don't think I quite understand why."

"That's the neatest part of all," Woody continued softly. "It's love. God loved us enough to send His Son to pay for our sin. You've probably heard of John 3:16. That verse puts it this way: 'For God so loved the world that he gave his one and only Son, that whoever believes in him shall not perish but have eternal life.' "

The last embers of the fire reflected the smile on Woody's face. "You're part of that world God loves, Jason. So am I. But it's still like the drowning man. He can't be rescued unless he reaches out and grabs the life preserver the lifeguard has thrown him. And you won't be saved unless you accept—by faith—what Jesus did for you."

◆ **TAKE A LOOK**
1 John 3:1; 4:16; Romans 5:8
No human mind or heart can ever understand all that's involved in God's love. One hymn writer put it this way:

> The love of God is greater far
>> Than tongue or pen can ever tell;
> It goes beyond the highest star
>> And reaches to the lowest hell.
> The guilty pair, bowed down with care,
>> God gave His Son to win;
> His erring child He reconciled,
>> And pardoned from his sin.
> Oh, love of God, how rich and pure!
>> How measureless and strong!
> It shall forevermore endure
>> The saints' and angels' song.*

▲ **TAKE A STEP**
First John 3:1; 4:16; and Romans 5:8 speak of that love.

> God demonstrates his own love for us in this: While we were still sinners, Christ died for us (Romans 5:8).

That's salvation in action! If love is the cord attached to the life preserver, who's holding the other end? But are you really aware that apart from Jesus Christ, you will drown in the "sea of sin"? Each person must grab salvation for himself. Nobody else can believe for you.

Close in a prayer of thanks that God draws us to Himself . . . and never lets go.

J ason was becoming more excited as Woody continued talking. "It seems like you're saying God loved us enough to send a life preserver, to send Jesus to pay for our sins on the cross. Okay, that makes sense; but how can I grab hold?"

Woody chuckled. "You've definitely got the right idea, buddy. Just knowing about God's plan for you isn't enough. You've got to do something about it."

"I know that, Woody. But what? I don't understand everything you're telling me, but I do know I've sinned. I've lied to my folks, cheated on tests, and been awfully mean to my little sister. I know those things are awfully bad. I don't want to be separated from God forever."

Woody's happiness showed in his voice as he answered his friend. "All you have to do is accept Jesus as your Savior," he replied. "You can do that by praying to Him right now. You can say something like this . . . "

◆ TAKE A LOOK / Acts 16:19-34

Thousands of people have asked the same question Jason was asking: "How can I have the salvation God offers?"

You'll see that the answer has always been the same when you read about the Philippian jailer in Acts 16:19-34.

▲ TAKE A STEP

"Believe in the Lord Jesus, and you will be saved" (Acts 16:31).

Knowing that Jesus is the Savior of the world doesn't bring salvation. Neither does simply admitting that you have sinned and need a Savior. These are facts you must understand and believe. But the faith that Paul speaks of also involves a personal, deliberate decision to forsake your sins and follow Jesus Christ as your Lord and King.

The prayer Woody led Jason to pray might be one you need to pray as well:

"Lord Jesus, I admit that I am a sinner.

"I am sorry for my sins, and I turn from them.

"I believe that You died for me, bearing my sins in Your own body.

"I thank You for Your great love.

"I want You to be my Savior.

"Come in as my Savior, Master, and Lord to cleanse me and to take control of my life. Amen."

If you have prayed this prayer and meant it, thank Christ now for the salvation He has given you.

The sinner's plea that God will hear

Q

How can I be saved?

A

Salvation is mine when I believe on Jesus as my Savior from sin.

TRUST

*R*ay felt a stab of fear when he realized a blanket of fog had suddenly rolled in over the airport. He had just gotten his pilot's license and hadn't logged much flight time yet. Now, with zero visibility and his fuel running low, the "crash" stories he'd heard from experienced pilots kept running through his mind.

Mentally Ray reviewed the practice flights when he had landed under radar controls, guided safely down by a firm, confident voice from the control tower. "I did it then; I can do it now," he thought as the controller's voice came through his headset.

"I'll take it from here," the voice said calmly. "Don't worry. I'll have you back on the ground in no time. Trust me."

As the controller in the tower issued instructions, Ray repeated them back. When he was sure he had heard correctly, he carefully set each instrument. Within a few minutes the plane's wheels touched the runway. Ray braked and taxied back to the hanger. "Total trust," he murmured to himself. "Something like that takes total trust."

◆ THINKING ABOUT TRUST

Ray was right. But trust is more than confidence. It is **confidence based on the character or reliability of another.** Ray trusted the controller because he knew the controller was well trained, well equipped, and experienced. He trusted the controller this time because he had trusted him before.

Like Ray's trust in the controller, this verse reminds us that our trust in God should be based on His reliability, not our own skill.

● KEY VERSE ON TRUST

Trust in the LORD *with all your heart and lean not on your own understanding* (Proverbs 3:5).

▲ LOOKING AHEAD

This week we'll probe what it means to trust God completely.

Isaiah 26:4 reveals one important reason why we can place our trust in God. Can you discover what it is?

"Our new associate, Dr. Hall, will be with you as soon as he gets out of his cap and gown."

*E*ddie gripped the side of the swimming pool with both hands. His knuckles were white, his jaw was locked, his little body was rigid with fear.

"Let go, Eddie," his father coaxed firmly. "I'll hold you up."

But Eddie only held tighter and shook his head.

"Eddie," his father reasoned, "you're five years old. It's time you learned to swim. Look at Rodney and Cliff—they're having a great time." Mr. Wilson pulled gently at his son's arm.

Eddie stiffened and pulled back, still shaking his head.

Mr. Watson climbed out of the pool and stood Eddie up on a nearby picnic table. "Eddie, do you remember how you used to jump off our table in the backyard when you were little? You'd say, 'Catch me, Daddy!' and then jump right into my arms. I never dropped you, did I? You trusted me to catch you and I did—every time. Well, learning to swim is like jumping off that table. If you trust me now and follow my instructions, you'll soon be splashing with your friends."

Twelve years later that incident ran through Eddie's mind as he stood in the center of the winner's platform at the state diving competition. He held up his trophy and winked at his proud dad.

◆ TAKE A LOOK
Deuteronomy 32:4; Psalms 117:2; 145:13

Eddie was one frightened little boy! Before he could learn to swim, he had to believe that "Dad can be trusted."

Most dads do their best to be trustworthy, to keep their word, to provide for their children's needs, and to protect them from harm. Because they are human, earthly fathers sometimes make mistakes. But God, our heavenly Father, never does. He is totally trustworthy. In Deuteronomy 32:4; Psalms 117:2; 145:13; and 2 Thessalonians 3:3, you will find words that describe God's trustworthiness (look for the word faithfulness). As you read, jot down four ways that God is faithful.

▲ TAKE A STEP
Our God is
a faithful God who does no wrong
(Deuteronomy 32:4).

Fear prevented Eddie from trusting his father—until Mr. Watson reminded his son why he was trustworthy. As you close your family time today, let each member tell of a time when he or she was hesitant to trust God.

He's totally trust-worthy, doubly depend-able

Q

How does God show that He is trust-worthy?

A

I can trust God because He faithfully loves His children and never makes mistakes.

Who—or what—will I put my trust in?

From his high school days on, Harry had witnessed to his friend Sam more times than he could remember. Sam was always interested but never really accepted the idea that he needed to know Jesus in a personal way. "Don't worry," he'd say. "I'll get around to it."

During college Harry kept praying for Sam, but still Sam never seemed interested. After all, why did he need Jesus? He was the quarterback of the football team, a straight-A student, and president of the student body. His family was well-off, so Sam had just about everything he wanted. To his way of thinking, life was pretty good just the way it was.

Then came the news he couldn't handle. With a shaking hand Sam phoned his friend. "Harry," he said, his voice coming out in great gulping sobs, "Mom and Dad . . . have been . . . killed in a crash. What am I going to do? Who in the world can I turn to?"

Q

Why do so few people trust God?

◆ **TAKE A LOOK**
Psalm 118:9; Proverbs 18:11; 28:26; Isaiah 31:1
Trust requires an object. Sam trusted the results of his own efforts—or his parents'—to get whatever he needed.

Look at Psalm 118:9; Proverbs 18:11; 28:26; and Isaiah 31:1. These verses will show you that Sam is no different from people who've lived in other times and places. You'll also learn what God says about those who don't trust Him.

A

Trust is misplaced when it is in any- thing— people, money, or things— apart from God.

▲ **TAKE A STEP**
Important people, wealth, oneself, weapons, others—there are many places you can put your trust other than in the living God. But what does God think about that?

This is what the LORD says: "Cursed is the one who trusts in man, who depends on flesh for his strength and whose heart turns away from the LORD" (Jeremiah 17:5).

Like Sam, many people don't realize their need for the Lord until . . . wealth is wasted, health fails, or a crisis hits. Even Christians must guard against trusting other people and other things.

Turn to the Key Verse for the week (page 96). Can you find a phrase in that verse that is the opposite of trusting the Lord?

What do you think it means to lean on your own understanding?

List three things that can help you—as a family and as an individual—to avoid "leaning on your own understanding."

*A*re you trying to keep the post office in business single-handedly?" Seventeen-year-old Debbie teased her older sister who was sealing a pale pink envelope.

"You wait a few years," Lois replied good-naturedly. "You'll do the same thing when your boyfriend is 200 miles away."

Debbie snickered, then looked serious. "Lois, what makes you trust Tim so much anyway? How do you know he's not dating some other girl and only coming back to you when he's home?"

Lois sensed the pain in Debbie's voice and reached for her sister's hand. "Oh, Deb, I know it was tough when you found out George was lying to you about dating other girls. Maybe you trusted him before you really got to know him. I trust Tim because I know the kind of person he is. I know his character and his personality, and I know he loves me. Someday you'll know and love someone so much that you'll trust him no matter how far away he is. Then you'll be supporting the post office too!"

◆ TAKE A LOOK
Psalms 9:10; 46:10; 100:3; Luke 24:27

Both Debbie and Lois had trusted their boyfriends. But Debbie's relationship with George deteriorated while Lois's relationship with Tim deepened. Why do you think this happened?

You've already learned this week that there's no such thing as trust without something or someone to trust in. And as Debbie and Lois discovered, it's the character of that object that makes the difference. Lois trusted Tim because she understood his character. And the better she got to know him, the more she trusted him.

That same principle holds true in our trust-relationship with the Lord. Read Psalms 9:10; 46:10; 100:3; and Luke 24:27 to learn how you can know and trust God better.

▲ TAKE A STEP

One way of getting to know God is revealed in Psalm 46:10:

Be still, and know that I am God.

Think about your daily routine. How often do you practice that verse? Does anything—a TV program, activity, job, or relationship—keep you away from God?

If God is all-powerful, all-knowing, all-wise, all-loving (and He is), could anything be more important than knowing, trusting, and obeying Him?

All that matters is who you know

How can I learn to trust God more completely?

A

Trust increases as I get to know God better and better.

Blessings are on the way— when you trust and obey

I n which of these situations could you trust God?
• "It's just not fair," Mandy said tearfully. "Coach told us no one could be on the team unless they made Cs or better on their report cards. But he lets Suzanne play even though she made two Ds. Just because she's a star player doesn't mean the rules should be changed for her. Mom, is that really fair?"
• "All they ever do is fight anymore," Link thought as he heard his parents' angry, bitter voices coming from the den. "What'll happen to us if Dad really leaves like he's threatening to do?"
• "God knows I live on a fixed income, and He knows the rent is going up," Mrs. Morris told her neighbor confidently. "It's no surprise to Him. So in times like these I do what I've always done: I just keep trusting my Lord. He'll see me through!"

◆ TAKE A LOOK / Psalms 32:10; 37:5-6; 115:11
Because believers know God's character, we know that no circumstance—not even one as bad as those mentioned—is too big for Him to handle. And our loving heavenly Father will reward our confidence in Him.

While we are on earth, we won't experience all the rewards God has promised us. The book of Hebrews tells about other believers who didn't receive what they had been promised before they died. Why? Because . . .

God had planned something better for us so that only together with us would they be made perfect (Hebrews 11:40).

The greatest reward of our trust in God will come when we see Jesus, but we can look forward to much right now. As you read the verses below, on the right list the blessing God promises when we trust Him:

Trusting God	**brings His children . . .**
Psalm 32:10	_____
Psalm 37:5-6	_____
	_____
Psalm 115:11	_____
	_____
Isaiah 26:3	_____
	_____

▲ TAKE A STEP
Proverbs 3:5-6 promises another benefit to those who trust God. Reward the first member of the family to find what it is with his or her choice of dessert tomorrow night.

Q

What blessings come from trusting God?

A

Trust in God brings the rewards of heaven— as well as blessings here and now.

PARENTS

*D*ear Mom and Dad,
"I appreciate you for all you've sacrificed for me.

"Mom, thanks for your special gift of love—for seeing me off every morning, for giving me lunch money out of the jar in the china cabinet, and for dressing me warmly for the long walk to school. Thanks for the ice cream cones and cherry colas (real ones) you bought me at the soda fountain.

"Dad, my dearest and best friend, I think back to the treasured times when you came home from work. I would open your lunch box, knowing you had saved me a cookie or two, a piece of gum, or half of your BBQ potato chips—small treats which meant so much.

"I remember every Sunday morning when I was little, how you flattened my cowlick with water so I would look like a little gentleman for church. You showed me how to stay close to God and you brought me up in His ways.

"Now, because of your example, I will do the same for my son.

"Love, your son, David"

◆ THINKING ABOUT PARENTS

Parents are **the special people God chose to influence and train you.** Whether your parents are loving and supportive, distant and cold, rich or poor, the relationship you have with them will always be one of the most important in your life.

So important, in fact, that one of God's basic laws deals with how children are to relate to their parents. God says simply:

● **KEY VERSE ON PARENTS**
Honor your father and your mother (Exodus 20:12).

▲ **LOOKING AHEAD**
This week in the opening stories five different people describe something they appreciate about their parents.

God gave parents specific instructions about their spiritual responsibilities. Restate them in your own words after you read Deuteronomy 6:4-7.

"Van Gogh's mother let him cut off his whole ear, and you won't even let me get mine pierced."

Parents, fear God— not your children

Q

How can parents please God?

A

Parents are responsible for teaching their children God's ways.

My parents gave 100 percent to my brothers and me as they raised us. From the day we were born, they brought us up according to Christian principles. They believed strongly in education and worked hard to support us emotionally and financially through college.

"As a teenager I can remember feeling that my parents were unfair because of their strict rules. Now I realize they loved me enough to protect me, and I appreciate the fact that they stood on God's promise: 'Train a child in the way he should go, and when he is old he will not turn from it' (Proverbs 22:6).

"My mother and I have grown to be best friends. Since I've married and moved away, I miss the special times we spent together. Mom and Dad, I just want to take this opportunity to say thank you for everything you've done. I love you with all my heart."

◆ **TAKE A LOOK / Deuteronomy 30:11-20; 32:46-47**

The most important job parents have is not to provide their children with clothes, food, an education, a car, or even an allowance. Their most important job is to raise their children in the ways of the Lord.

The Old Testament book of Deuteronomy is a book of law. It contains God's principles for living, which can bring His blessing for individuals, families, and nations—if they are obeyed. It also describes the disasters—or "curses"—which come on those who refuse to obey God's commandments.

Near the end of these instructions, God gives a profound warning that all parents and children should take seriously. Read those solemn words now in Deuteronomy 30:11-20 and 32:46-47.

▲ **TAKE A STEP**

God's commands about the life that pleases Him are not optional. Parents have the responsibility to teach their children God's ways. They must also discipline their children while they are young so that they will not walk in rebellion.

"They are not just idle words for you—they are your life" (Deuteronomy 32:47).

Close your family time by talking about this question: Is it more loving for parents to be strict and insist that their children obey while they are young, or to allow them to go their own way and just hope they'll turn out okay?

What do you appreciate most about your parents' rules? What rules would you like to discuss with your parents?

*M*y parents' discipline taught me never to discipline in anger. On one memorable occasion when I was eight years old, several of my friends discovered what a delicious sound it made when dirt clods were thrown over the fence into the neighbors' pool. I joined in the fun. That evening my father confronted me with this stern question: 'Did you throw dirt into the neighbors' pool?'

"I lied. He knew I was lying. But rather than spank me in anger at that moment, he did a very wise thing. For the next 24 hours he did his homework, ferreting out exactly what happened. The next night, without a hint of anger in his voice, he asked me, 'Who else besides you threw dirt in the pool?'

"My defenses crumbled, I burst into tears, and the spanking that followed was received as an act of love.

"Many times since, I too have delayed punishment for my own children just long enough to insure it was given in love, not anger—and with wonderful effect."

◆ TAKE A LOOK / 1 Samuel 3:8-18; 4:10-11, 14-22

God doesn't simply suggest that parents discipline their children in His way; He commands them to do so (Proverbs 22:6).

When the Prophet Samuel was a young child, God spoke to him. But Samuel didn't recognize God's voice; three times he thought the old priest Eli had called him. Eli realized God was speaking to Samuel and told him to respond, "Speak, Lord, for your servant is listening."

Samuel did as he was told and God spoke to him—the first of many messages He would give this great leader. But have you ever paid much attention to the rest of the story? Have you ever thought about the message God gave Samuel?

Find out what that important message was by reading 1 Samuel 3:8-18. Then read 4:10-11 and 14-22 to learn the tragic ending of this story.

▲ TAKE A STEP

Eli's family was judged because of the sin he knew about; his sons made themselves contemptible, and he failed to restrain them (1 Samuel 3:13).

True love disciplines. That means parents must be consistent, fair, and loving as they discipline. They fear the Lord, not their kids.

Can you give some real-life examples of beneficial discipline from your experience?

The rod applied is God's design

Q

Why is parental discipline important?

A

Parents are responsible to discipline their children in obedience to God.

PARENT
Here's a helpful family project: Use a concordance to find all the verses in the book of Proverbs dealing with disciplining your child. (Look up the words child, children, son, *and* parents.)

What you are is what they'll be

Q

What are some of the important things parents do?

A

Parents teach their children by example and by praying for them.

I didn't notice it when I was growing up, but our family lived a simple life. Our house was small and plain, and we always bought secondhand cars. But life was filled with meals together, prayer before we all left each morning, and great Ping-Pong games in the basement. And we had plenty of time to talk with Mom and Dad.

"I can remember countless times hearing Dad pray that the Lord would guide, protect, and use each of us that day. And God answered those prayers.

"Though my life has changed, one thing remains the same: the values my parents demonstrated. Following the example of my parents, I know the importance of keeping God first in my life, praying for my family, and making home a great place to be."

◆ **TAKE A LOOK / 1 Samuel 2:1-11**

Discipline is not the only responsibility parents have. It is also the parents' responsibility to teach their children God's ways.

All four introductory stories this week have shown us that parents teach by example as well as by what they say.

Above all, parents have the great privilege of praying for their children. Hannah's son Samuel was a direct answer to her prayers. She gave her son back to God to serve Him all his days.

"I prayed for this child, and the LORD has granted me what I asked of him. So now I give him to the LORD. For his whole life he will be given over to the LORD" (1 Samuel 1:27-28).

Hannah didn't stop praying for Samuel even after she took him to serve in God's house. Read Hannah's great prayer of praise to God in 1 Samuel 2:1-10.

▲ **TAKE A STEP**

All the parents you've read about this week entrusted their children to the Lord, as Hannah did, and prayed for them.

Ask your parents if they are praying for you. And be sure and tell your parents what to pray about—the math test, the teacher who doesn't like you, the tryout for the cheerleading squad. Can you sense that God is answering some of those prayers even now?

Also, parents, if your own parents are believers, let them know you appreciate their prayers for you—and your children. They are still one of your most valuable spiritual resources!

***O**ne of the most important things my parents did for me was to teach me what a Christian marriage should be.*

"Both my mom and my dad have made a commitment to Christ as their Lord and Savior, so each has a personal relationship with Him. Because their commitment to Christ is their number-one priority, their marriage is based on His principles. And that focuses our whole family on the Lord.

"My parents' relationship not only gave me the love and security I needed as a child, it also prepared me for my own marriage.

"So the greatest gift my parents gave me is one they continue to give—their growing love for each other."

◆ **TAKE A LOOK / Philippians 2:3-4**

If someone hid a camera in your home and then showed the film to your Sunday school class, would you be embarrassed by the way you treat your parents?

We've talked a lot this week about the duties of parents, but now it's time to talk about the duties of children. If you don't know how to honor your parents, Philippians 2:3-4 gives you easy-to-follow instructions.

▲ **TAKE A STEP**

Selfishness is probably the number-one reason why children and teenagers don't honor their parents. But real Christian love must begin with those closest to you—and that's Mom and Dad.

After you read this verse again, answer the following questions (no fudging, please). Then you'll be able to see exactly how God expects you to honor your parents on a day-by-day basis:

Do nothing out of selfish ambition or vain conceit, but in humility consider others better than yourselves (Philippians 2:3).

Do you ever . . . think you know more than Mom and Dad? . . . grudgingly do only what you have to? . . . argue, pout, or complain when you don't get your way? . . . act rudely and sarcastically when you are corrected? . . . mock your parents behind their backs? . . . forget your chores until Mom or Dad does them? . . . lie to your parents by not telling the whole story? . . . think you should get paid for doing your chores?

In short, do you really honor your parents?

On my honor I will honor my parents

Q

How can I honor my parents?

A

Parents can be honored by the way I treat them every day.

MATURITY

*H*ave you ever wanted to be like Peter Pan and never grow up? In this scene featuring Peter and Wendy's mother, which occurs after the children have returned from Never-never Land, Mrs. Darling explains to Peter that she'd like to adopt him:

"Would you send me to school?" he inquired craftily.

"Yes."

"And then to an office?"

"I suppose so."

"Soon I should be a man?"

"Very soon."

"I don't want to go to school and learn solemn things," he told her passionately. "I don't want to be a man. O Wendy's mother, how horrible if I was to wake up and feel there was a beard!"*

◆ THINKING ABOUT MATURITY

All of us have a part that doesn't want to give up childhood. But in every way except one, maturity—**developing physically, intellectually, emotionally, and spiritually**—comes at the cost of growing older.

Human beings mature physically at about the same rate. But spiritual maturity isn't always related to growing older. The apostle Paul says the whole body of Christ must be built up . . .

● KEY VERSE ON MATURITY

Until we all reach unity in the faith and in the knowledge of the Son of God and become mature, attaining to the whole measure of the fullness of Christ (Ephesians 4:13).

"I'm too old for baby limas!"

▲ LOOKING AHEAD

From our definition of maturity above (in boldface type) and this week's Key Verse, how would *you* define *spiritual maturity?* Write it on a sheet of paper, and leave room to add to it as the week goes on.

*Excerpted from *Peter and Wendy* by J. M. Barrie. Copyright ©1911, Charles Scribner's Sons; copyright renewed ©1939 by Lady Cynthia and Peter L. Davies.

*S*handa hated shopping with her mother. "Why does it take so long?" she complained for the fifth time. Mrs. Pearson never simply picked up an item and put it in the cart. Instead, she read every label and unit price.

But Shanda really got annoyed when they came to the produce section. There her mother examined the tassels on each ear of corn, pressed the ends of the melons, hefted the lettuce to feel its weight, squeezed the avocados, and smelled the strawberries.

"Come on, Mom!" Shanda whined. "Let's go home."

"Shanda, I want to get the most tasty vegetables and fruits I can find—not underripe, but not too mature either," her mother replied. "And speaking of maturity, you need to quit complaining like an impatient baby. I'll be ready when I'm ready."

◆ TAKE A LOOK / Numbers 13:26–14:4

Shanda's impatient attitude made her seem more like a two-year-old than a ten-year-old. She simply wasn't as mature as she thought.

Some people are not as spiritually mature as they think they are either, a condition that can have tragic results.

After freeing the Israelites from slavery in Egypt, God intended to help them conquer the land of Canaan and take it as their own. Twelve men went ahead to spy out the land. When the spies returned, ten reported that they could not conquer Canaan. Their spiritual immaturity kept them from seeing God's plan. As you read Numbers 13:26–14:4, look for the name of one spy whose trust in God demonstrated his spiritual maturity.

▲ TAKE A STEP

Of the twelve spies, only Caleb and Joshua believed God would do as He promised. As a result, that entire generation died before any Israelites ever entered Canaan. If they had been spiritually mature, they would have trusted and obeyed God. The New Testament encourages us to trust and obey God,

that you may stand firm in all the will of God, mature and fully assured (Colossians 4:12).

In today's story, what clues indicate that Shanda lacked maturity?

On a scale of 1-10 (10 being the highest), rate your own maturity. (Try measuring it by how often you complain about your parents' decisions.) Write your number on a slip of paper and then compare it with the number your mom or dad wrote down for you!

Try to be mature, but not overripe!

Q

Does everyone mature at the same rate?

A

Maturity, which is evident when I trust and obey God, comes at different rates for different people.

Maturity —the ability to see behind the scenes

Q

What is spiritual maturity?

A

Maturity means I consider how my decisions will spiritually affect others as well as how they will affect me.

But, Daddy, the manager says some waitresses pull in $50 a night in tips. And just because I'd serve drinks doesn't mean I'm going to drink." Lucy was earnestly trying to make her father agree that taking a job in the town's newest and fanciest restaurant was a good idea.

"Lucy, it simply wouldn't be a good situation for you. You would have to work late every night, drive home alone, and then get up early for classes the next morning. Right now, doing well in college is more important than making a lot of money. I'd rather you find a different job."

"Dad, every time I try to make a decision on my own, you and Mom interfere," Lucy retorted. "After all, I am 18 years old. I'm supposed to be able to do what I want."

"You could," Mr. Kramer replied gently. "And some young people do. But that's a mark of immaturity, not maturity. A mature person considers wise counsel—even if it comes from parents."

Lucy looked at her father for a long moment. "Dad, you're right. My grades are important. I need to do well at school. And it would be hard to be a witness for Jesus while serving someone a drink. I was just trying to convince myself that this job was for me, but it's not. I'll look somewhere else."

◆ TAKE A LOOK / Romans 14:19–15:2

Yesterday we learned that trusting God and doing His will without complaining is one way to measure spiritual maturity. Lucy's decision shows another way. See how the Bible describes it by reading Romans 14:19–15:2.

▲ TAKE A STEP

But solid food is for the mature, who by constant use have trained themselves to distinguish good from evil (Hebrews 5:14).

Though Lucy was old enough to make her own decisions, she was mature enough to take her father's advice. As she thought seriously about her values and the truth of God's Word, she was able to "distinguish good from evil."

As you close your family time today, add the phrases "knowing and doing God's will without complaining" and "distinguishing good from evil" to the definition of spiritual maturity you began on Day One. What other phrase might you add from Romans 14:21?

*S*ometimes I don't think I can stand it," Mrs. Russell sighed, "wondering every week if I'll have money to buy groceries."

Mrs. Thrasher understood what her friend was saying. A single mother with a limited income has a hard time stretching the budget to meet ever-increasing expenses.

Mrs. Russell sipped her coffee and continued. "Two years ago when John died and the kids and I were on our own, I prayed that I would learn to depend on God to meet my needs. Day by day He's answering that prayer. I feel closer to God than I ever have.

"He's really stretching my faith," she continued. "When there's no more money, a Christian friend will give me a gift. A friend repaired my washing machine. Someone loaned me a car to drive when mine was at the garage—so many things. But it seems God always waits until the last minute before He sends the help. I think it's so I'll know for sure that He did it." She paused and smiled. "Do you suppose that's God's sense of humor?"

◆ **TAKE A LOOK / James 1:2-8; Romans 5:1-5**

Whether she realized it or not, Mrs. Russell was becoming spiritually mature. She held to her faith without wavering. As she trusted God to meet her needs in spite of her circumstances, she was practicing perseverance.

You'll see how perseverance helps God's children become spiritually mature as you read James 1:2-8 and Romans 5:1-5.

▲ **TAKE A STEP**

Perseverance must finish its work so that you may be mature and complete, not lacking anything (James 1:4).

We human beings will go out of our way to avoid trials or suffering. We'd much rather live on "easy street." But God's Word and the experiences of God's children who have gone before us clearly show that a certain amount of suffering lies on the road to spiritual maturity. James teaches that we become more mature when we persevere through those trials.

Add the phrase "perseverance in trials and suffering" to the definition you began on Day One. Then share with one another a situation in which you needed to persevere. If you're in the midst of that situation right now, close with a family prayer for the strength and courage you'll need to see it through.

At the end of your rope? Tie a knot and hang on!

Q

What helps me to mature spiritually?

A

Maturity is gained by persevering through trials and suffering.

Q

A

PARENT
Encourage your child to become a prayer partner with a grandparent or older person in your church who can offer support and advice.

*Y*ou'd better listen carefully to what I'm saying, Gordon," Mr. Mallock said sternly, "because your future depends on it."

Gordon's eyes were pinned to the floor as his father spoke. He knew he had tested his parents to the limits these last few months. What he hadn't realized was how hurt they were. This morning the principal had informed Mr. Mallock that Gordon was suspended for a week for taking beer on a school field trip.

Mr. Mallock continued. "You'll soon be 18—legally able to decide where you want to live. I hope you'll continue to live with us—at least until you're out of college. But as long as you live in our home, you must abide by our standards of behavior.

"Mom and I love you with all our hearts, but we've never condoned drinking. So if you choose that kind of behavior, you'll have to leave. From now on, your behavior indicates your choice."

◆ TAKE A LOOK / Luke 8:4-9, 11-15

Gordon's parents had trained their children to know the Lord and obey His Word. So Gordon knew what his parents expected. But over the past few months he had chosen to go along with the crowd. As a result, he became disobedient both to the Lord and to his parents. And he stopped maturing spiritually.

Jesus told a parable that gives us three reasons why people don't mature spiritually. See if you can find them in Luke 8:4-9, 11-15.

▲ TAKE A STEP

God's children grow when they feed on God's Word. But God's Word won't take root in a life filled with "thorns."

Can you think of some "thorns" that keep you from growing? Examine several areas of your life such as entertainment, academics, and relationships.

Worldly concerns can squeeze God's Word right out of a person's life. But those who are maturing spiritually are represented by the good seed.

"[They] hear the word, retain it, and by persevering produce a crop" (Luke 8:15).

Perhaps you know a Christian who—like Gordon—deliberately rejected the godly principles he or she had been taught. How important do you think God's Word was to that person?

Share a time when God's Word kept you on the right track spiritually. How important is God's Word to you right now?

IN CHRIST

*W*hat?! Are those leaves growing on the ceiling?" 13-year-old Brandt asked in amazement. He'd come to London, England, for a visit with his aunt and uncle. It didn't take long to learn that things were different here. As they drove from the airport—on the "wrong" side of the road—Brandt had been wide-eyed at the large intersections with no traffic lights. "Roundabouts," his uncle had called them. Now here was a ceiling covered with leaves!

"Oh, that's our grapevine," Aunt Nancy laughed, opening the doors to the special room. "Come out and look." The sun shining through the glass roof and the mass of leaves gave the room a cool, green glow. As he peered up, Brandt noticed clusters of tiny grapes nestled among the leaves. Open-mouthed, he spun on his heels, looking at all four walls and the ceiling. "How did it get in here?" he asked. Where are the roots?"

◆ THINKING ABOUT BEING "IN CHRIST"

The Bible is full of descriptions of God's children. But one you might overlook is the little phrase "in Christ." Christians are "new creatures *in Christ*" (2 Corinthians 5:17); we are "wise *in Christ*" (1 Corinthians 4:10); and we are "approved *in Christ*" (Romans 16:10). In fact, that phrase is used over 150 times in the New Testament!

Being "in Christ" is **being united with Him, having His eternal life in us so that we live now and forever by His power.**

The apostle Paul tells us . . .

● KEY VERSE ON BEING "IN CHRIST"

If anyone is in Christ, he is a new creation; the old has gone, the new has come!
(2 Corinthians 5:17).

▲ LOOKING AHEAD

Why do you think the story of Brandt and the grapevine was chosen to introduce this week's topic? Read John 15:1-8 to see if your guess was right.

"God bless the fruit, and I suppose the vegetables, of our labor."

The life of a branch is in the vine

Brandt looked at the four corners of the room. "Where is the main vine?" he asked his aunt. "I don't see where it comes into the room."

"I know," she replied. "It's hidden so well that you literally have to go outside to see it. Over here." She opened a door and motioned to the corner where the sun porch joined the main house.

"That's a grapevine?" Brandt said in amazement. "It's almost as big as a tree!"

Indeed it was. Standing in a well-lit corner, the vine was about 26 inches around at its base. It grew straight for the height of the porch, then angled across. A pane had been removed so it could grow through.

"It was planted when the house was built," Aunt Nancy noted, "but I've no idea how long it took to reach this stage."

"A long time, I'll bet," Brandt replied absentmindedly. "But what I want to know is what made it turn and go inside?"

◆ **TAKE A LOOK / John 15:1-4; Ephesians 3:16-19**

When he looked around the room, Brandt was puzzled because all he saw were branches and leaves. He knew there must be a vine somewhere.

And sure enough, there it was—invisible from inside the room but completely supporting and nourishing all the lush branches and juicy fruit.

Being in Christ is exactly like being a branch on a vine. Just as Brandt couldn't see the vine, we can't actually see Jesus. But as branches, we're nourished, supported, and kept alive by His life, not our own.

Reread John 15:1-4. Then read Paul's prayer for believers in Ephesians 3:16-19. Pick a verse from each passage that you think describes the source of a believer's strength in Christ.

▲ **TAKE A STEP**

Jesus Himself is the Vine, His followers are the branches, and God the Father is the Gardener. Believers who want to please God must "abide" or remain in Jesus, the Vine:

"No branch can bear fruit by itself; it must remain in the vine. Neither can you bear fruit unless you remain in me" (John 15:4).

The life of the branch comes from the vine as it draws water and nutrients from the soil. As Christians, what is our food and water? How are we "fed"?

Q

Who is my source of strength in Christ?

A

In Christ God is my source of strength.

*B*randt stared at the grapevine. "This is weird. How did it get over to the roof?" he asked, looking up and down the trunk. "How did it turn and go into the sun room?"

"Mr. Williams did it," his aunt replied. "He's 74 years old now, and he's been the gardener at this house all his life. He's retired now, but he still comes here once a week because he loves this grapevine. To him it's a work of art.

"He told me once that he planted this vine when he was a young man. In a few years he tied a cord between the vine and the room so that it could inch its way across. Little by little, he's trained it to cover the entire ceiling."

Brandt was puzzled. "How do you 'train' a grapevine? Is it like taking a puppy to obedience school?"

◆ **TAKE A LOOK / John 15:6-8; Hebrews 12:10-11**
Mr. Williams's goal was for his vine to produce grapes—grapes to eat fresh from the vine; some for making jams, jellies, and juice; and others to dry for raisins.

For one vine to be that productive, he couldn't allow it to grow haphazardly. So, when it was ready, he gently tied strings to it that guided its growth. Some branches he cut away. And as time passed, the vine grew where he had trained it to go. As a result, Mr. Williams became well known for his grapevine and its fruit.

As the Master Gardener, God often ties "strings" to His branches. Through trying circumstances and difficult situations, He molds and shapes us so that we will bear fruit for Him. Read about God's training process in John 15:6-8. Hebrews 12:10-11 defines "the fruit" that God's daily discipline produces.

▲ **TAKE A STEP**
Why is the God of the universe interested in the fruit your life in Christ produces? Jesus gave this answer:

"This is to my Father's glory, that you bear much fruit, showing yourselves to be my disciples" (John 15:8).

Two kinds of fruit produced in a believer's life are righteousness (obeying God's commands in His strength) and peace. Does your life demonstrate those types of fruit? What other "spiritual fruit" is God producing through you?

The finest fruit in the universe

Q

What does God expect from those in Christ?

A

In Christ I bear fruit that brings glory to God.

PARENT
Discuss the purpose of discipline with your child. How does each of the following help to produce fruit: Practicing an instrument? Doing homework? Exercising regularly? Having devotions?

The fruit that feeds the world

Q

How can I bear more fruit in Christ?

A

In Christ I have a fruitful life as I become more and more like Him.

Have I got a surprise for you!" Aunt Nancy announced next morning as she set a tray of hot buttered toast on the breakfast table. From her apron pocket she whisked a small, dark jar.

"What is it?" Brandt asked in a puzzled tone. Then the light dawned. "From the grapevine—it's jam from the grapes. Mmm, it smells good," he exclaimed as he inhaled the aroma. Quickly he spread a spoonful on a piece of toast. "Oh, yum, it tastes as good as it looks. Can I have another piece?"

As Brandt continued to eat, Aunt Nancy told him about the grapes. "You wouldn't believe how much that vine produces each summer. We eat grapes every day, we give them away, we make jams and jellies and juice. I think this one grapevine could feed the whole neighborhood."

"I don't know about the neighborhood," Brandt interrupted, "but it's feeding me! Aunt Nancy, can I have a jar of this jam to take home? Mom won't believe how good it is unless she tries it!"

◆ TAKE A LOOK / Galatians 5:22-23; Ephesians 5:9; Colossians 1:10

The fruit from Mr. Williams's grapevine brought him fame in his neighborhood. In a similar way, God wants the fruit of our lives in Christ to bring Him glory.

Mr. Williams's grapevine didn't bear bananas, oranges, or apples—only grapes. Although the verses in John 15 we've been reading this week only speak about "spiritual fruit" in general, a Christian's life may have a variety of fruit. You'll discover the many different character qualities the fruitful Christian life will produce as you read Galatians 5:22-23; Ephesians 5:9; and Colossians 1:10.

▲ TAKE A STEP

Many people think bearing fruit in the Christian life means winning people to the Lord. That's part of it, but God goes one step further. He knows that people will be drawn to Him when they see believers doing "every good work" (Colossians 1:10) because they are led by His Spirit and demonstrate lives of

love, joy, peace, patience, kindness, goodness, faithfulness, gentleness and self-control (Galatians 5:22-23).

Find out how you can bear fruit by rereading John 15:4. Look carefully at each of the above words in bold type. Do they describe the "fruit" in your life today?

*T*hat week when the gardener came, Brandt had a dozen questions: "Exactly what kind of grapevine is this? Is it hard to grow? Does it need special soil?"

The old man assured Brandt that with patience he too could train a vine to spread into a sun porch and eventually produce wonderful grapes. "But I'll tell you something," he concluded slowly. "I hope your vine doesn't see the trouble mine has seen."

A grapevine in trouble seemed odd to Brandt. "What do you mean, sir?" he asked politely.

Mr. Williams pointed to a hump in the base of the vine. "My vine has been through a war—World War II, that is, when London was bombed. The whole side of this house was hit and collapsed. Almost cut the vine off. When the war ended and I got back to gardening, I didn't have much hope for it. But the root was deep and still alive. Spring of '45 it was when I saw green shoots again. Seems curious, but we gardeners don't give up."

◆ TAKE A LOOK / Ephesians 6:12; Hebrews 2:14; 1 Peter 5:8; 1 John 3:8

Fruit-bearing branches are sometimes attacked by enemies. Insects of all kinds, infested soil, drought, and bad weather can affect their production. In Mr. Williams's case, the vine itself was attacked.

People who are in Christ also have an enemy who seeks to ruin the fruit. Find out who he is and what will happen to him by looking up the verses below:

His Identity	His Fate
Ephesians 6:12	Hebrews 2:14
1 Peter 5:8	1 John 3:8

▲ TAKE A STEP

Satan, God's enemy, tries to undo the work of the Master Gardener by attacking the branches that are bearing fruit. But those "in Christ" know that nothing can separate them from God's love, care, and protection.

Spend a few minutes memorizing the verse below. Then the next time you feel like a branch about to break under the weight of problems and trials, repeat it to yourself for encouragement:

Set your mind on things above, not on earthly things. For you died, and your life is now hidden with Christ in God (Colossians 3:2-3).
Can you think of a better hiding place?

I'm in the Gardener's capable hands

Q

What happens when trouble comes to those in Christ?

A

In Christ I am safe from harm, even though I may be attacked by God's enemy.

MARRIAGE

I think they're dumb, even if they are my brother and your sister," 12-year-old Chris whispered to Todd as they lugged the large, silver punch bowl down the stairs. "You wait—Chip will turn out just like my other brother, Craig. We used to go fishing a lot, and he even came to all my ball games. But since he married Melanie, he hardly ever comes around. This marriage business stinks."

The boys were helping their families prepare for a wedding the next day. Though Chris was pretty disgusted over it, Todd was more hopeful.

"I've never had a brother, so I'll get something out of this deal," he joked. "But you know, there must be something to marriage, or else we wouldn't be here."

"I don't mean that," Chris retorted. "It's just that marriage changes everyone. Craig's different. He's not any fun anymore. Whenever he comes over, Melanie's with him. It's just not the way it was, and now it's going to happen again with Chip. I can't stand it."

◆ THINKING ABOUT MARRIAGE

In one respect, Chris is right: Marriage does change things. But if it's done in God's way, the changes are for the better.

Marriage is the **publicly recognized, legal union of a man and woman as husband and wife.** Though some people may think marriage is outdated, God hasn't changed His mind about His design for the human race. In fact, He performed the first "wedding":

"Because your mother and I are still married. That's why you don't get child support."

● **KEY VERSE ON MARRIAGE**
Then the LORD God made a woman from the rib he had taken out of the man, and he brought her to the man (Genesis 2:22).

▲ **LOOKING AHEAD**
When husbands or wives no longer view marriage the way God does, they may get divorced. Do you have friends who are experiencing divorce? Close your family time with a prayer for them.

W hile the rest of the McCarthy family was excitedly preparing for the wedding rehearsal, Chris was mired in self-pity because he was "losing" his brother to a wife. "Aw, Chip, why do you have to get married?" he whined as they stood in front of the bathroom mirror combing their hair. "Why don't you wait until you finish college?"

"I didn't think you'd really miss me, little brother," Chip teased. "Just think, now you'll have Mom and Dad's full attention, you won't have to split the last piece of cake, and you can have the hair dryer all to yourself! No, really it's been great growing up here. Mom and Dad are super folks, and you're not so bad for a little brother. But, I just can't explain it . . . I want to be with Amy every minute. Hey, someday you'll find out for yourself!"

◆ TAKE A LOOK / Genesis 2:15-25

Our goal this week is to understand marriage the way God designed it. To do this, we'll spend the next few days focusing on one passage of Scripture. Read Genesis 2:15-25 now to find God's purpose and plan for marriage.

▲ TAKE A STEP

God declared that everything He created was beautiful and good. But there was one problem—something that was not good. Did you catch it in this verse?

The LORD *God said, "It is not good for the man to be alone. I will make a helper suitable for him" (Genesis 2:18).*

The first problem that the first man experienced was loneliness. Marriage was God's solution to that problem.

God's purpose in making woman was not to make someone less capable, less intelligent, or less spiritual than Adam. Instead, God wanted to bring Adam happiness and joy, to give him a helper who would make him all that he could be.

You may have thought a helper was a kind of servant, but the Hebrew word for helper means "one who assists another to reach complete fulfillment."

Think about the verses in Genesis. Find one that indicates Eve was Adam's spiritual equal before God. Find a verse explaining that Eve was so much a part of Adam that he would have felt lost without her.

How do these verses help you understand how Chip felt about Amy?

The math of marriage: 1 + 1 = ONE

Q

Why do people get married?

A

Marriage is the relationship God designed for a man and a woman to complete each other.

PARENT
God does call some people to remain single. Discuss with your child some opportunities and options a single person has for serving God that a married person might not have.

Some marriages stick together like super glue!

Q

What's the most important ingredient in a marriage?

A

Marriage, as God designed it, is based on total commitment to one another.

PARENT
Test the priorities in your marriage by asking yourself, "If I knew without a doubt that I had only one year to live, would I do anything differently in my marriage?"

After the pastor had given each member of the wedding party instructions, the rehearsal started. As the organist began playing the first song, Chip's palms suddenly got sweaty. "What am I doing?" he thought. "I'm only 21 and Amy's only 20. What if I don't get a good job when I graduate? Maybe we should have waited."

As she stood with her father at the back of the church, Amy was thinking too. "What if he hates the way I cook? What if I can't work and keep house too? And—oh dear—what if we have a baby? Maybe we should have waited."

But when the organist ended the prelude and the soloist began to sing, those doubts vanished. Chip and Amy, separated by the length of the church, looked at each other and thought exactly the same thing: "Darling, I'd give my life for you. Nothing will ever separate us."

◆ TAKE A LOOK / Genesis 2:20-24
God's purposes for marriage—that each partner should "complete" the other, and that one plus one equals one—have never changed. Can you discover in Genesis 2:20-24 God's specific procedure for carrying out His plan?

▲ TAKE A STEP
For this reason a man will leave his father and mother and be united to his wife, and they will become one flesh (Genesis 2:24).

Verse 24 is the key to marriage as God meant it to be. The first requirement is to leave all other relationships. This doesn't mean a couple must abandon their parents or break all their friendships. But it does mean that the character of those relationships should change. A guy can't spend all his free time with his hunting pals. A girl can't keep running home to Mama.

The second part of God's plan involves being united. The King James translation reads, "A man shall cleave unto his wife." This means the couple should cling together like glue.

One word that summarizes the idea of "leaving and cleaving" is commitment. Talk about what the word commitment means. Look it up in a dictionary if you need to.

Review Chris and Amy's story and find the phrase that describes their commitment to each other. Look up Ephesians 5:25. How does the verse help you to understand better that kind of commitment?

Do you, Christopher, take this woman to be your lawful, wedded wife, to have and to hold, to love and to cherish, in sickness and in health, till death do you part?"

"I'm glad Chris and Amy chose the traditional vows," Mrs. McCarthy thought as her husband squeezed her hand. Like Amy's parents across the aisle, the McCarthys were thinking about the day they too had repeated those vows. They remembered their own thrills and nervous thoughts about starting life together. And they recalled with a secret smile their wedding night when, for the first time, they physically expressed their love for each other.

"But marriage is so much more than that," Mrs. McCarthy mused. "It was the good times and the hard times, the joys and the heartaches—even our little Danielle's death. It took all that to make us really one." As she reached over to stroke her husband's arm, her hand caught the tear that fell from his cheek.

◆ TAKE A LOOK / Ephesians 5:24-33

What does it mean to become "one flesh"? That phrase describes the sexual relationship of a man and a woman in marriage. But it's more than that. It's two people sharing everything they have—not only their bodies, but their feelings and thoughts, their joys and sorrows, their successes and failures, their hopes and fears. As the husband and wife leave other relationships and unite in every way, the two merge into one.

In many ways this is a mystery we may never understand completely. But it happens! You'll find a better description of the mystery of marriage— and another mystery as well—in Ephesians 5:24-33.

▲ TAKE A STEP

The deep, tender relationship that God designed for marriage is patterned after the love Jesus Christ has for His church. Look again at Genesis 2 and use what you've learned to fill in the blanks below.

• Christ left His heavenly Father and became a man. A man leaves his _____ and _____ to cleave to his wife.

• The church is united with Christ as His bride. A man is _____ with his wife with no thought of _____ .

• Jesus shares everything with us. What was ours became His: Our sin and punishment became His. And His life becomes our life. In the same way, a man and his wife become _____ .

What's mine is mine and yours and ours

Q

What does it mean to become "one flesh?"

A

Marriage is more than a physical relationship; it pictures the loving commitment Jesus has for us.

ANSWERS
father mother;
united . . .
separating; one.

There's one opinion that really matters

Q

What does God think about divorce?

A

Marriage can—and will—last "till death do us part" when it grows according to God's guidelines.

"**T**hose kids don't know what they're in for," Mr. Bartlett muttered bitterly as he and his wife left the wedding. "What'll they do when they find out marriage is only a trap?" Tears welled up in Mrs. Bartlett's eyes, but she bit her lip and said nothing.

Mr. Bartlett continued: "Either they'll stay married and be miserable, or they'll call it quits. And I might as well tell you now—I'm filing for a divorce. I have to live my own life. Everyone I talk to thinks it's better for the children if I leave. So I'm not going to put it off any longer."

After a long silence, Mrs. Bartlett spoke quietly, her voice quivering. "You seem to have gotten lots of opinions about this already. But have you considered God's opinion? His is really the only one that matters."

◆ TAKE A LOOK
Malachi 2:13-16; Matthew 19:3-9

Nearly half of all marriages end in divorce. Two people, who are really one in God's sight, are suddenly torn apart. Homes are disrupted, family members devastated.

You've probably heard some of the excuses people give for divorcing. Like Mr. Bartlett, they may feel they're no longer in love and have drifted apart. Others may say that they want to find happiness and they're tired of the responsibilities, or that they're in love with someone else.

Many people sincerely believe it's okay to get divorced. But sincerity doesn't make it right when God says it's wrong. Divorce is not part of God's design for marriage—a fact you'll learn by reading Malachi 2:13-16 and Matthew 19:3-9.

▲ TAKE A STEP

Has God changed His mind to suit a sinful world? Here's the answer in His own words:

"I hate divorce," says the LORD *God of Israel (Malachi 2:16).*

God forgives sins—even divorce. But He wants Christians to live according to His standards, not their own desires or the world's customs. If husbands and wives will obey God's principles about relationships with others, it is possible to have the love-filled marriages He intends.

On a notecard, write a reminder to pray daily for your parents' marriage. What can you as their child do to help?

If you live in a home that has experienced divorce, realize that God still loves you—and your parents. You, too, can still pray for your parents.

RIGHTEOUSNESS

What does it take to get into heaven?"
Mr. Bowen's question caught the attention of the
high school students in his Sunday school class. Elaine glanced around
uneasily. Sandy stopped fidgeting. Allan looked squarely at Mr. Bowen.

"I thought it was about time we got down to basics," said Mr. Bowen.
"Who can tell me the one word used in the Bible to describe what a person must have to get into heaven?"

Answers came quickly: "Forgiveness," "Salvation," "Jesus."

"Well," Mr. Bowen replied, "those are all good answers. But the one word I'm looking for describes what you get when Jesus saves and forgives you. It's a quality that makes you fit to enter heaven."

The class was puzzled. They all knew a person had to accept Jesus to get into heaven. What was Mr. Bowen getting at?

Mr. Bowen smiled. "Let's find the answer by looking in the Word. Romans 5:19 is a good place to start."

◆ KEY VERSE ON RIGHTEOUSNESS
For just as through the disobedience of the one man the many were made sinners, so also through the obedience of the one man the many will be made righteous (Romans 5:19).

● THINKING ABOUT RIGHTEOUSNESS
God is holy. That means He will not dwell in the presence of sin. Anyone who lives with Him in heaven must also be holy.

Righteousness is the **standard of conduct God has set requiring humans to be perfect**, without sin. Yet the Bible says (and we all know) that everyone sins— no one is perfectly righteous.

▲ LOOKING AHEAD
How can we become righteous enough to enter God's presence? Romans 3:23 tells us that everyone sins—no one can enter heaven because of his own righteousness. Read Romans 3:21-22 to see where righteousness comes from.

"I'm a perfect little angel while I'm asleep, Sir. It's being awake that gives me trouble."

Good works that look like filthy rags

Q

Is right-
eousness
the same
as doing
good
works?

A

Righteous-
ness is not
measured
by my
good
works, but
by God's
holiness.

PARENT
*Help your child
assess different
ways to be
measured—
by grades,
competitions,
yearly check-
ups, etc. Then
discuss how
spiritual
growth can be
measured.*

For weeks Terri had been quietly witnessing to her classmate Leila, encouraging her and patiently answering Leila's many questions. But when Terri mentioned the fact that everyone is a sinner, Leila became upset.

"Wait a minute!" she fumed. "I've never stolen anything. I've never murdered anybody. I've even given money to charity and done volunteer work at the community center. The good things I do outweigh the bad things fifty to one. I'm as good as you are. So how can you call me a sinner?"

"I'm not calling you a sinner," Terri replied gently. "God is. If you just compare the two of us, you probably are much better. But God doesn't compare human beings. And He doesn't have a scale to weigh a person's good deeds against his bad deeds. You see," she explained, "God's standard is total perfection."

◆ TAKE A LOOK
Psalm 53:3; Proverbs 20:9; James 2:10; 4:17

In Jesus' day the Pharisees were the most righteous people around. They devised clever ways to keep God's law, thinking that their "good deeds" would add up to righteousness. And they thought they were better than just about everybody else. But Jesus said this about their good works:

"Unless your righteousness surpasses that of the Pharisees and the teachers of the law, you will certainly not enter the kingdom of heaven" (Matthew 5:20).

Reading these verses will make it clear that no one is completely righteous: Psalm 53:3; Proverbs 20:9; James 2:10; 4:17. How do those verses make you feel?

▲ TAKE A STEP

Like Leila, many people think that if their good works outweigh the bad ones, God will let them into heaven. But God doesn't decide on that basis. He is a holy God who cannot tolerate any sin—or sinful being—in His presence. The requirement for being with Him is total perfection, and no human being measures up to that.

Tomorrow and the following day we'll see how God made it possible to meet His standard of righteousness. The first step is to see ourselves as God sees us—sinners who need help.

Why do you think people like the Pharisees—or Leila—have a hard time seeing themselves as God does? Have you ever admitted that you are a sinful person?

L ong ago a man was called to serve in the army during wartime. Because of a hardship in his family, he couldn't go. But his brother, who had not been called, volunteered to serve in his place and was accepted as a substitute. Unfortunately, the brother was killed in battle.

Sometime later, the young man received another notice calling him to serve in the army. He wrote back: "I have already served." Amazed at his arrogance, the commanding officer demanded that he report for duty or face arrest and court martial. Instead, the man took his case to court.

After both sides testified, the judge gave his verdict: "This man is legally free. His brother volunteered to be his substitute and was accepted as such by the army. As far as the law is concerned, it is as if this man himself had served and died. The army has no claim on him. He is free."

◆ TAKE A LOOK / Romans 5:17-21

Because of our sin, we can never be righteous enough on our own to reach God's standard of perfection. So is the situation hopeless?

No! Just as the young farmer had a substitute to take his place in the army, we have a substitute who lived a righteous life for us before God. You'll see who—and how—when you read Romans 5:17-21.

▲ TAKE A STEP

For just as through the disobedience of the one man the many were made sinners, so also through the obedience of the one man the many will be made righteous (Romans 5:19).

Adam was the "one man" whose sin brought death to all. Jesus is the "one Man" whose life of perfect obedience brings righteousness to all who believe. From all eternity Jesus was and is the Righteous One.

In His death, Jesus paid for our sin. In His life, He was perfectly righteous in all He said and did. He lived the kind of life everyone must live who wants to be in God's presence. It's two sides of the same coin: In His life as well as in His death Jesus Christ was our substitute.

You've probably thanked Jesus many times for dying in your place. But have you ever thanked Him for living the perfect life you couldn't possibly live—for not giving in to temptation, for suffering hardship, for completely obeying God's law? Thank Him now for doing all that and more— as your substitute.

He's our substitute in life and death

Q

Whose righteousness pleases God?

A

Righteousness that pleases God was lived by Jesus Christ.

Why should God let you into heaven?

Q

How can I become righteous?

A

The righteous-ness of Christ becomes mine by faith.

PARENT
C. S. Lewis's
The Horse and
His Boy *is
about a com-
moner and a
prince who
switch identi-
ties. Discuss
how the com-
moner might
benefit from
having the
royal privileges.
What privileges
do we have as
children of
the King?*

We can pull it off. I know we can! Just think what fun it'll be. She'll never know the difference."

"Yeah, well, in the last movie I saw where guys switched identities, one of them wound up in really big trouble," Jake mumbled.

Though only cousins, Brandon Elliot and Jake Carlson looked enough alike to be twins. They were notorious for their practical jokes. Now, after living in another city for five years, a friend of theirs from ele-mentary school, Emily Taylor, had come back to visit. Brandon thought it would be fun to pretend to be Jake and ask Emily for a date.

"I'll wear some of your clothes, drive your car, try to act like you. I'm sure I can convince her I'm you. Why, before the night is over, I might even believe it myself!"

◆ **TAKE A LOOK / Romans 10:4;
1 Corinthians 1:30; Philippians 3:9**

No matter how hard Brandon tried, he couldn't be Jake. Even if you believed with all your heart that you were different, people still see the "same old you."

But in order to enter God's presence, we must truly become different people. We must have the righteousness that comes only from God—the perfect righteousness of Jesus Christ.

Romans 10:4; 1 Corinthians 1:30; and Philippians 3:9 will show you that Christ is our righteousness, and that His righteousness can become ours only by faith.

▲ **TAKE A STEP**

The blood of Jesus Christ removes, or cleanses, sin. The righteousness of Christ provides the perfec-tion God demands.

We must recognize that our own "righteous-ness" (all our good works combined) is not good enough to earn God's approval. We must also understand that our own sins deserve God's wrath. Then we can have both His forgiveness and His righteousness simply by faith. Then 2 Corinthians 5:17 becomes true about us:

*If anyone is in Christ, he is a new creation;
the old has gone, the new has come!*

Imagine you are at heaven's gate and God asks why He should let you in. If you don't know, complete this sentence: "I can enter heaven because I believe Jesus has _____ my sins and given me His _____ ."

*W*hy did you lie about that?" Alan protested to his friend. "Sometimes I think you lie more than you tell the truth."

"So I have some fun by telling a little lie now and then. Big deal!" Josh grinned back.

"Josh, it really isn't funny," Alan retorted. " 'You shall not lie' is one of the Ten Commandments, and Christians are supposed to obey God's laws."

"Aw, Alan, loosen up and live a little. You've heard enough sermons to know that nobody can keep God's laws perfectly. We all sin in some way or another. That's why Jesus had to die—to pay for our sins. So He's already paid for it. He'll forgive me."

"That doesn't sound quite right," Alan said slowly. "Sure, it's true that Jesus died to pay for our sins, and He does forgive us. But He didn't go around just doing whatever He wanted. You're acting like God canceled the Ten Commandments!"

◆ TAKE A LOOK / Romans 6:11-22

Josh was right: God does forgive sin. But Josh was wrong in thinking a believer can live any way he wants to. In fact, when a Christian truly understands what Jesus did for him, he will express his love for God by keeping His commandments.

This is love for God: to obey his commands.
And his commands are not burdensome
(1 John 5:3).

Sinful acts . . . unrighteous deeds. What place do they have in a believer's life? Romans 6:11-22 explains that such do not belong in a Christian's life at all.

▲ TAKE A STEP

Only the perfect righteousness of Jesus makes us fit to enter God's presence. We acquire this righteousness by faith. But we must also realize that God hasn't canceled His commandments. It doesn't please Him when we live just as we please. Instead, He desires that we do good works and obey His commands. As Paul told his young friend Timothy, we are to

pursue righteousness, godliness, faith, love,
endurance and gentleness (1 Timothy 6:11).

With his habit of lying, Josh was holding on to a "pet" sin. In view of the Scriptures you've read today, what does his attitude tell you about his love for God?

Do you have a pet sin, which reveals the same thing about your life? What will you do about it in order to "pursue righteousness"?

God hasn't canceled the Ten Commandments!

Q

What good are my own works of righteousness?

A

Righteousness in my life expresses my love for God.

PLAY

*S*even-year-old Shelley was crying softly when her mother came in to kiss her goodnight. "What's the matter, honey?" Mrs. Stephens asked as she sat down on the bed. "Does something hurt?"

"No, I'm okay," she sniffed, but then burst into tears. "Oh, Mom, do I have to go back to camp tomorrow? I don't want to."

"Why, Shelley, I thought you enjoyed being with your friends. What's changed your mind?"

"Well, I like the crafts and the stories. And swimming is fun. But I hate the games we play, Mommy. I'm no good at them."

Shelley wiped her tears with the sheet. "Today the ball came right to me but I missed it, and everybody laughed. The next time it was my turn to catch the ball, I missed again, and some of the kids got mad. They said I was giving the game away. I don't want to play anymore. They don't like me. Can't I stay home . . . please?"

◆ THINKING ABOUT PLAY

From babies playing peek-a-boo to granddads on the golf course, people of all ages enjoy **sports or games for recreation or amusement.** But when the desire to win takes away from the fun, everybody loses.

The Bible doesn't really talk about playing, although it does refer a few times to various sports. But whether working or playing, the Bible does encourage us to:

"Who's gonna stay here and do my homework?"

● KEY VERSE ON PLAY

Do nothing out of selfish ambition or vain conceit, but in humility consider others better than yourselves (Philippians 2:3).

▲ LOOKING AHEAD

Have you, like Shelley, ever been frustrated or hurt while playing? If you were at camp with Shelley, how would you help her? (This week's Key Verse may give some clues.)

Here's a Bible game that may not be as easy as it looks—but it will start your mind to thinking. In this paragraph are hidden the names of 15 books of the Bible. One is highlighted to get you started. It's a real lulu. Kept me looking so hard for the facts that I missed the revelation. I was in a jam especially since the names were not capitalized. The truth will come to numbers of our readers. To others it will be a real job. For all it will be a most fascinating search. Yes, there will be some easy to spot; and others hard to judge, so we'll admit it usually results in loud lamentations when we can't find them. One lady says she brews coffee while she puzzles over it. Re**mark**able, isn't it!

◆ **TAKE A LOOK / Romans 12:2-3, 9-11**
If you haven't found all 15 names of the Bible books hidden in that paragraph, work as a team to find the rest. Don't compete against each other: cooperate. Work together to "beat" the puzzle. That way, nobody wins, but nobody loses either. Everybody just does his best . . . and has fun in the process!

Play—especially team sports—can be highly competitive. Winning is often the most important goal. But the more we focus on winning, the harder it is to have fun.

How does Romans 12:2-3, 9-11 encourage you to change the "winning is everything" philosophy?

▲ **TAKE A STEP**
Be transformed by the renewing of your mind. . . . Honor one another above yourselves (Romans 12:2, 10).
Fierce competition in games that are supposed to be fun can often bring out the *beast* rather than the *best* in us. Otherwise "nice" people will delight in others' failures and become puffed up over their own accomplishments. And it's all done in the name of winning.

Many times the games we play—and the way we play them—teach us values that don't honor God or help us grow spiritually or emotionally. Instead of cooperating, we criticize.

Perhaps you or some member of your family is involved in a competitive sport. Think for a moment about the way you view the people who don't make the team or those who stay on the bench. How will you put to work the verses you just read in the next game you play?

Who likes to play games nobody loses?

How can play be fun when nobody wins or loses?

A

Play is more fun when I remember that people are more important than winning or losing.

I'm a winner when I help others win

Q

How does helping others win help me win too?

A

Play in which I help someone else win makes me a winner too.

PARENT
Games that teach younger children cooperation instead of competition can be found in The Cooperative Sports & Games Book *by Terry Orlick.*

*W*hen American Indians chose sides for their games, they made sure no one was humiliated by being picked last. Why not try one of their methods the next time you and your friends choose sides for a team game.

One approach was to have the chief sit inside a circle. All the players' sticks were placed in a heap in front of him. (You could use name tags or wooden popsicle sticks with the players' names on them.) Blindfolded, the chief picked sticks two at a time and placed one on his left and one on his right until all the sticks were gone. Players then ran to the two piles of sticks, found their own, and joined that team.

Another way was for the chief to place strips of two different colors of paper in a small pouch or covered basket. Each player drew one slip of paper and was assigned to a team according to the color he chose.

◆ TAKE A LOOK / Romans 15:1-7

Unless you're a sports superstar, you've probably stood in line hoping you wouldn't be picked last. That's not a fun feeling, is it?

How you treat your playmates is important. It's not whether you win or lose, but how you play the game that counts. God loves everyone—not just superstars. And He gives all His children room to fail and opportunities to grow.

Early Christians had a problem knowing how to treat other believers who didn't "play the game" the same way they did. After you read Romans 15:1-7, discuss how it applies to the way you treat the people you play with.

▲ TAKE A STEP

Competition is striving to win for yourself or your team; cooperation is working together so everyone wins.

As Christians we are told that . . .

Each of us should please his neighbor for his good, to build him up (Romans 15:2).

Playing with others can be an occasion to develop skills, strive for success, and enjoy real fun. Think about the games you play at home and with others. Do they help build up your playmates? Are participants allowed to make mistakes without feeling inferior?

Together, try to think of a game you could play that isn't based on winning or losing, but is "just for the fun of it."

*H*ere's a fun summer activity you might want to try. Organize a neighborhood scavenger hunt and picnic. Arrange the judges in advance—perhaps an older couple who would rather not go on the actual hunt. Then send out several groups to bring back items such as:

1. The biggest piece of wood they can find—or carry
2. The oldest nickel
3. The smelliest sock
4. The heaviest rock
5. The most worn-out shoe
6. An old tire
7. The oldest riding toy
8. Last Sunday's church bulletin

When the teams return at a predetermined time, the "judges" will inspect each item and award points. The team with the most points gets to be first in line at the picnic table or the ice cream bucket!*

◆ **TAKE A LOOK / Acts 18:1-4, 18-19, 24-26**

Have you ever thought you might like to tell someone about Jesus, but you didn't quite know how? It's sometimes hard to tell a total stranger about Jesus. That's why a neighborhood get-together centered on an activity like the one above is a great way to start. In this way your family can get to know other neighborhood people, build some friendships, and have fun together.

The apostle Paul was no stranger to "friendship evangelism." By reading Acts 18:1-4, 18-19, 24-26 you'll see how Paul established relationships before he witnessed.

▲ **TAKE A STEP**

"Tentmaking" is hard work. But whether you're at work or play, your witness is more effective when it's based on friendship with the other person. With that foundation laid, you can then take this advice from the apostle Paul:

Make the most of every opportunity. Let your conversation be always full of grace, seasoned with salt, so that you may know how to answer everyone (Colossians 4:5-6).

How can you "make the most of every opportunity" to talk to your friends about Jesus? And by the way, two great books of games you and your family may want to buy or check out of the library are *Fun 'n Games* by Rice, Rydberg & Yaconelli, and *More New Games* from the New Games Foundation.

The way I play has something to say

Q

How can the way I play help me witness for Jesus?

A

Play provides opportunities for me to build friendships before I share the gospel.

*Taken from Fun 'n Games, Wayne Rice, Dennis Rydberg and Mike Yaconelli. ©1977 by Youth Specialties.

Learn to play— play to learn

The Last Detail" is an observation game that's fun to play with just about anyone, in any age group, at any time. Start by facing each other (one-to-one or team-to-team). Remain still for two or three minutes. Try to observe and remember as much as you can about the person facing you.

Then turn your backs to each other and change six details about the way you look. (For instance, untie a shoestring; change a watch from one arm to the other; tilt a ribbon, hat, or bow in the opposite direction.)

Once rearranged, turn back to face each other and see whether you can spot all the changes in your opposite player—down to the very last detail.

What skills can I develop as I play?

A

Play gives me an opportunity to practice spiritual sportsmanship.

◆**TAKE A LOOK / Romans 12:3-17; 13:1**
Playing games of all kinds can give you an opportunity to develop skills you'll always find useful. Some games can increase your memory, your concentration, and your ability to observe, reason, and think. Others can increase your general knowledge.

As you play sports or do physical exercise, you also build strength, stamina, and coordination. But have you ever realized that play can increase some important spiritual skills as well?

People who play together know the importance of practicing good sportsmanship. As you read Romans 12:3-17; 13:1, think about how Paul describes what we usually mean when we speak of good sportsmanship.

▲ **TAKE A STEP**
If you play according to those "rules," you'll build your "spiritual muscles" and practice good sportsmanship at the same time!

Of course, the key is realizing that every person in God's family is unique and has a special role to play. Everyone is equally important. In fact, when we play together,

Each member belongs to all the others
(Romans 12:5).

Conclude this week's family time by making a poster titled "The Way We Play." Write out in your own words one observation from each of the 16 verses you read today. (For instance, your first sentence might be: "Be honest about yourself.") Print them neatly on a letter-size sheet of paper or poster board. Add a border or design and post it on your family bulletin board or make copies for each family member.

FREEDOM

On October 30, 1956, the citizens of Hungary overthrew their communist government. Two days later, Soviet troops surrounded their country. The new government asked other free countries for help. No help came. On November 4, the invading army attacked and crushed the new government. In the following months, thousands of people who had worked for freedom were executed or imprisoned.

This poem expresses the viewpoint of one of those prisoners:

> Death sits with us everyday
> in the court, in the cell.
> And as we raise the cold water
> to our mouths and the hard bread
> and the few dry beans, and the dead soup
> we are learning a new thanks—
> pronouncing a real benediction.
> We can tell you more about freedom now.*

◆ THINKING ABOUT FREEDOM

What comes to mind when *you* think about freedom? Like many people, you may think of freedom of speech, freedom to choose leaders, and freedom to practice religion without being hindered. But true freedom also has a spiritual meaning. True freedom—**being released from sin, guilt, and fear of death**—is found only through Jesus Christ.

● KEY VERSE ON FREEDOM

"If the Son sets you free, you will be free indeed" (John 8:36).

▲ LOOKING AHEAD

This week we'll probe the deeper meaning of freedom. As you look at a world map, locate several countries where you've heard that Christians may be suffering for their faith. Then take time to pray for the believers in those countries today.

"... and he huffed, and he puffed, and he blew the house in.... Obviously a nonsmoker."

*Reprinted from THE SECRET TREES by Luci Shaw, by permission of Harold Shaw Publishers.

In chains as a prisoner of sin

C hris fidgeted all during history class. As the bell rang, he darted into the rest room and hurriedly pulled out his lighter. He lit a cigarette, took a long drag, and then leaned against the door.

He'd been like this for two years—nervous and miserable in class, unable to concentrate. When the bell rang he would hurry to the smoking area or the rest room for a smoke. Only then did he feel he could relax.

Chris had tried to stop smoking. Once he'd even thrown a whole pack down the toilet. But he couldn't stand it—he soon rushed to the convenience store and bought a whole carton.

It made no difference that his friends called the cigarettes "coffin nails." For Chris, they were chains he couldn't break. His habit was his master.

What does it mean to be a slave to sin?

◆ **TAKE A LOOK**
Proverbs 5:22; Romans 6:16; John 8:31-36

We human beings like to think we're free as the wind, and always in control. But freedom isn't our natural condition. Spiritually, human beings are not born free.

Chris's slavery to his habit is only one illustration of the various forms of bondage human beings experience. You'll learn who's the "master" behind all wrong behavior as you read Proverbs 5:22; Romans 6:16; and 2 Timothy 2:24-26. Discover Jesus' solution to this condition as you read John 8:31-36.

A slave to sin is under the control of sin.

▲ **TAKE A STEP**

God's Word teaches that human beings were born slaves of sin:

We were in slavery under the basic principles of the world (Galatians 4:3).

And as you discovered in 2 Timothy 2:26, it is Satan who has taken people captive to do his will.

Chris found it impossible to break the chains of his sinful habit on his own. It is absolutely impossible for us to escape the slavery of sin on our own. But Jesus has set us free. His life within us gives us power over sinful attitudes and actions in our daily lives.

Sometimes what we call "habits" are really the chains of sin. Can you identify your "bad habits"? What does God's Word say about them?

How would you feel if you had to stop those habits? Would you have a tough time like Chris did when he tried to stop smoking?

*T*odd was sitting with a group of his friends watching the Piedmont High football team beat Creston.

Chris, sitting next to him, reached in his pocket for his lighter and cigarettes. He offered one to Todd.

Todd shook his head. "No thanks, Chris. I quit."

Chris looked surprised, then said sarcastically, "Oh, yeah, I remember. You're going to be Mr. Do-Right now that you're into all that born-again stuff. You must have whole lists of things you can't do."

Ralph chimed in: "Yeah, can't smoke, can't chew, and can't go out with girls that do. I wonder if there's anything left he can do!"

Several of their friends started to chuckle, and Todd could feel his face turning red. "Well actually, it's not that I can't do those things anymore," he replied. "I really don't want to."

◆ TAKE A LOOK / Romans 6:5-18

When someone offered him a cigarette before, Todd—like Chris—hadn't been able to say no. But when Todd became a Christian, he knew that he was saved from the penalty of sin. And he also learned that God works in our lives to free us from the chains of sin.

God's goal for His children is that we become more like Jesus. He changes us from the inside out, chipping away at our sinful attitudes, actions, and habits.

In Romans 6:5-18 the apostle Paul describes this process as "putting to death the old self." To help you understand this important passage, try reading it from more than one translation of the Bible. You might enjoy the Living Bible or even the Amplified Bible.

▲ TAKE A STEP

As a Christian, Todd learned that it's not our willpower or determination that frees us from sin. It's God's power working in us so that we no longer want to sin. As Paul wrote,

Now that you have been set free from sin and have become slaves to God, the benefit you reap leads to holiness (Romans 6:22).

Is there some sin in your life that you'd like to conquer? Confess it specifically to the Lord; ask Him to take away your desire to do it. Then, if you're tempted to do that again, remember that Jesus can keep you from sinning—if you let His power work through you.

Freedom: the ability to say no and let sin go

Q

How does Christ set me free?

A

Freedom means God's power is working in me to keep me from sinning.

My freedom ends where yours begins

Q

*What
are the
responsi-
bilities
of my
freedom?*

A

*Freedom
includes the
responsibility
to put
others'
needs before
my own
rights.*

PARENT
*Discuss some of
the "rights"
movements men-
tioned on this
page. Begin by
asking: Does this
movement
encourage
people to
indulge their
sinful, selfish
natures?*

Stephanie was stepping out of her car when she heard it—the pulsating beat and gyrating rhythm rocking the air around the apartment building. That deafening sound couldn't be coming from her apartment—could it?

Stephanie charged up the stairs two at a time. She opened the door to confront her brother Mark, who stood defiantly in front of his new stereo.

"Mark, turn that down!" she yelled. "They'll call the police!"

"They can't do that. I have a right to listen to music I like!"

"But Mark—" Just then someone pounded on the door. It was the landlord, red-faced and angry.

"Just what do you think you're doing?" he bellowed. "If I ever hear that thing again, you—and it—will be out on the street."

◆ TAKE A LOOK / Galatians 5:1, 13-15

Agree or disagree: Mark had the freedom to play his stereo as loudly as he wanted.

Agree or disagree: The tenants in the building had the right to normal peace and quiet.

The truth we must understand is that no one individual has absolute freedom. Mark's right to play loud music ended where the other tenants' rights to peace and quiet began.

Galatians 5:1, 13-15 points out a Christian's freedom should be ruled by love and concern for other people.

▲ TAKE A STEP

Women's rights . . . children's rights . . . equal rights . . . abortion rights . . . gay rights—individuals and groups are constantly clamoring for their "rights." But before you jump on anybody's bandwagon—or even toot the horn for your own rights at home or at school—use God's Word to judge the merit of the cause:

Do not use your freedom to indulge the sinful nature; rather, serve one another in love (Galatians 5:13).

Give an example of a time when you limited your rights for another person's benefit, such as giving up working on a favorite hobby to help someone else. Parents, describe some of the ways your rights changed when you became an adult, married, and had children. For instance, you gained the right to set your own house rules; but you also gained the responsibility to provide for your own house.

*I*t was against the law to teach children about God. But one woman's love for her two children led her to take the risk. She wanted her little ones to know the true and living God—despite the danger.

All went well until the children started school. What they were taught there conflicted with what they had learned from their mother. But even though they were very young, they refused to agree with their teachers who said there was no God.

The teachers tried to persuade the children in every way they could. Then they threatened them. The teachers allowed other children to mock the "little Christians." Still the children would not give up the faith their mother had taught them.

Then the teachers went to the authorities. They accused the mother of false, anti-government teaching, and of being an unfit parent. Soon her children were taken from her and put in a state-operated orphanage. She never saw her children again.

◆ TAKE A LOOK / Romans 13:1-8

One of God's tremendous blessings for Americans is our form of government, which protects our freedoms and our families. Without it, we might not be able to worship freely, gain an education, choose our own careers, vote as conscience leads, or raise our children as God directs.

In Romans 13:1-8, the apostle Paul explains our relationship with the "governing authorities." As you read, look for two things every citizen must do.

▲ TAKE A STEP

As believers, we are to submit to the authorities and pay our taxes. Jesus taught that we should give our government the obedience and respect due it. Paul wrote to Timothy,

I urge . . . that requests, prayers, intercession and thanksgiving be made for everyone—for kings and all those in authority (1 Timothy 2:1-2).

Christians should pray for their government leaders. Why not pray now for your elected officials—city, county, state, and nation. But first, what other actions could your family take to help protect freedom? Remember, to take freedom for granted is to risk losing it. Remember also that not all countries allow their citizens the freedoms we enjoy. If you know people who have lived in a country with restricted freedom, why not invite them for a meal. Ask them why they left their country and what they enjoy most now.

Freedom is possessed by those who defend it

Q

How can I help protect our national freedom?

A

Freedom is protected when I pray for my leaders and work to keep human laws in line with God's laws.

PARENT
Did you vote in the last election? What would our country be like if all Christians answered no?

CHILDHOOD

D *o you remember how you thought about God when you were very*
young? Some children shared these impressions of God. God is
. . . *so big He is everywhere.*
. . . *so small He can fit in my heart.*
. . . *invisible (but He doesn't sleep at night).*
. . . *putting angels around my bed so nothing can squeeze through.*
. . . *smarter than my teacher, 'cause He listens to us all at the same*
    time. My teacher says, "One at a time," or "I can't hear you."
. . . *as big as Daddy.*
. . . *coming real soon, so I look out the window.*
. . . *something, but I don't know what.*

◆ THINKING ABOUT CHILDHOOD

God could have designed human beings to develop more rapidly
than we do. Instead, each person on the planet is in **a dependent
period of growth for many years.** We call this stage of life
"childhood."

It's easy for adults to forget a lot about their childhood. Some
grownups even look down on children as "unimportant little people." But as Christians, all of us—grandparents, parents, and children too—need to understand that children are important to God.

"I can never remember whether children
are to be seen and not heard or the
other way around."

● KEY VERSE ON CHILDHOOD
Sons are a heritage
from the LORD, *children*
are a reward from him
(Psalm 127:3).

▲ LOOKING AHEAD
This week the
thoughts of a girl named
Sara and of her mother
will help us answer some
questions about child-
hood.

When does God get
interested in a child's
development? Find the
answer in Psalm 139:13-
16. Then try to remember
your earliest thoughts
about God and share
them with one another.
How have your ideas
changed?

Don't worry, Mommy. The Bible says God will keep us safe," Sara said positively.

Mrs. Casey simply didn't know what to say. She and her husband never thought much about God, and they had never taken their children to church. But ever since Sara had started going to the Bible club at Mrs. Gibson's house, she seemed to be talking about God—and trusting Him—more and more. Now with this recent crisis in her sister's family, Mrs. Casey felt she should say something to Sara.

"Honey, Aunt Martha and Uncle Philip are good folks, but they couldn't stop that flood. We're just glad no one was hurt."

"Oh, I know, Mommy. I thanked God for keeping them safe. God will look after us too—even if a flood comes to our house. I know He will. He promises that in His Bible."

As Sara ran out to play, Mrs. Casey wondered. "What if there really is a God we can trust? Life would be so different . . . "

◆ **TAKE A LOOK / Matthew 18:1-4; Mark 10:13-16**

When a child asks questions about God, adults may say, "Wait until you're older." But like Sara, children often have the desire and the ability to trust God wholeheartedly. They have the faith and humility to believe what God says. That's what Jesus tells us in Matthew 18:1-4.

Jesus' own disciples had a wrong attitude toward children. Perhaps they were thinking, "They're too young," or "They can't really understand." But Jesus' response demonstrated once and for all that God wants children to be with Him.

As you read Mark 10:13-16 notice how Jesus reacted when His disciples tried to turn the children away. How would you have felt if you had been one of those children?

▲ **TAKE A STEP**

Jesus was indignant and rebuked the disciples by saying,

"Let the little children come to me, and do not hinder them" (Mark 10:14).

He wanted the disciples to understand that a person is never too young to accept and believe in God.

Jesus has never changed His mind about children. Do you think knowing that fact would give Sara confidence in her situation? How could it help you in some of the situations of your life?

What did Jesus mean when He said to become like a child?

Childhood is a time when we demonstrate the ability to trust God completely.

One warning you don't want to overlook

Q

What warnings did Jesus give about children?

A

Childhood is an impressionable time when faith is easily damaged.

PARENT
If you have some destructive attitudes toward your child, confide in your pastor, a close friend, or a counselor. Help is available.

As they spoke by phone, Mrs. Casey couldn't understand how her sister Martha could be so calm.

"Martha, don't tell me God is looking after you. Your whole house is gone and everything in it. How can you keep saying 'all things work together for good'?" Mrs. Casey burst into tears. She continued to sob as her sister replied.

"Miranda, God has taken care of us. Sure, our possessions are gone. But those things don't have any eternal value. God is meeting our needs through His people in the church every day."

"Well, I think you're foolish," Mrs. Casey sobbed.

Just around the corner, Sara's eyes grew wide as she heard her mother's irritation. "Maybe God isn't as good as Mrs. Gibson says," she thought. "Maybe He can't keep us safe after all."

◆ TAKE A LOOK / Matthew 18:6-9

Sara loved and trusted her mother more than anyone in the world. To believe in something her mother doubted seemed like disloyalty. As the fear and frustration in her mother's voice sank into Sara's mind, a seed of doubt was planted. Rather than strengthening her daughter's faith, Mrs. Casey damaged it.

Yesterday we learned that Jesus said we must become like children to enter His kingdom. But Jesus also gave strong, serious warning to anyone who causes a child to sin. Read that warning in Matthew 18:6-9.

▲ TAKE A STEP

Adults influence children in many ways—both for good and bad. That influence is so important that every adult should be concerned about it.

"If anyone causes one of these little ones who believe in me to sin, it would be better for him to have a large millstone hung around his neck and to be drowned in the depths of the sea" (Matthew 18:6).

Every adult needs to think carefully about those words. But verse 5 also describes a wonderful privilege adults have.

After you read that verse again, let each person share a memory or an experience when he or she received Jesus' love through an adult. If you can remember enough details, put your experience in the form of a story. Or make it a mystery by having other family members guess who helped you understand Jesus' love.

Sara ran to answer the doorbell. Timmy Gibson was standing there with his mother.

"We brought some stuff for your cousins," Timmy declared as he lugged a large shopping bag into the living room. Mrs. Gibson was right behind him carrying another load.

"Sara told us you were going up to see your sister," Mrs. Gibson said to Sara's mother. "We felt God wanted us to help them get back on their feet. A few other families in the church pitched in too."

Sara's face brightened as she and her mother looked at the sheets and blankets in one of the bags. "Oh, Mommy, look. This blanket is exactly like the one Jennifer lost. And blue is her favorite color. I think God must really love Aunt Martha and Uncle Philip."

Then she turned to Mrs. Gibson. "I told Mommy God would look after my aunt and uncle, and He is, isn't He?"

◆ **TAKE A LOOK / Matthew 18:10-14**

Christian adults represent God to children by almost everything they say and do. Sara believed God's promise to supply all our needs. When Timmy and his mom brought household goods for her relatives, she saw their actions as a demonstration of God's love.

But the actions of adults are not the only way children can understand God's love. In the same chapter you read from yesterday, Jesus tells a parable illustrating just how precious children are to Him. You can read that "earthly story with a heavenly meaning" in Matthew 18:10-14.

▲ **TAKE A STEP**

In that parable, Jesus showed how great God's love for children is. He compared God to a man who had a hundred sheep. One of them got lost, so the man left the rest and searched for the lost one.

What does that tell you about how much God loves you? How interested is God in your problems and fears? If you're an adult, what does that story tell you about the kind of love you should have for children?

Close your family time by letting each family member draw a picture of the "lambs" in your family. Write this verse underneath and memorize it this week:

"Your Father in heaven is not willing that any of these little ones should perish"
(Matthew 18:14).

God really cares for His little lambs

Q

Can children really understand God's love?

A

Childhood is a time when we can understand God's love for us through His Word and the loving actions of others.

Be a child and lay aside your pride

Q

What can adults learn from children?

A

Childhood pictures the kind of humility God wants me to have toward Him.

Yes, He does love them," Mrs. Gibson smiled, drawing Sara into her arms. "God cares about your aunt and uncle—and He cares about you too."

Mrs. Casey was pretending that she wasn't listening while Sara and Mrs. Gibson talked. Then her ear caught Mrs. Gibson's words and she couldn't help but interrupt. "That may be fine for a child, but it can't be that easy. We grownups have to look out for ourselves."

"A great king once had this to say," Mrs. Gibson replied softly: " 'My heart is not proud, O Lord, my eyes are not haughty; . . . but I have stilled and quieted my soul; like a weaned child with its mother . . . is my soul within. Put your hope in the Lord both now and forever.'" She continued, looking at Mrs. Casey, "Miranda, that king knew the peace that Sara knows too. He knew that a loving, kind God is interested in His children. That same God loves you too. May I tell you about Him?"

◆ TAKE A LOOK / Matthew 18:1-6

Adults can learn a lot from children! Even the disciples who had once rebuked parents for bringing the little children to Jesus later asked a very important question. You might be as surprised as they were by His answer when you read Matthew 18:1-6 again.

▲ TAKE A STEP

When they asked, "Who is the greatest in the kingdom of heaven?" the disciples were thinking along the lines of an earthly kingdom where people have positions of power and wealth.

Perhaps they thought they'd hear names like Moses, Elijah, Daniel, or John the Baptist. They may even have hoped to hear their own names mentioned!

But by using a child as an example, Jesus pinpointed pride as a problem human beings have. Then He stated one quality everyone needs to become a citizen of His kingdom:

*"Whoever humbles himself like this child
is the greatest in the kingdom of heaven"
(Matthew 18:4).*

How is a little child humble?

A child who believes in Jesus knows that God is powerful and strong. He or she depends on God for everything and is quick and willing to obey.

How could Mrs. Casey learn humility from her daughter Sara? How would you rate your own humility?

GENESIS

*M*r. *Townsend looked at the textbooks spread out on his daughter's desk. No wonder Andrea was upset over what she was being taught —especially in science class!*

"Daddy," Andrea said as she put her pen down, "when you and I talked about evolution last year, I realized there aren't many facts to back it up. And after we studied the book of Genesis together, I saw how the Bible explains the way things really happened. But just look at these pictures!"

Andrea pointed to a series of drawings across the bottom of two pages. From a slumping apelike creature on one side, the figures gradually became more like standing human forms.

"This book never says that these are just artists' ideas of human development," Andrea said angrily. "And Mr. Biggs teaches this stuff like someone was there with a camera millions of years ago. It's not even honest!"

◆ THINKING ABOUT GENESIS

Andrea was serious about her studies and wanted all the knowledge her teachers could provide. But she realized she was being taught theory instead of truth.

As the first book in the Bible, Genesis is one of the most important books ever written. In the Hebrew language its title is *bereshith*, which means "in the beginning." The English title, Genesis, which comes from the Greek word *geneseos*, means "history of origin." Genesis is truly the **book of beginnings.** It reveals truth about beginnings no one was around to observe.

"I'd be a lot better off if God had created more heaven and less earth."

● KEY VERSE OF GENESIS

This is the account of the heavens and earth when they were created (Genesis 2:4).

▲ LOOKING AHEAD

Read Genesis 1 aloud. As you do, make a list of all the "beginnings" you find there. You may be surprised!

Super truth supernaturally revealed

Q

Why is Genesis an important book?

A

Genesis reveals "beginnings" we couldn't know or understand any other way.

PARENT
While our study focuses on the first chapters of Genesis, we hope you'll read the entire book. Two chapters a day and you'll be done in a month!

*A*ndrea was upset with what her science teacher taught about the origin of life.

"He won't even consider any viewpoint other than evolution," she declared. "When I asked him if he'd ever read the Bible, he just laughed and said it was all a myth, so why should he read it!"

"That sounds like it was quite a discussion," Mr. Townsend commented. "What did you say then?"

"I said that archaeological discoveries have shown the Bible is accurate about the historical people and places it mentions, so why shouldn't it be accurate about creation too. And I told him a lot of people think evolution is a myth, so why don't schools present both viewpoints fairly and let people make up their own minds. Then some kids clapped, and Mr. Biggs said we didn't have time to discuss it any longer."

◆ **TAKE A LOOK**
Genesis 1:1; Isaiah 44:24; 45:18; John 1:1-2

Andrea recognized that what Mr. Biggs was teaching as scientific fact was really only an unproved theory.

Scientific evidence involves a procedure that can be performed again and again, proving that it is true. Since no human being will ever be able to create a universe or make one evolve, human beings will never be able to prove how the universe began. But in the book of Genesis God reveals that He caused the universe to come into existence.

In the beginning God created . . . (Genesis 1:1).

Read Genesis 1:1 and think about the importance of those words. Then read Isaiah 44:24; Isaiah 45:18; John 1:1-2; and Colossians 1:16.

Can a person believe the Bible is the Word of God and not believe that God created everything?

▲ **TAKE A STEP**

Yesterday you discovered that Genesis reveals the beginnings of the universe, the solar system, and life itself.

As we mentioned, the scientific method proves a truth by duplicating it. Now read Isaiah 65:17 and 66:22-24 to see how and when God will prove to rebellious people that He is indeed the Creator.

Close your family time by discussing how the issue of beginnings is handled in the school you attend. Is evolution presented as a fact? Is creation even mentioned as a possibility? How does it make you feel to realize that teachers and textbooks might not be presenting the truth?

You really showed old Biggs," Hank commented to Andrea the next day. "I hope you two get in another discussion today."

"Hank, I don't argue with Mr. Biggs for the fun of it. Nobody's ever going to prove it one way or the other."

"Wait a minute," Hank replied slowly. "Are you saying that you don't really believe all that stuff about creation?"

"Sure I believe it—with all my heart. And I believe it for three reasons," she said, holding up three fingers. "First, because the Bible says God created everything. Second, it doesn't go against real scientific facts. And third, it explains why people are here at all. But whether you believe in creation or evolution, it's all based on faith."

"Hey, wait, you're losing me. Evolution is scientific. The Bible is religion. How can you say evolution is based on faith?"

◆ **TAKE A LOOK / Hebrews 11:3**

Genesis reveals that God created all things supernaturally.

And God said, "Let there be light," and there was light (Genesis 1:3).

One moment there was no light. The next moment there was! One instant there was no life, the next instant there was!

In six days God created the heavens and the earth. We accept this by faith because God has told us so, not because we have seen it for ourselves—as you'll learn when you read Hebrews 11:3.

▲ **TAKE A STEP**

No one was present at creation to see everything that happened, but God has revealed that He did it. Because Christians know that God is trustworthy, we can put our faith in what He has said about how things began.

However, people who do not believe that God created the world try to find other explanations for how things began. One of the most common explanations today is called the theory of evolution.

Even though the theory of evolution has not been scientifically proved, it is taught as fact in many school systems. When you hear someone claim that human beings came from another kind of animal, or that it took billions of years for life to evolve on earth, just remember, that's a theory, not a fact.

God the Creator was there at the beginning

Q

What does Genesis teach about creation?

A

Genesis reveals that God created the universe supernaturally.

PARENT
If your child is being taught evolutionary theory, we recommend reading DRY BONES AND OTHER FOSSILS by Gary Parker.

The bite that brought a bitter reward

H ank enjoyed talking with Andrea. *"Okay, Brain,"* he teased, *"I read the first four chapters of Genesis like you told me to. But it sure leaves out a lot—like what they did every day, what kind of people they really were, and how they felt about what happened."*

"You're right," Andrea replied. *"But one thing's certain—they weren't cavemen like those pictures in our science book. They started out perfect, with 100 percent use of their brain power. Can you imagine how wonderful they must have been?"*

"Yeah," Hank nodded as his imagination began to work. *"But I still have a question: Why do people think Eve ate an apple?"*

◆ TAKE A LOOK / Genesis 3

As Hank discovered, the first part of Genesis doesn't give a detailed picture of how Adam and his descendants lived. Sadly, it shows that human beings—who were created to have constant fellowship with God—instead listened to the lies of His enemy, disobeyed Him, and brought death into the world.

Take time now to read Genesis 3. What sad "beginnings" do you find?

How do you know God still loved Adam and Eve even though they caused tragedy in His creation?

Why do you think their disobedience has been called "the fall of man"?

▲ TAKE A STEP

The LORD God made garments of skin . . . and clothed them. . . . The LORD God banished him from the Garden of Eden (Genesis 3:21, 23).

God spilled the blood of an innocent animal to "cover" their sin. That pictures how, many years later, He would spill the blood of His own Son to cleanse the sin of all people. Then God banished Adam and Eve from the beautiful garden so they couldn't eat of the Tree of Life and live forever in their sin. They accepted God's love. Have you?

Oh, by the way, do you know the answer to Hank's question: Why do people assume Eve ate an apple?

One reason is that the Latin words for both *apple* and *evil* are very similar. When the Bible was translated into Latin in the fourth century A.D., the word for evil appeared in the phrase "tree of the knowledge of good and evil." From that time on, many people associated an apple with the fruit Eve ate.

Q

What does Genesis teach about the human race?

A

Genesis reveals that people are not what God intended them to be because sin came into the world.

Andrea's next "assignment" for Hank had been to read Genesis 5–11. And he had a million questions. She just wasn't prepared for the first one.

"Andrea, wouldn't there have had to be dinosaurs on the ark?"

"Hmm! What do you think?" she grinned.

"Well, we know dinosaurs were real—all those fossils in the Smithsonian museum prove that. It seems to me that Noah would have taken a pair on the ark. Maybe they just didn't adapt real well after the Flood. Do you think that's possible?"

"Well," Andrea answered, "the pieces do seem to fit if you consider the Flood . . . "

Just about that time, Mrs. Loomis called the class to order. In a few minutes, Andrea opened a note from Hank. It said, "We never have enough time to talk. Can I come over sometime so we can finish this conversation? I really want to know more."

◆ **TAKE A LOOK / Genesis 7:11–8:5, 13**

Genesis teaches that God sent a flood to destroy all humanity—except for Noah and his family (eight people) and two each of the unclean animals and seven each of the clean animals. (During Old Testament times God's people were allowed to eat only certain "clean" animals. Leviticus 11 explains clean and unclean animals.)

Some people wonder if it was possible for a flood to cover the entire earth, but the Bible says that's exactly what God caused supernaturally in the days of Noah.

As you read Genesis 7:11–8:5, 13, imagine Noah stepping out to find a different kind of world. He no longer recognized places and landmarks. Everything had been changed by the tremendous flood. Perhaps even the climate was different.

Discuss how you would have felt if you had been one of Noah's sons. Safe in the ark—a huge, barge-like boat—Noah and his family were the only human beings on the planet to survive the supernatural flood. What do you think you would have felt and done when you left the ark?

▲ **TAKE A STEP**

Close your family time today by reading 2 Peter 3:3-7. Which people today make the following claim?

"Everything goes on as it has since the beginning of creation" (2 Peter 3:4).

In verse 7 what does God say will happen to them ?

The world that is, is not the world that was!

Q

What does Genesis teach about the world we live in?

A

Genesis describes a time when God judged the world with a flood.

PARENT
For further reading on the Flood, see THE WORLD THAT PERISHED by John Whitcomb. Both you and your older child will find it informative.

ATTENTIVENESS

As the child climbed up in her chair for a haircut, Rose's mind was on the company that would be coming for dinner. Had she made enough lasagne? Did she have enough bread? As she began to cut the child's lovely blond curls, she decided to buy some extra rolls—just to be on the safe side. With her mind wandering, Rose snipped the curls and finally blew the hair into soft waves framing the child's face.

When she finished, she motioned the mother over and handed the child a mirror. "There now, don't you look pretty?" she cooed. "This is a very popular cut with little girls."

"Little girls?" the child's mother exclaimed. "**Little girls!** Mark is a boy! Didn't you hear me introduce him to you?"

Too late Rose noticed the cowboy boots. This customer was gone for good, all because she failed to pay attention.

◆ THINKING ABOUT ATTENTIVENESS

Be honest now—you've probably been told more than once by a parent or teacher to quit daydreaming and pay attention!

As Christians we are to be sensitive and attentive to other people and their needs, not self-centered and wrapped up in our own concerns. We are to **listen with our eyes, ears, and hearts.**

Not only that, but we are to pay close attention to God's Word and allow it to change our attitudes and actions.

● KEY VERSE ON ATTENTIVENESS

My son, pay attention to what I say; listen closely to my words. Do not let them out of your sight, keep them within your heart (Proverbs 4:20-21).

▲ LOOKING AHEAD

In Proverbs 13:1, 18 and 15:5, 32 you'll find another word that could be translated "Pay attention." After you've found that word, reread those same verses to find three words that are the opposite of paying attention.

"While I was watching my P's and Q's, the other twenty-four letters got away from me."

Mrs. Peterson was having the ladies from her garden club over for their monthly meeting. The house was cleaned and straightened, and the refreshments were ready.

She was putting the finishing touches to her makeup when seven-year-old Mandy walked in. "Oh, Mom, you look so pretty. Is it time for the ladies to come?"

Before she could answer, the doorbell rang and Mrs. Peterson turned to go downstairs. "Mom, wait, you—" Mandy called.

"Mandy, go on next door. Whatever it is will have to wait."

"But Mom . . ." Mandy stopped at her mother's stern look.

Two hours later, Mrs. Peterson caught a glimpse of herself in the hall mirror as her guests left. Immediately she knew what Mandy had tried to tell her. Her dress was unzipped about six inches in the back. If only she had paid attention!

◆ TAKE A LOOK / Psalm 19:7-14

Mrs. Peterson was certainly embarrassed, but sometimes lack of attentiveness can be much more damaging. Numerous auto accidents occur because a driver wasn't paying attention. Students fail tests because they didn't pay attention in class. Children sometimes put themselves in danger because they don't listen carefully to instructions. But by far the greatest damage is done in the lives of people who ignore God's instructions for living.

God wants His children to follow His instructions. As you read Psalm 19:7-14, make a list on a separate sheet of paper six things God's Word does for an attentive believer. This will be easier to do if you work together as a family, with someone reading each verse aloud. Four things are found in verses 7-8, one is in verse 11, and the last is in verse 12.

▲ TAKE A STEP

God's Word says that whoever pays careful attention to His commands will stay out of trouble or danger; but it also tells us that attentiveness brings rewards:

By them [God's truths] is your servant warned; in keeping them there is great reward (Psalm 19:11).

Close your family time by sharing an occasion when being attentive to a parent brought an unexpected reward. Then list as many rewards as you can think of for being attentive to God's Word. Time limit: three minutes!

Just leave me alone; don't bother me now!

Q

To whom should I be attentive?

A

Attentiveness to God and His Word will encourage me to be attentive to others.

PARENT
You do your child no favors by repeating instructions three or four times before making him or her obey. Announce that from now on, a one-warning policy is in force in your family.

Pay attention to the one who loves you most

Q

What are the benefits of attentiveness?

A

Attentiveness to the Lord on a one-to-One basis brings the reward of personal fellowship with Him.

The table was set for two, the stereo was playing soft music, and the candles glowed.

"Say, what's this? Are we celebrating something, honey?" David teased as he hugged Denise. Then he dramatically handed her five roses, one for each year of their marriage. Her eyes sparkled, but then she became wistful.

"What's the matter, honey? Are you okay?"

"Yeah, but I was just wish—"

". . . wishing we had a baby to share this moment with," he completed her sentence. "Am I right?" he asked softly as he reached for her hand.

Denise made a face. "How did you know what I was thinking?"

"Silly," he replied, drawing her into a hug. "You know I can read your mind. Besides, I was—"

Denise interrupted: " . . . thinking the same thing?" she giggled. "Well, maybe next year there'll be a high-chair at our table."

◆ TAKE A LOOK / Ephesians 1:17-21

David and Denise knew each other's facial expressions, tones of voice, and moods. Their attentiveness to each other had brought them so close that it sometimes seemed that they thought and felt as one person instead of two.

The apostle Paul wanted the Christians in the city of Ephesus to know Jesus Christ in that same close, personal way. As you read his prayer for them in Ephesians 1:17-21, find three words in verses 18 and 19 that describe the rewards of knowing Christ intimately.

▲ TAKE A STEP

Paul describes the rewards of truly knowing Christ in this prayer:

I pray also that the eyes of your heart may be enlightened in order that you may know the hope to which he has called you, the riches of his glorious inheritance, . . . and his incomparably great power for us who believe (Ephesians 1:18-19).

A future with Him forever! Fellowship with Him now! God's power at work in your life!

Even though your family has a daily time of worship and growth, it's also important that each individual take time to love the Lord and listen to Him in a personal devotional time. If that's not your habit, start it today!

By the way, which three words did you choose from Ephesians 1:18-19? We picked *hope, riches,* and *power.*

I t's too soon for summer to end!" Wendy thought as she dawdled into her next class—social studies with Mr. Rogers. In only two more hours she could go home, grab her bike, and go for a long ride. She was so pre-occupied with leaving school that she jumped when Bart poked her. "Hey, Space-cadet, clear your desk. He's giving out the tests."

"Test? What test?" Wendy whispered frantically.

"The unit test, dummy. The one we've been reviewing for all week."

Just then Mr. Rogers placed a copy of the test on Wendy's desk. There was no way she could pass! If only she had been paying attention!

◆ TAKE A LOOK
Isaiah 42:20-25; Hebrews 2:1-4; 12:25

Wendy endangered her grade because she didn't pay attention. But when God's children are not attentive to His Word, they place themselves in spiritual danger.

In Old Testament times the nation of Israel suffered the consequences of inattentiveness and disobedience to God's Word. Isaiah 42:20-25 describes the result.

After you've read those verses, read a similar warning found in Hebrews 2:1-4; 12:25.

▲ TAKE A STEP
We must pay more careful attention, therefore, to what we have heard, so that we do not drift away (Hebrews 2:1).

Wendy's mind drifted away from her studies and she failed the test. God's Old Testament people were taken into captivity because they drifted into disobedience. We are warned to be careful not to drift away from God's teachings.

What is spiritual drifting? Here are eight characteristics:
- laziness about spiritual matters;
- lack of spiritual purpose;
- self-pity;
- pride;
- murmuring and complaining;
- impure thoughts and actions;
- hatred of correction;
- bitterness toward God or others.

If you see yourself in any of those phrases, grab the anchor of God's Word and be attentive to His commands. It's the difference between life and death!

Without anchor or oar, adrift on the open sea

Q
What happens when I'm not attentive to God's Word?

A
Failure to be attentive to God's Word can cause me to drift away from Him spiritually.

Seeing needs through others' eyes

At the family reunion Granny Hamlin sat quietly rocking as various grandchildren and great-grand-children stopped to chat. From time to time she chuckled, "I'm the most spoiled old lady in the world, but I sure do love it!"

At the other end of the pavilion, playpens and portable cribs accommodated the newest generation of Hamlins. Older sisters and cousins helped their aunts care for the infants and toddlers.

As food was brought in, the grandmothers organized it on the long tables, checked the serving utensils, and carefully folded the foil, plastic wrap, and bags that would be needed later. Even the granddads pitched in, emptying bags of ice and filling cups.

As the day wore on, people moved from table to table to catch up on all the family news and to reminisce about old times. Every member of the Hamlin family got plenty of attention that day!

Q

How can I be more attentive to others' needs?

A

Attentiveness to others demonstrates God's love for them and my love for Him.

◆**TAKE A LOOK / 1 Thessalonians 3:12; 5:12-18**

It's easy to be sensitive to people when you don't have anything else to do. But being attentive to others can be—and should be—an everyday concern. And as it did in the Hamlin family, attentiveness to others should cross the lines between all ages.

Being sensitive and attentive is an excellent way of sharing God's love. In Galatians 6:2 the apostle Paul encourages us to . . .

Carry each other's burdens, and in this way you will fulfill the law of Christ (Galatians 6:2).

How many other ways to be attentive to the needs of others can you find in 1 Thessalonians 3:12; 5:12-18?

▲ **TAKE A STEP**

Paul prayed that the love between believers would increase and overflow. Have you ever noticed how your love for even the most difficult people expands when you take an interest in them?

Think of a person you have difficulty getting along with. As you review 1 Thessalonians 5:12-18 ask: "Do I hold _____ in high regard? Am I patient and encouraging with _____ ? Do I do all I can to get along, or do I do things to aggravate _____ ? Do I pray for _____ ? Am I thankful for _____ ?"

When you give someone that much attention, you'll find God increasing your love on a daily basis.

APPEARANCE

*H*iring you to slide these advertisements under each door was a great idea," Mrs. Saxon remarked as her daughter Ronda came into the apartment. "Mr. Towns's cleaning business will get new customers when people start using the coupons on the flyer." Then Mrs. Saxon changed the subject. "But I thought it would take you longer to go to all 120 apartments. Did Bethany help?"

Ronda and her friend Bethany glanced at each other. "No, I just worked real hard," Ronda replied slowly.

Later Ronda looked at the 10 dollars Mr. Towns had paid her. Oh, if she only hadn't listened to Bethany. "No one will ever know," Bethany had said as she dropped the last 50 flyers into a trash can. Now Ronda felt awful. Her mother and Mr. Towns both thought she was a trustworthy person. But it wasn't like that. She had cheated Mr. Towns and had lied to her mother. The situation wasn't what it appeared to be.

◆ THINKING ABOUT APPEARANCE

As human beings we get information through our senses. But sight, smell, touch, taste, and hearing do not always show us the reality of what we experience. As in Ronda's case, appearance— **the outward aspect of a person or thing**—may be deceiving.

Only God knows and understands all things the way they really are. He has a different way of seeing things.

● KEY VERSE ON APPEARANCE

"*The* LORD *does not look at the things man looks at. Man looks at the outward appearance, but the* LORD *looks at the heart*" (1 Samuel 16:7).

▲ LOOKING AHEAD

This week we'll think about the difference between the way things appear to be and the way they really are.

Has your appearance ever deceived others as Ronda's did? Did you fool everyone? Did you fool anyone? On the basis of 1 Samuel 16:7, who wasn't fooled?

"*I should've known I was in trouble when you started saying it's what's inside your head that counts.*"

God isn't impressed by the outer "me"

Q

Why does God look on the heart rather than the appearance?

A

Appearance sometimes covers up the true motives of the heart.

PARENT
Good grooming is important. Sometimes courses on manners and grooming for young teens are taught in local churches or community centers.

B ecca paused by the mirror, but as she raised her hand to her hair, the mirror reflected her mother's frown.

"You won't do anything to help me, will you?" Becca snapped rudely to her mother. "You know how badly I want to be elected to the homecoming court."

"Yes, I know," Mrs. Benson replied softly. "What I'm wondering is whether you know why."

"Well, just think what it will mean if a Christian is homecoming queen."

"But dropping out of youth group and giving up your work at the children's home to take a modeling course doesn't show much commitment. You might deceive yourself, you might even fool me, but God knows your motives. I'm just not sure you do."

◆ TAKE A LOOK / 1 Samuel 16:1-13

Ours is the era of the "body beautiful." In our nation we spend millions of dollars on cosmetics, fitness clubs, diets, and beauty aids. We idolize movie stars. We dress for success.

But God is not as interested in our outward appearance as we are. He is more concerned with the condition of the heart.

God revealed His preference for pure motives and right attitudes when He sent the prophet Samuel to anoint one of Jesse's eight sons to be the future king of Israel. Read that story for yourself in 1 Samuel 16:1-13.

▲ TAKE A STEP

People are impressed by appearance. But in time, strength fails and beauty fades. What lasts is the inner beauty that comes from knowing Jesus Christ.

Jesus once spoke strongly to the Pharisees, a group of men who appeared to be holy and good. He told them:

"You hypocrites! You are like whitewashed tombs, which look beautiful on the outside but on the inside are full of . . . bones . . . . Outside you appear . . . righteous but . . . inside you are full of . . . wickedness" (Matthew 23:27-28).

Appearance is often a thin covering over what's inside. Discuss the motives behind Becca's desire to improve her appearance.

Think about the last few items of clothing you've purchased. Are there hidden motives in the way you dress and act?

A widow attends a seance hoping to "make contact" with the "spirit" of her dead husband.

• A Christian attending a rock concert feels an atmosphere of oppression in the auditorium.

• A man who is anxious about a business deal he is making consults an astrologer for advice based on his horoscope.

• A ten-year-old boy is home alone when the power goes off during a fierce storm. At first he is terrified, but then he asks God to protect him. Later, he reports to his parents that he felt as though a guardian angel was right there with him.

• A group of witches claims Satan gives them power. They prepare potions, read fortunes, and cast "good" spells, although they sometimes use a "curse" for revenge or punishment.

◆TAKE A LOOK / Ephesians 6:12; 1 Peter 5:8

If you're like a lot of people, you may be saying, "There's nothing to that. They must be making it up." In some cases, you might be right. But not always.

There is an invisible spirit world that exists alongside the physical world we live in. But just because something is supernatural doesn't always mean that it's good.

The Bible teaches that there are real beings that we cannot see. Those spirit beings who are faithful to God are called angels. Those who followed Satan in his rebellion against God are called demons. Though Christians do not see evil spirit beings, we are in a war with them, a fact you'll see in Ephesians 6:12 and 1 Peter 5:8.

▲ TAKE A STEP

There is more to this old world than meets the eye. All is not as it appears to be. As Christians,
Our struggle is not against flesh and blood, but against the rulers, against the authorities, against the powers of this dark world and against the spiritual forces of evil in the heavenly realms (Ephesians 6:12).

Organizations and individuals that promote ideas and actions that are opposed to God's laws are backed by evil spiritual forces—even though they may appear to be good.

Can you identify any organizations or individuals in your community that have an appearance of good but actually go against God's Word? Close by reading Ephesians 6:11-18 to find out how this spiritual warfare can be won.

What you see might not be all you get

Q

Are there real things I can't see?

A

Appearance in the physical world is matched by an unseen spiritual world.

God reveals what we cannot see

Q

How can I understand what's real if I can't use my senses?

A

Appearance is sometimes made clear by the special revelation of God's Word.

I'm not sure those boys of ours are telling us the whole truth," Mrs. Johnson commented to her friend Mrs. Norris. "There's more to this than meets the eye."

"I know what you mean," Mrs. Norris agreed. "When I mention that church camping trip, Nathan starts giving me one-word answers, almost like he's thinking about every word before he speaks. It's like they're hiding something, hoping we won't find out."

About two weeks later, Mr. Norris called Nathan into the kitchen. "Nathan, your mother and I want to know why you and Mack were at the beach last month instead of at the church camp where you were supposed to be."

A startled expression crossed Nathan's face and he ducked his head. He and Mack had been so careful! How in the world did his dad find out?

◆ TAKE A LOOK
Deuteronomy 29:29; Romans 16:25-26

Nathan and Mack gave the appearance of having camped in the mountains with their youth group. But the reality was different. How did their parents learn the truth?

The answer is simple! An outside source of information revealed it to them. One of Mr. Norris's business associates saw the boys on the beach and casually mentioned it to Nathan's dad. Without his "special revelation," Nathan's parents may have suspected that things weren't the way they appeared to be, but they would never have known for sure.

In a far greater way, God's Word is a special revelation to help us understand that "there's more to life than meets the eye." His revelation explains that, in addition to the physical world we see, there is a spiritual world we cannot grasp with our physical senses.

As you read Deuteronomy 29:29 and Romans 16:25-26, you'll learn why God reveals Himself to mankind.

▲ TAKE A STEP

God has revealed things about Himself . . . *So that all nations might believe and obey him* (Romans 16:26).

Many people who appear to be happy are really in need of spiritual truth. Because of God's revelation we know that He is at work in our lives. Can you think of someone in your neighborhood, at work or at school that you can share God's revelation with today?

I don't like it," Mr. Blackburn told his wife. "Stamping the kids' wrists so they can re-enter the amusement park seems innocent enough now, but the Bible speaks of a time when God's enemy will require everybody to receive a mark on their forehead or hand. If people get conditioned to things like this, they may not recognize real spiritual danger when it actually confronts them.

"Regina and Daniel will have to get written passes if they go out of the park," Mr. Blackburn continued. "I want them to learn to see beyond appearances and judge things spiritually."

◆ TAKE A LOOK / 1 Corinthians 2:6-16

Mr. Blackburn did not judge only by appearances. Instead, he looked beneath the surface of a situation and saw a meaning no one else did. Was he right, or was he way off track?

This week we've learned that people, circumstances, and situations are not always exactly what they appear to be. God has revealed that there is a spiritual realm that is not apparent to our five senses.

What does that mean to your daily life? Does everything have a "spiritual" meaning?

Jesus once warned His listeners to look beyond their own understanding. He said:

"Stop judging by mere appearances, and make a right judgment" (John 7:24).

You'll find out how you can do that by reading 1 Corinthians 2:6-16.

▲ TAKE A STEP

Every one of God's children has God's Spirit within his or her life, and He doesn't go by appearances. The Holy Spirit knows there's a war for the souls of people going on in that unseen, spiritual realm.

As you read God's Word and learn to listen to the Holy Spirit, you too will start seeing beyond appearances. You will begin to see that people are hurting and in need. You will begin to spot the depravity that often fills movies, books, magazines, and music. And sometimes you will see God's love in action.

Close your family time today by sharing some times when you've seen into the spiritual meaning of a situation. Then ask God to open your spiritual "eyes" so you can see the people around you differently. Plan to share what you "see" at dinner on Sunday.

My eyes can "see" what they didn't see before

Q

How can I see beyond mere appearance?

A

Appearance can turn to understanding as God's Spirit within helps me.

PARENT
Discuss how some people seek to take advantage of others. Teach your child now about reading the fine print in business dealings and contracts. Discuss the wisdom of always getting sound advice before making major decisions.

HOLY SPIRIT

*F*or the past 200 miles all the little towns had looked almost alike—not very interesting to a second grader from the big city. But suddenly Gregory sat up straight. This town was different! A mobile home they drove past looked like somebody had pried the roof off with a can opener. A huge oak tree lay uprooted beside the road. And why in the world didn't that house have a roof?

As the Morrisons drove slowly through the town, Gregory's eyes got bigger. Here was a grain silo broken in half. There was a whole row of buildings with all the windows blown out. On either side of the road piles of rubble lay where houses once stood.

"Mom, what happened?" Gregory asked in a whisper.

"Hmm, I remember reading that a tornado touched down here about a week ago," Mrs. Morrison replied. "This town was practically destroyed—and it took less than five minutes."

"You can't really understand how bad it is from the news pictures, can you?" Mr. Morrison commented.

"It's awful," Gregory said. "Like a giant walked through without looking. I hope we never have a tornado in our town."

◆ THINKING ABOUT THE HOLY SPIRIT

The Holy Spirit, **who lives within every child of God**, is somewhat like the wind in that story: Although He is never seen, His power can be felt everywhere in the world. Jesus made this promise to His disciples regarding the Holy Spirit:

"So He can go to public school with you. That's why the Holy Spirit's invisible."

● KEY VERSE ON THE HOLY SPIRIT

"You will receive power when the Holy Spirit comes on you; and you will be my witnesses" (Acts 1:8).

▲ LOOKING AHEAD

In John 16:7, Jesus told His disciples that it was good for Him to return to heaven. The disciples probably couldn't see why that was true. Can you? Read John 16:5-16 to find out what Jesus meant.

Voodoo? Ron couldn't believe it! This time they were really going too far.

His friend Paul continued trying to persuade Ron to come with them. "Look, it's no big deal. All the guys are going. None of us really believes that old lady is really a voodoo mamba. We're just going for the fun of it. Besides, you talk about spirits yourself, Ron. I've heard you say something about a 'Holy Spirit' or something."

"That's not the same at all," Ron said emphatically. "You guys are messing around with real evil spirits."

"Well, what about this Holy Spirit? Why's it so important?"

"Not it, Paul. He. The Holy Spirit is God Himself." Roger was eager to explain to his friend. "Why don't we go get a pizza and talk. Just stay away from that voodoo stuff. It's nothing but trouble."

◆ **TAKE A LOOK**
John 4:24; 2 Corinthians 3:17-18
As Ron explained to Paul, the spirits of evil angels—which the Bible calls demons—are at work in the world even though we don't see them. Nor do we see the good angels who do God's work in the world.

Both angels and demons are created beings who happen to be spirits. But the Holy Spirit is different. He is not a created being. Instead, He is the Creator of all life. The Holy Spirit is God Himself. After Jesus returned to heaven, He sent the Holy Spirit.

Reading John 4:24 and 2 Corinthians 3:17-18 will show you that the Holy Spirit is God.

▲ **TAKE A STEP**
Now the Lord is the Spirit (2 Corinthians 3:17).
The Holy Spirit does not have a body, but He is a Person who is with every child of God at all times.

Think about the Holy Spirit this way: Imagine you are alone in a house except for another family member who is in another room. He doesn't always talk and you don't see him. But he is always there. And just knowing he is there and feeling his presence makes a difference in what you do and say!

What difference does it make to know that God Himself lives in the same "house" you do—even though you can't see Him?

He's always there— my invisible Lord

Q

Who is the Holy Spirit?

A

The Holy Spirit is God Himself and is always with God's children.

PARENT
One of the obvious domains of deceiving spirits is the occult. Make your child aware that evil spirits are behind witchcraft, voodoo, seances, and many other forms of "spiritism."

Sweet heavenly dove has come from above

Maria ran her finger down the smooth, gold-edged pages of the new Bible Sondra had given her. She traced the outline of a dove stamped right in the center of the cover.

"Sondra, why is this dove here? Is it some secret code for Christians?"

Sondra chuckled. "Kind of! It's a Christian symbol, but it's not a secret code. Tell you what: I'll give you some verses to read tonight, and tomorrow you tell me what the dove symbolizes."

That night Maria read the verses Sondra had listed for her. The next morning she was beaming when Sondra came into homeroom. "The dove stands for the Holy Spirit, doesn't it! Now, what's my next assignment?"

◆ **TAKE A LOOK**
Acts 2:1-4; Genesis 1:1-2; Matthew 3:13-17

You too may have seen the dove used as a symbol on Bibles, stationery, or jewelry. And like Maria, you may have wondered, "Why a dove?"

Before His crucifixion, Jesus told His disciples that He would send the Holy Spirit to them (John 14:16-17). After Jesus returned to heaven, the disciples waited in Jerusalem until the Day of Pentecost, when the Holy Spirit came upon them.

As you read about the coming of the Holy Spirit in Acts 2:1-4, you will discover one symbol for the Holy Spirit (what is it?), but you won't find any mention of a dove. To see why the dove symbolizes the Holy Spirit read Genesis 1:1-2 and Matthew 3:13-17.

▲ **TAKE A STEP**
At the time of creation,
The Spirit of God was hovering over the waters (Genesis 1:2).

In the Hebrew language, the word *hovering* is an expression that means "outstretched wings." At the baptism of Jesus, the Holy Spirit visibly descended on Jesus with that same motion.

Just as the Holy Spirit filled the disciples at Pentecost, giving them power to live for God, He fills believers today and gives them power to live for Jesus. Does it surprise you, then, that the dove is such a beloved symbol of the Holy Spirit?

Why not try your hand at drawing a picture combining a flame of fire and a descending dove. Keep it in your room to remind you of your study this week!

When did the Holy Spirit come?

The Holy Spirit came at Pentecost to give all God's children power for living and for serving Him.

N atalie," Jenna asked solemnly, "can anybody be that perfect? Douglas sounds too good to be true."

Jenna, who had never met Douglas Jerome Austin in person, was good-naturedly teasing her roommate. Natalie had just received a letter from her fiancé and excitedly read Jenna a poem Douglas had written. In fact, all Natalie seemed to talk about these days was Douglas.

"Oh, he's so wonderful," she would say at the end of a phone conversation. "He can tell how I'm feeling just from my tone of voice." Or, "Douglas is so dedicated. His supervisor says he's a hard worker, and I'm sure he'll be promoted soon." Or, when she received a new photograph of Douglas in a letter, "Look, Jenna! I just love his dimples."

Jenna smiled. Maybe after the wedding Natalie would find another topic of conversation!

◆ TAKE A LOOK / John 16:5-15

Natalie talked about Douglas so much that Jenna felt she knew him. But what really amused her was how Natalie already thought of herself not as Natalie Reeves, but as Mrs. Douglas Jerome Austin. She practiced her future signature again and again.

Have you ever wondered why the Holy Spirit doesn't have a name? Or if He does, why the Bible doesn't tell us what it is?

Well, just as Natalie could hardly think or speak of anyone but Douglas, so everything the Holy Spirit does points to Jesus Christ—not to Himself. His work is to help us put Jesus first in our lives. The Holy Spirit personally wants to go unnoticed so we will focus more on our Savior, Jesus Christ.

Reread Jesus' explanation of the Holy Spirit's work in John 16:5-15.

▲ TAKE A STEP

"He will bring glory to me by taking from what is mine and making it known to you" (John 16:14).

When the Holy Spirit works in a believer's heart, He fills the mind with worshipful thoughts of Jesus Christ. Do you recall a time when you really knew the Holy Spirit was working in your life?

After you share, ask Him to help you write a "praise chain." Have each family member in turn write on a sheet of paper a sentence of thanks to Jesus for who He is or what He has done. After each person has had at least three turns, pray your praises back to God.

There's only one topic of conversation— Jesus!

Why did the Holy Spirit come?

The Holy Spirit came to glorify Jesus rather than Himself.

Q

What does the Holy Spirit do?

A

The Holy Spirit works constantly in my life to make me more like Jesus— if I let Him.

PARENT
A child's personality and abilities may make him feel "different." Just as the Spirit reassures us that we "belong" in His family, you may need to give that child an extra reassurance.

Glen looked at the heavy gold watch glittering in his palm. He was sure he'd never seen such an impressive pocket watch.

"My father gave it to me when I turned 21, just as his father had given it to him," Mr. Sanders explained. "Now it's yours to wear and pass on someday to your son."

Tracing the outline of the intricately lettered "S" on the case, Glen realized that he would be the fifth Robert Glen Sanders to own this watch. If he'd ever doubted it before, he knew now that he was truly his father's son.

"Dad," Glen spoke quietly, "am I the only adopted son to inherit this?"

"As a matter of fact, you are. But you're as much a Sanders as Grandpa and I are—and the others before. You're my son. There's no difference at all."

◆ TAKE A LOOK
Ephesians 1:13-14; Romans 8:9-11, 15-16

Glen's watch was a sign that he was a certified member of the Sanders family. You'll discover the "proof" Christians have of being God's children by reading Ephesians 1:13-14 and Romans 8:9-11, 15-16.

▲ TAKE A STEP

When a person turns from sin and trusts in Jesus for salvation, the Holy Spirit comes to live within. His presence is a guarantee that a person has eternal life.

The Holy Spirit works constantly in the lives of believers. He

(a) makes us aware of God's love,
(b) teaches us about Jesus,
(c) helps us pray,
(d) gives us special abilities to do God's work, and
(e) works to make us more like Jesus in character and conduct.

Close your family time by matching each of those benefits with one of these verses.

_____ Romans 8:26

_____ Galatians 5:16, 22

_____ John 14:26

_____ Romans 5:5

_____ 1 Corinthians 12:4, 7

SPIRITUAL GIFTS ·

I *t was a head-on collision. He didn't have a chance. John Martin was dead on arrival at City Hospital. His wife, Marie, and his sons, Jason and Johnny—ages two and six—suddenly were left alone.*

Over the next few days friends from the church cared for the children, brought food, cleaned the house, and helped Marie arrange the funeral. They supported her with their presence. A young woman, who also had recently lost her husband, spent long hours with Marie. She understood Marie's fears, her anger, and her sorrow.

On the day of the funeral Marie was consoled by her pastor's words, even though her grief was great.

As the days and weeks went by, people pitched in to help Marie pick up the pieces of her life. Several men repaired her roof, a lawyer in the church took care of John's will and the insurance. The pastor's wife dropped in often for morning coffee, and friends' husbands were glad to include the boys in outings with their children.

It seemed every time Marie turned around, someone was helping, giving, encouraging. She was glad to be a part of the family of God.

◆ THINKING ABOUT SPIRITUAL GIFTS

What Marie and her children experienced was a family lovingly working together for the good of a member who was grieving. Some helped by encouraging, others by giving, and many others by praying. They were all using their spiritual gifts.

A spiritual gift is **a talent, ability, or aptitude given by the Holy Spirit to benefit the whole family of God.** The Bible instructs us to:

● KEY VERSE ON SPIRITUAL GIFTS
Follow the way of love and eagerly desire spiritual gifts (1 Corinthians 14:1).

▲ LOOKING AHEAD
Make a list of the spiritual gifts you find listed in Romans 12:6-8; 1 Corinthians 12:8-10; and Ephesians 4:11-13. Did God leave out anything we need to live for Him or serve Him?

"You're in luck. Viewing happens to be my area of expertise."

Fully equipped and ready to grow

Q

Who receives spiritual gifts?

A

Spiritual gifts are given to each member of God's family.

PARENT
If you are interested in learning more about spiritual gifts, ask your pastor to recommend a book on the subject.

A son was born to a poor mother who fed her seven children water instead of milk. Her child suffered the effects of that early malnutrition all his life.

When the child was three years old, he could pick out chords on the harpsichord, and at five he was writing music. By age seven, his father was booking concert tours all over Europe for his son, who by that time played both violin and piano. During one tour, he met the famous composer Johann S. Bach and sat on his lap to play a duet.

As the boy grew older, he wrote composition after composition, including sonatas, minuets, and operas. Nothing could stop the music that flowed from him.

By the time he was 30, he had lost his earlier popularity. His music went unrecognized and his income dwindled. But still he wrote.

Though he died a pauper at age 35, you know him today because of his great gift for music. His name is Wolfgang Amadeus Mozart.

◆ TAKE A LOOK
1 Corinthians 12:7-11; Romans 12:6-8
Just as Mozart's gift for music was there when he was born, every person who is "born" again into God's family possesses a spiritual gift. Spiritual gifts give believers the ability to express, display, or communicate Christ's love in some way. The apostle Paul explained it this way:

To each one the manifestation of the Spirit is given for the common good (1 Corinthians 12:7).

Spiritual gifts have two primary uses. Some are mainly for communicating and teaching God's Word. Others are for seeing and meeting people's needs.

As you read 1 Corinthians 12:7-11 and Romans 12:6-8, identify one gift a pastor or preacher might have. Look for another that a worker in a shelter for the homeless might have.

▲ TAKE A STEP
Do you know the spiritual gifts of each person in your family? Hand out a piece of paper to each person, who can then list the names of the other family members. Review the gifts listed in Romans and try to match one gift to each name. Then compare to see if any of the lists match!

And after you've identified some spiritual gifts in your family, discuss how they are used to help other family members. How do you use your gift?

Martha first noticed it in English class, a dull, throbbing ache in her right foot. It seemed to be coming from her big toe. She could hardly wait until class was over to strip off her shoe and look at it. Sure enough, the whole side of her big toe was swollen and ugly, and there was a yellowish cast to the skin.

Wearily Martha limped home after school. "Mom, my foot feels like it's going to fall off, it hurts so bad." She began to cry. "Something awful is wrong. I feel bad all over."

Mrs. Kensington eased off Martha's sock. "Oh, honey, it's an ingrown toenail and it's gotten infected. We'll have to go to the clinic."

After Dr. Masters had drained the infection around the toenail and Martha was feeling better, she laughed. "I can't believe one little toe made my whole body ache. From now on, I'll keep on my toes to take care of my toes."

◆ **TAKE A LOOK / 1 Corinthians 12:12-27**

As Martha discovered, a toe may seem small and insignificant, but when it hurts, the pain can spread to the entire body. It's like that in the body of Christ, too.

Though we are individual members of God's family, Christians do not function alone. We are all part of a living organism called the "body of Christ" (see 1 Corinthians 12:13). Though we have different functions in that body, we work together; in fact, we're dependent on each other. No one can really stand alone.

You'll discover just how important the different parts of the spiritual body are as you read 1 Corinthians 12:12-27.

▲ **TAKE A STEP**

Now you are the body of Christ, and each one of you is a part of it (1 Corinthians 12:27).

Spiritual gifts are given to every Christian so the whole body can function well together. That means we should not look down on any person— or their spiritual gift—as being unimportant. Each Christian has been given a different gift, and each one is special.

Think for a moment about some Christians you know who often go unrecognized. Perhaps it's the lady at church who always makes "goodies" or the deacon who's always repairing things. Take time right now to write a note of appreciation to one of these special people just to say thanks.

Is there one part you could do without?

Q

Should I use my spiritual gift(s) for myself?

A

Spiritual gifts help Christians work together as a "body."

Geared up to go and lubricated with love

Q

How should I use my spiritual gifts?

A

Spiritual gifts are most beneficial when they are used with love.

Mrs. Tyler looked pensively at her daughter Lyn. "She's so uncaring and cold," she thought sadly. "Why can't she be as beautiful on the inside as she is on the outside?"

Lyn was a lovely girl, and exceptionally talented. She had won the senior award as best student and had received a scholarship to study art at State University. Her paintings and drawings had already received city-wide recognition.

Just then the phone rang. Mrs. Tyler answered and listened to the caller with shock and concern on her face. She hung up and turned to Lyn. "Honey, that was Mary Johnson. Her mother just died and she must leave to fly home. She needs someone to watch her twins until her husband gets home tomorrow night. Do you think you could help out? It would mean so much."

"Oh, Mother, you know how obnoxious those kids can be. Besides, I've got so much to do—I just can't. How can you even ask?"

With an injured look on her face, Lyn left the room. And with a heavy heart, Mrs. Tyler shook her head.

◆ TAKE A LOOK / 1 Corinthians 13

Lyn was blessed with many gifts. But in one thing she was sadly lacking.

The Bible tells us that we may have all kinds of gifts and talents—such as knowledge, musical talent, prophecy, faith, generosity, and self-sacrifice. But without one key ingredient, all these gifts are meaningless.

Read 1 Corinthians 13 to discover what puts all those spiritual gifts "in gear."

▲ TAKE A STEP

In 1 Corinthians 13, Paul reveals that love is the key ingredient that everyone can have—and can share.

If I . . . have not love, I am only a resounding gong. . . . If I . . . have not love, I am nothing. If I . . . have not love, I gain nothing (1 Corinthians 13:1-3).

When we exercise spiritual gifts without the motivation of love, our lives are hollow and meaningless. Used with love, spiritual gifts bring blessing to all God's family.

Paul described love so beautifully. How would you describe love? Write your own poem or paragraph describing love. But don't let it end with words. How will you exercise your spiritual gift with love today? Be specific!

*T*eddy was depressed. His day started off badly with the algebra test. Then in band class, Mr. Evans had yelled at him for playing off key. But the worst part of the day had come after school at the soccer game.

One of his teammates had passed him the ball. There was no one between him and the goal when he took off down the field. Then, within kicking distance of the net, he'd tripped over his own feet. A groan went up from the stands. Now as he thought about his awful day, Teddy felt like a first-class klutz.

Just then the phone rang. It was Mrs. Johnson. She told Teddy about her mother's sudden death and explained that she needed someone to watch the twins.

"I'll be glad to come," he replied instantly. "Sure am sorry about your mother, but your little guys will be okay with me. Don't you worry about a thing."

◆ TAKE A LOOK / 1 Corinthians 12:21-31

Teddy may not have been a mathematical genius. Perhaps he wasn't a great saxophone player. And he'd certainly never make the championship soccer team. But Teddy did have one very special quality: He had the spiritual gift of mercy that expressed itself in a willing, helpful heart.

Teddy may not have considered his spiritual gift to be very spectacular, but Teddy's gift was important in God's sight because

God has combined the members of the body and has given greater honor to the parts that lacked it, so that there should be no division in the body, but that its parts should have equal concern for each other (1 Corinthians 12:24-25).

First Corinthians 12:21-31 explains how the individual members can work together in the body of Christ.

▲ TAKE A STEP

As you study 1 Corinthians 12–13 and Romans 12:6-8, ask the Holy Spirit to show you what your gift is. Pay attention to the kinds of things others ask you to do and the compliments they pay you.

Do you enjoy sending cards to those who are sick and struggling? Do you like to teach God's Word? Do you find yourself telling people about Jesus?

Depending upon how you answer those questions, you may have the gift of mercy or encouragement, teaching or evangelizing. Keep your Christian life active and you'll soon find your niche!

It may not be spectacular, but it sure is fulfilling!

Q

How can I recognize my spiritual gift(s)?

A

Spiritual gifts can be recognized by asking the Holy Spirit to reveal them.

WITNESSING

*S*ure is foggy this morning," Ed thought as he jogged along Main Street. "I can barely see my hand in front of my face."

Just then, an elderly woman started across the intersection. Ed watched, horror-struck, as a red pickup truck roared out of the fog. At the last second the driver swerved, but it was too late. The truck sped away, leaving the injured woman lying on the pavement.

After the ambulance had taken the woman to the hospital, the police questioned Ed. "What kind of truck was it? What color? Did you see the driver? Did you get a glimpse at the license plate?"

Later, TV reporters interviewed Ed. That night the six o'clock news announcer introduced Ed with these words: "And here's Ed Austin, the only eyewitness to this morning's hit-and-run accident. Ed, tell us in your own words exactly what happened . . . "

◆ THINKING ABOUT WITNESSING

Because Ed had seen the accident, he had information no one else had. He had a responsibility to pass it on. When the driver was arrested, Ed also testified in court.

Ed was a witness—**someone who tells others about an event he has seen or experienced.** As Christians, we too have something we must tell others. It's not about an accident or a crime. It's about a Person.

Before He returned to heaven, Jesus told His disciples:

● KEY VERSE ON WITNESSING

"You will receive power when the Holy Spirit comes on you; and you will be my witnesses" (Acts 1:8).

▲ LOOKING AHEAD

This week we'll explore how Jesus expects us to be His witnesses, by looking at the life of the apostle Paul, whose story is told in the book of Acts. As someone reads Acts 9:1-22, you'll hear how Saul (later called Paul) became a believer. Who witnessed to him?

"Wouldn't it have been easier just to call Channel Three Eyewitness Newscam?"

***T**wo weeks ago the Hawk River had overflowed and people had been evacuated. But finally the rains had stopped and life was getting back to normal.*

One evening, twelve-year-old Derek Baxter was walking home from a convenience store. As he stepped onto the Hawk Bridge, he hesitated. The wooden planks under his feet felt different. He stopped in disbelief. Half of the bridge was gone!

Horrified, Derek turned quickly and ran back to the store. "Mr. Simon! Mr. Simon! The bridge is out! Hurry—Get the sheriff!"

◆ TAKE A LOOK / Romans 10:9-15

Derek knew dozens of cars traveled that highway and lives were in danger. Because he was the only witness to the broken bridge, he couldn't simply walk away. He had to give a warning.

As Christians, we know that a serious danger lies ahead for people who don't know Jesus. We too have an urgent message to deliver.

The apostle Paul witnessed everywhere he went, telling all kinds of people about Jesus. He had a deep love for his own Jewish people, but he knew God also had called him to witness to the Gentiles (those people who were not Jewish). God had said:

"I have made you a light for the Gentiles, that you may bring salvation to the ends of the earth" (Acts 13:47).

Paul's goal was that all people would come to know Jesus as their Savior.

You'll discover what was needed to get the job done as you read part of a letter Paul wrote to some fellow Christians in Romans 10:9-15.

▲ TAKE A STEP

What do you think life would be like if you had never met another Christian? What if you are the only Christian your friend or neighbor ever meets?

Right now, have each member of the family put an extra pair of shoes in an unusual place— bedroom slippers in the kitchen, sandals on the seat beside you in your car, a pair of boots on the coffee table—to remind you to put "feet to your faith" and witness to your friend or neighbor.

You can also discuss specific people that you would like to witness to in some way. Plan what you will do or say. Then close with a prayer that God will give you that opportunity—today.

Does somebody's life depend on you?

Q

Why should I witness?

A

Witnessing warns people of the danger they're in unless they know Jesus as their Savior.

PARENT
Encourage your child to witness to his or her friends and classmates by inviting them to church. Your willingness to provide transportation shows that you believe it's important to witness.

Come on, Mr. Simon, quick! Before a car comes!" As words tumbled from Derek's mouth, Mr. Simon simply stared at him. Then he chuckled.

"That's real good, Derek, real good. I almost fell for it. But I've got work to do. Now scoot."

Almost sobbing, Derek ran from the store. He remembered all the times he had told Mr. Simon some tale or another, only to laugh when the old man fell for his joke. But what could he do now?

Just then he saw the headlights of a car down the highway. Quickly Derek ran to the road, ripped off his shirt, and began waving it wildly over his head. As the car drew near, he yelled as loudly as he could, "The bridge is out! The bridge is out!"

The car passed, and Derek ran after it sobbing. Suddenly the driver braked, reversed, and turned, quickly maneuvering his car to block the highway. "I'll get help," he shouted as he ran toward the store.

◆ **TAKE A LOOK / Acts 14:1-7; 17:1-10**

Derek did his best to warn Mr. Simon about the danger, but the storekeeper wouldn't believe him. He turned Derek away because he thought the boy was joking.

Many Christians are afraid to witness because they think people will reject what they say. And that might happen. Not everyone you share the good news about Jesus with will immediately believe it. Some may argue. A few will laugh. Others won't even talk about it. A few might even get angry. But some will be eager to hear what you have to say.

You'll see the kind of reception Paul and his co-workers experienced as you read Acts 14:1-7; 17:1-10.

▲ **TAKE A STEP**

Some people accepted Paul's message. Others rejected it. And it's no different today. Though he wanted all people to believe in Christ, Paul knew his responsibility was to witness as God wanted him to. He was later able to say:

"I have declared to both Jews and Greeks that they must turn to God in repentance and have faith in our Lord Jesus" (Acts 20:21).

Paul was a good witness because:
1. He built friendships; and
2. He didn't try to explain everything all at one time.

Those are good tips for you too.

Q

Will everyone accept my witness?

A

Witnessing won't always result in belief, but it is most effective when I build friendships as I share the Good News.

*A*s winner of her state's science fair, she had an opportunity to spend a month aboard a marine research vessel.

It would be hard to find anybody who knew more about ocean exploration programs than Sally. She had studied the structure of bathyscaphs and submersibles. She had studied marine life common to tropical seas, that which was found in arctic seas, and what could be found on coral reefs.

Finally, Sally was on board the ship. As the vessel left the port, she thought about the report she would give her science class back home. "It's almost indescribable," she thought. "How can I ever really put these feelings into words?"

◆TAKE A LOOK / Galatians 1:11-24
Part of Sally's assignment was to report back to her classmates what she witnessed on the trip. Sally prepared in advance. She read books, took notes, and studied accounts of previous expeditions. When she was finally on the boat, she knew what was happening at each stage and was able to write a good report for her classmates.

If we are to be effective witnesses for Jesus Christ, we too should be well prepared. The apostle Peter, who practiced what he preached, wrote:
Always be prepared to give an answer to everyone who asks you to give the reason for the hope that you have (1 Peter 3:15).
The apostle Paul, whose life we've looked at this week, also spent time preparing to witness. Find out how long it took him to prepare—and where he went to do it—by reading Galatians 1:11-24.

▲ TAKE A STEP
Maybe God won't take you into the Arabian Desert, as He did Paul! But He does expect us all to know how to tell others why we believe in Him.

A good way to start is by writing out your testimony. Explain how you realized that you needed Christ as your Savior, how you came to know Him, and what it means to be His child.

Share with each other during your family time on Sunday. Then when God brings along someone else for you to share with, you'll be prepared.

Families with older children might also enjoy taking a course in evangelism or apologetics. Or ask your pastor or youth leader to suggest a book you can study together as you prepare to answer questions when you witness.

Was the apostle Paul the first Boy Scout?

Q

Should I prepare to witness?

A

Witnessing is a responsibility that I can prepare for.

Someone's watching you every day, everywhere

*M*ary worked at the Kentwood Nursing Home, lovingly caring for even the most difficult patients. She was kind and cheerful to everyone, even when someone was grouchy or rude.

One day Christie, another nurse, saw Mr. Trumple knock the spoon out of Mary's hand and jerk his head away. "Why didn't you just give up on him?" Christie asked. "Just let him go hungry if he doesn't cooperate." Then she paused.

"You know," she continued thoughtfully, "for most of us, working here is just a job, but you really love these old people. And it shows in everything you do. What's your secret anyway?"

◆TAKE A LOOK / Acts 16:16-34

Mary didn't realize it, but she had witnessed to her co-workers long before Christie asked her that question. As she went about her work, her life showed that Jesus lived in her. People saw—and experienced—God's love in Mary's attitudes and actions.

The familiar story of Paul and Silas in the Philippian jail is found in Acts 16:16-34. After you read it, tell what Paul and Silas did—or didn't do—to show love and consideration for the jailer. How do you think their actions led to his salvation?

▲ TAKE A STEP

When the prison doors fell, Paul and Silas could have escaped and been free men. But they knew the Philippian jailer's job—and perhaps even his life—was at stake. So they stayed where they were.

Because Paul and Silas put the jailer's needs before their own, they got an opportunity to witness to the jailer and his entire household. By the next morning they all sat at breakfast rejoicing because

He [the jailer] had come to believe in God—
he and his whole family (Acts 16:34).

When you let Jesus live through you, then you—like Mary and Paul and Silas—will attract people who will ask: "What's different about you?" or "What must I do to be saved?"

Share with the family a time when someone noticed something different about your life. Explain what you were doing and why you think they noticed. What did you say in response? Would you say anything else now? How did their questions or compliments make you feel?

Q

What kind of witnessing can people see in my everyday life?

A

Witnessing goes on every day as I let Jesus live His life through me.

END TIMES

Mr. Packer was almost asleep when he heard a mumbled cry from Eric's room. He rushed to Eric's bed and found him tossing and turning, thrashing his arms over his head.

"Wake up, son," his dad said, gently grabbing the waving arms. "Wake up, it's only a bad dream. You'll be okay."

Slowly ten-year-old Eric sat up and rubbed his eyes. "Oh, Dad, that was an awful dream. There was a war and only a few people were still alive. I was one of them, and I was hiding in a cave. Boy, that was some nightmare! I'm glad it wasn't real!"

As Eric lay back and Mr. Packer pulled the blanket over his son, Eric looked intently at his father. "I'm sure glad I know Jesus is coming again. He'll take care of everything, just like the Bible says."

◆ THINKING ABOUT THE END TIMES

Nations today have the power to destroy the world, so thinking about the worldwide destruction doesn't stretch our imaginations too far. But nearly 2,000 years ago, God's Son Jesus spoke of the time when God will make all things new—even the heavens and the earth. And best of all, Jesus promised that He Himself would return, and then His people would live with Him forever.

No one knows exactly when Jesus will come again, but God has given His children some clues to look for and some promises to claim about the end times, or **the time immediately preceding the return of Jesus Christ.** One of those promises is found in Matthew 28:20.

● KEY VERSE ON THE END TIMES

"I am with you always, to the very end of the age" (Matthew 28:20).

▲ LOOKING AHEAD

This week we'll see how the Bible describes the period of time before Jesus returns.

Like Eric, you may sometimes feel afraid about the world situation. After you reread Matthew 28:20, discuss how that promise can give you courage in difficult times.

"I'll bet it waits 'til after the geography test."

In times like these, He's as good as His Word!

Q

How do I know Jesus is coming again?

A

The end times will climax in the return of Jesus, who will come as He promised.

PARENT
If you'd like more information about the return of Christ, ask your pastor to recommend appropriate books.

Curtis had been waiting at the corner a long time. He was bored, tired, and very thirsty.

"Hey, Curtis!" a voice called from a car stopped for the light. "Want a ride? We'll take you home." It was Dirk, a classmate.

"No thanks, my dad told me he'd pick me up here."

"He probably forgot. Come on," Dirk coaxed.

"No, he promised he'd come. I'd better wait."

Curtis watched gloomily as his friend's car pulled away.

Soon a black pickup pulled up to the curb. "Hey kid, you all alone? Get in. I'll drive you home."

Curtis knew strangers could mean trouble. "No thanks," he stammered. "My dad is on his way. I'll wait for him."

Just then, the familiar station wagon pulled up, and the man in the pickup moved away. Curtis opened the door and climbed in beside his dad. "I'll bet you thought I wasn't coming," his dad smiled. "The radiator hose broke out on Highway 31, and I had to fix it. I'm really sorry."

"Aw Dad, I knew you'd come. You promised," Curtis replied happily. "I would have waited all night. But Dad, can we get something to drink?"

◆ TAKE A LOOK
John 14:1-3; Acts 1:11; Hebrews 9:28

Even though his father was delayed, Curtis knew his dad would eventually keep his promise. So he did as he was told and waited.

Jesus also promised His followers that He would come back to earth again. You can find those promises in these Bible verses: John 14:1-3; Matthew 26:64; Acts 1:11; Hebrews 9:28; and 1 Thessalonians 4:16.

▲ TAKE A STEP

Even though centuries have passed since Jesus went back to heaven, He will return. And even though He did not say specifically when He will return, He will keep His Word to us:

"I will come back and take you to be with me that you also may be where I am" (John 14:3).

In order to *believe* what Jesus said, we must *know* what He said. Let each family member choose one of the verses you looked up for today's reading and memorize it this week. After working on your verses separately, encourage each other by saying them to one another at a mealtime next Sunday!

*P*astor Barker had finished his sermon and was about to close the Sunday evening service. "Are there any other announcements before we dismiss?" he asked. Then Virgil Smith stood up.

"Pastor, Jesus spoke to me this afternoon," the elderly man said in an excited voice. "He said, 'Virgil, I'm coming back this Tuesday. Tell everyone to be ready.' And He said to go out to . . ."

As Mr. Smith continued, people began to whisper. Some were amazed; others were embarrassed for the old man; a few even chuckled.

Six-year-old James Higgins whispered: "Mom, is it true? Did God speak to Mr. Smith? Is Jesus really coming back on Tuesday?"

"Shh, I'll show you what the Bible says later," she whispered back. "Look, Pastor Barker's going to say something. Let's listen."

◆ TAKE A LOOK / Matthew 24:3-14, 23-31, 36

Everybody would like to know when Jesus is returning. Some, like Mr. Smith, even feel that God has given them a special message, the "inside information" so to speak.

Other people have been so convinced of a specific time that they have left their homes and jobs to wait. But they've all been wrong. And they've looked pretty foolish to scoffers who don't believe Jesus will return at all.

Jesus' own disciples wanted to know when He would return. You'll learn that the answer He gave them is important for us today as you read Matthew 24:3-14, 23-31, 36.

▲ TAKE A STEP

When Jesus spoke to His disciples about His own return, He plainly stated:

"No one knows about that day or hour, not even the angels in heaven, nor the Son, but only the Father" (Matthew 24:36).

He continued the thought by saying, "The Son of Man [another title for Jesus] will come at an hour when you do not expect him" (Matthew 24:44).

But Jesus did describe many "signs" or general conditions that would exist in the world before His return. Without reviewing, can you remember any from the verses you just read?

After you review those verses, discuss which of those general signs you read about in newspapers or see on television.

Don't pick a date— you may still have to wait

Q

Does anyone know when the end times will be?

A

The end times will be identified by certain signs that Jesus explained.

How much worse can this world get?

What will happen during the end times?

The end times will be times of great evil as self-centered people increasingly turn away from God.

*A*t age 80, Mr. Sandridge thought a lot about how the world had changed in the last 20 years or so. It seemed to him to be getting worse and worse.

For instance, when 17-year-old Fred asked to use the car, his dad refused. So Fred stole his dad's credit cards, his mother's diamond ring, and the car, and he hasn't been heard from since! Mr. Sandridge just shook his head over such selfish rebellion.

Another thing Mr. Sandridge didn't understand was modern television. "Why do you kids watch that filth?" he'd ask his grandchildren and great-grand-children.

But the younger people paid no attention to him. "Who does he think he is, talking about 'signs of the times'?" they whispered. "What does he know anyway? Just ignore him."

And they did.

◆ TAKE A LOOK
1 Timothy 4:1; 2 Timothy 3:1-7; 2 Peter 3:3-5

Mr. Sandridge was right in thinking that the spiritual condition of the world was getting worse, not better. From his long experience, he was able to see how the prophecies about the end times were being fulfilled.

Though no one knows exactly when Jesus will return, the Bible does speak about the condition of the world before He does. You'll find some of those "signs of the times" listed in 1 Timothy 4:1; 2 Timothy 3:1-7; and 2 Peter 3:3-5.

▲ TAKE A STEP
The verses you read describe a society full of self-centered, violent people who scoff at anything pertaining to God. Such people are

. . . *lovers of pleasure rather than lovers of God (2 Timothy 3:4).*

And we are warned,

"Have nothing to do with them" (2 Timothy 3:5).

Mr. Sandridge's great-grandchildren didn't realize that instead of being out of touch with reality, the old man was actually in tune with God's Word.

Do you think any of the signs you read about today are being fulfilled? Try to give a specific example from the news or from your own observation. Don't be surprised if you begin to think that we are indeed living in the last days!

Marcia Tyler enjoyed keeping house for Mr. O'Harris. But since he had been away for nearly a year life seemed really dull.

One day Marcia decided she would give a dinner party for her friends. So she prepared the special dishes she always served Mr. O'Harris's guests. She hired extra help and even bought a new outfit. This would be her night!

At the party the guests became quite careless. They marred the floors and broke several crystal goblets. But no one cared. They were having a great time.

Suddenly, the heavy front door creaked. "That's strange," Marcia thought. "All my guests are already here."

As the mystery guest walked in, the look on his face made Marcia begin to tremble.

Mr. O'Harris had returned unexpectedly!

◆ TAKE A LOOK
Matthew 24:44-51; 25:1-13

Marcia certainly had no problem understanding why she was looking for a job the next day. But imagine for a moment what Mr. O'Harris thought. Here was his trusted servant sitting at his table and eating his food, totally unconcerned about him or his property.

Just as Marcia should have faithfully looked after Mr. O'Harris's property, Christians have a responsibility to follow Jesus' instructions until His return. Jesus told several parables to remind His followers to be ready at all times for His return.

Two of them are found in Matthew 24:44-51 and Matthew 25:1-13. Read one parable—or both, if you have time—and look for the specific verse(s) that warns us to be ready for our Master's return.

▲ TAKE A STEP

What should you do to get ready for Jesus' return? The apostle Peter answers that exact question this way:

You ought to live holy and godly lives as you look forward to the day of God and speed its coming (2 Peter 3:11-12).

Check your life for things you should be doing (but aren't) and things you are doing (but probably shouldn't be).

What would you do differently if you knew Jesus would be returning one year from today? What would you do differently if you knew Jesus was returning two weeks from today?

Will you be ready when the Master returns?

Q

How can I prepare for the end times?

A

The end times will not catch me unprepared if I live every day for Jesus.

PARENT
If your family continues to study the end times, make a folder for newspaper and magazine articles related to the signs of the times. You'll be surprised at how quickly you will fill it up.

EDUCATION

*W*ell, we're about ready to decide," Mr. Knowles announced as the family finished dessert and Mrs. Knowles poured another cup of coffee. Kip and Jennifer glanced at each other. The twins knew that because their parents wanted them to have the best education possible, they wanted to place their children in another school. As third-graders, they were glad to be included in the family discussion.

Mr. Knowles reviewed the possibilities. "We can let you stay where you are now, but Mom and I aren't happy about that," he said. "You're soaking up a lot of teaching that opposes what we believe.

"Another possibility is to send you to the church school. But it's 30 miles away and costs more money than we can afford.

"Or we could home school, as we've talked about before. Mom and I are leaning that way, but we want to know what you think."

"But Dad," Kip interrupted. "There's one more choice." Mr. Knowles looked puzzled. "Not going to school at all," Kip grinned. "I'd vote for that any day!"

◆ THINKING ABOUT EDUCATION

Like parents all over the world, Mr. and Mrs. Knowles want the best possible education for their children. But exactly what is a good education? How can you get one?

The word *education* is not used in the Bible. But all our educational experiences should help us reach God's goal for our lives. And God is very clear about what that goal is.

"Ask Mom for Paulo's Alphabet Soup. Tell her it's educational."

● KEY VERSE ON EDUCATION
Love the LORD your God with all your heart and with all your soul and with all your strength (Deuteronomy 6:5).

▲ LOOKING AHEAD
Education is the lifelong process of learning.

As you read Proverbs 4:5-9; 9:10, what should your main goal in life be? How actively are *you* pursuing that goal?

*T*hat might not be a bad idea," Mr. Knowles replied when Kip made his suggestion about not going to school at all, and Kip could hardly believe his ears. He didn't think for a minute that Dad would seriously consider no school at all!

Mr. Knowles continued. "Suppose you want to be a pilot. It would save time if you worked directly with an expert pilot and spent the next 10 or 15 years learning all he knows . . ."

But Kip didn't let Mr. Knowles finish that thought. "But Dad, I don't know what I want to do yet," he protested. "I'm only in the third grade. Besides, I was only teasing. I like school."

◆ TAKE A LOOK / Acts 7:17-33

Kip's dad knew he was teasing. But Dad wanted Kip to think about the purpose of education.

A real education is much more than spending time in school. And it's more than simply preparing for a certain kind of job. The great English poet John Milton said this: "The end, then, of learning is to repair the ruins of our first parents by regaining to know God aright, and out of that knowledge to love Him, to imitate Him, to be like Him."

Do you know what Milton meant? Even more important, do you know any teachers who would agree that the goal of education is to love God and be like Him?

Many people believe education is supposed to equip people to make money. But if Milton is right, that's not the purpose of education at all. A glance at one of the most highly educated men in the Old Testament will help you understand what really matters to God.

In Acts 7:17-33, we learn that Moses was 80 years old when he became the leader of God's people. Where do you think he received the better education: in Pharaoh's court, or in the Midian desert learning to know God?

▲ TAKE A STEP

Moses may have been the best-educated man in Egypt. But that counted for little until he really came to know, worship, and rely on the true and living God. He had to learn the importance of depending on God for instruction.

"Lean not on your own understanding" (Proverbs 3:5).

Reread the quotation from Milton. What can you do to make your education meet Milton's goal and fulfill God's purpose?

Diplomas don't always equal education

What is the purpose of education?

Education is meant to draw me closer to the Lord God.

People need to read God's Book

*T*he b-r-o-wn cat j-u . . . j-u-m-p-e-d on the . . . chore."

What? Six-year-old Robbie scratched his head and studied the word. "Cats don't jump on chores," he thought. He peered at the strange word again and carefully sounded it out letter by letter: "C-h-a-i-r . . . c-h-a-i-r . . . chair! The brown cat jumped up on the chair!" His voice rang with excitement as the new word became another friend in his growing vocabulary.

"Hey, Rob," his father said, poking his head around the door, "You're doing a great job with your reading. When I was your age I couldn't have read that sentence."

"Why not, Dad?" Robbie asked.

"When I started school, I was afraid to ask questions, and I really didn't learn how to read. When I went into second grade I was really scared. Everybody in the class could read but me!"

◆ TAKE A LOOK
Deuteronomy 6:4-9; 31:13; Psalm 78:2-8

Like many young students, Robbie couldn't solve his problem alone. If you were Robbie's parents, what would you do to help? Just as the Bible doesn't mention the word education, it doesn't say anything about learning to read either. But it does give some very clear indications of who's responsible for teaching—and educating—children and where that training should take place. You'll discover the who and where of good education as you read Deuteronomy 6:4-9; 31:13; Psalm 78:2-8.

▲ TAKE A STEP

Talk about them when you sit at home and when you walk along the road, when you lie down and when you get up (Deuteronomy 6:7).

"Parents are their children's first and most influential teachers. What parents do to help their children learn is more important . . . than how well-off the family is." That quotation from a publication of the United States Department of Education underlines what God has said all along: Education primarily happens in the home.

Through daily conversations, household routines, and obedience to God's Word, parents teach their children values that really count.

Can you identify how education happens in your home? What is taught when you "sit at home"? When you "lie down"? When you "get up"? How are you learning that Jesus Christ is the center of all life?

Q

Where does education take place?

A

Education happens best in my home.

PARENT
You can obtain many informational booklets from the government. Check your local library for the CONSUMER INFORMATION CATALOG published quarterly by the General Services Administration.

Robbie couldn't believe his ears. His dad hadn't learned to read in first grade! "What happened when you got to second grade?" he asked.

"Well, as I recall, the teacher divided the class into three reading groups—the Lions, the Tigers, and the Cougars," his father explained. "I was in the Tigers, but everyone knew ours was the slowest group, so we were secretly called the 'Turtles.' Sometimes we even called ourselves 'Turtles.'"

"Were you dumb, Dad?" Robbie asked.

"No, but sometimes I felt dumb," his father replied. "My parents knew I was okay and maybe I just needed some help. So they found a retired school teacher to tutor me in phonics. It wasn't long before I was right up there with the best readers in the class. And since then I've read just about everything I could get my hands on. Because I learned to read, I've been able to keep on learning even though I finished college years ago. For me—and for most everybody—reading is the key to a real education."

◆ TAKE A LOOK / 2 Peter 1:5-9

Having the best parents in the world or attending the finest schools in the world will not make you or anyone else an educated person. You have to do that for yourself by having a desire to learn, by disciplining yourself to study, and by cooperating with your teachers.

Education didn't begin when you started kindergarten. It doesn't have to stop when you receive a high school or college diploma. You'll find God's syllabus on how to have a continuing education in 2 Peter 1:5-9.

▲ TAKE A STEP

The foundation of education (or "knowledge" as Peter might refer to it) is not a school or a teacher. It is faith in God and the ability to see the world and everything in it as His creation.

To be well educated means you are always interested in learning something new—wanting to increase your skills and knowledge—and then using all you've learned to worship and bring glory to God.

Read Psalm 25:4-5 aloud together. If you think the verses are appropriate as a student's prayer, pray them together now:

Show me your ways, O LORD, teach me your paths; guide me in your truth and teach me, for you are God my Savior (Psalm 25:4-5).

It's never too late to educate

Q

How much education is enough?

A

Education is a lifelong process founded on faith in God and His truth.

Tear down the walls that keep Jesus boxed in

Q

What is the most important thing I can learn?

A

Education's highest goal is learning to know Jesus Christ.

PARENT
Remember your child's main goal should not be simply to get a good job or learn a new skill. Begin at an early age to encourage your children to dedicate their lives to God's service.

On Walt's recent trips home from college, he'd been spending so much time working, seeing his girl-friend, and sleeping that he barely had time to tell his folks hello. And he had no time at all for worshiping with the family.

"Sorry I can't make it," he'd say Sunday after Sunday as he left the house before his parents left for church.

Sadly, Mr. Faber watched Walt's attempts to run his life without God at the center. Finally Walt's dad knew he had to talk to his son.

The opportunity came when Walt's car broke down, and he called his dad for help. After they'd arranged for a tow truck and were heading home, Walt began opening up. "You know, Dad," he said, "everything seems to be going wrong lately. I need a good job, but I can't decide what I want to do. I can't make enough money with just a part-time job. I feel like I've hit a brick wall."

◆ **TAKE A LOOK / John 17:3; Philippians 3:10; Matthew 6:25-34**

Walt had hit an invisible wall—one he had made himself. He had tried to control the areas of his life such as job, friends, and education, and leave a few "spiritual" areas for God to control. But it wasn't working, and Walt was miserable.

Mr. Faber reminded Walt of the peace he used to have when Christ was the center of his life—and of the turmoil he had now that he was trying to be in control. He gently encouraged Walt to recall that the goal of his education was not simply to get a good job, but to equip him to glorify God.

That night Walt thought long and hard about what his dad had said. He took his Bible from the bottom of the stack of books by his bed and turned to the verses his dad had suggested. You might like to read them too: John 17:3; Philippians 3:10; and Matthew 6:25-34.

▲ **TAKE A STEP**

"Seek first his kingdom and his righteousness, and all these things will be given to you as well" (Matthew 6:33).

The most important part of your education is not learning how to make money, have a job, or control your own life. It's learning to know Jesus Christ better. Do you ever feel frustrated like Walt? If so, what invisible "walls" in your life are keeping Jesus from being the center?

BIBLE

*H*ere is a true-false test to take as a family. Once you find the key, you shouldn't have any trouble getting every answer right!

T   F   1. The Bible, though one Book, is made up of many books.
T   F   2. The Bible was written by God.
T   F   3. The Bible was written by men.
T   F   4. The Bible is like a flashlight, compass, and sword.
T   F   5. The Bible, though thousands of years old, is alive today.

If you get a bit confused, the "key" is simple—they're all true!

◆ THINKING ABOUT THE BIBLE

Have you ever watched TV with the sound turned off and tried to guess what the actors were saying? (Try it!) It's not easy.

History is like that. Go back as far as you like—all the way back to the beginning—and you will discover that "in the beginning God . . . " (Genesis 1:1). God has no beginning, and will have no end. History is really just His story! But without an explanation of history, we might never know its meaning.

In many ways, the Bible is the "sound track" of history. **It shows us circumstances and events from God's point of view**, especially the events surrounding the birth and life, death and resurrection of Jesus Christ.

God has many things He wants us to know that we could not learn simply by reading a history book. So He gave us His Book!

● KEY VERSE ON THE BIBLE

All Scripture . . . is useful for teaching, rebuking, correcting and training in righteousness, so that the man of God may be thoroughly equipped for every good work (2 Timothy 3:16-17).

▲ LOOKING AHEAD

In case the quiz at the top of the page is still puzzling you, just relax. By the end of the week you'll know why each statement is true. Best of all, you'll know why there's no better "compass" to guide your life than the unchanging Word of God.

"Once upon a time . . . long ago . . . before TV . . ."

And now a Word from our Creator

Q

How did God give us the Bible?

A

The Bible came from God's mind to human authors.

*P*aul and his sister Melanie watched intently as their hamster Henry raced around his exercise wheel.

"I wish hamsters could talk," Paul sighed. "I wonder what Henry is thinking about. Maybe we could learn 'hamster talk.' "

"Don't be silly," Melanie said matter-of-factly. "That's impossible. Anyway, what would you say to a hamster?"

"I'd tell him I like him . . . and that I want to take care of him and play with him every day."

"I'll bet if Henry could talk," Melanie responded, "he would say 'Let me out! Let me out!'"

"But the cage protects him. Without the cage the cat next door would catch him! Boy," Paul sighed, "I wish hamsters could talk."

◆ **TAKE A LOOK / Jeremiah 1:1-10**

How exactly did we get our Bible? Did God magically breathe words onto scrolls for angels to deliver to earth? The apostle Peter tells us how the Bible did—and did not—have its beginning:

> For prophecy [God's Word] never had its origin in the will of man, but men spoke from God as they were carried along by the Holy Spirit (2 Peter 1:21).

God did not use the language of angels, the sound of thunder, or the roar of the ocean to speak to us (though He could have). Instead, He used human language—real people writing His words.

The men who wrote God's words were ordinary people: shepherds (like Moses and David), farmers (like Amos), doctors (like Luke). But "carried along by the Holy Spirit," and using their own individual writing styles and personalities, they wrote down the truth God wanted us to know—truth from God's mind to their pens to your Bible!

Jeremiah was one such man that God used. Though Jeremiah wrote the words you will read in Jeremiah 1:1-10, see if you can discover by reading those verses who was in fact doing the speaking and "moved" Jeremiah to write what he did.

▲ **TAKE A STEP**

Paul couldn't free his hamster, because he couldn't give him instructions or warn him of danger. But in the Bible your Creator communicates with you, giving instruction and warning of danger. He tells you of His love for you. The question you must ask yourself now is this: "Am I really listening to what God has to say?"

*Y*ears ago missionaries contacted a savage tribe cut off from civilization by thick jungle and high mountains. The missionaries knew these violent people needed to have the Word of God, and hear about the love of God that could change their lives. But not a single word of the Bible was available in their language.

Slowly the missionaries began learning to speak and write the tribe's language, a task that took many years. But at last the day came when a small portion of the Bible was ready to read in words the tribespeople could understand.

The tribal leaders listened closely as the missionary read. Suddenly, an angry whisper was heard. What was wrong, the missionary wondered? Was the translation bad? Finally, the chief spoke: "How is it," he asked, "that your God knows how to write so accurately about our tribe?"

◆ TAKE A LOOK / 2 Kings 22:8-13; 23:1-3

God's accurate description of the sinful minds, hearts, and actions of the tribespeople made them curious to know more about the God who already knew them so well! As God's Word spoke to them, they learned:

The unfolding of your words gives light; it gives understanding to the simple (Psalm 119:130).

A similar thing happened in the days of Josiah, king of Judah. Through neglect and sin, the temple of God had been abandoned. But King Josiah ordered the temple to be repaired. During the clean-up, a wonderful discovery was made amid the dust and debris. Find out what it was by reading 2 Kings 22:8-13; 23:1-3.

▲ TAKE A STEP

When the Book of the Law (all the Old Testament that had been written to that point) was brought out and read to the king, Josiah instantly "saw the light"! He realized that he and his people were not obeying the Lord. But once they saw their sin, the people repented.

Has the entrance of the light of God's Word made as much difference in your life as it did in the lives of those tribespeople? Or in the lives of King Josiah and his people? What do you do when God's Word shows you something that is not exactly as it should be? Do you ignore it . . . or are you willing to let God help you change? If something you've recently read in the Bible has shown you an area in your life that needs change, thank God for showing you what's needed, and ask Him to help you do it!

God wrote the book on me, so He must know me

Q

Why did God give us the Bible?

A

The Bible tells me what God wants me to know and do.

PARENT
Let each family member share a time when he or she felt that God communicated in a specific way from the Bible.

The flashlight that never needs batteries

The boys had been hiking the Appalachian Trail for six days—traveling in pairs, moving at their own pace, meeting each night at a designated point. Everything was going well. That is, until Terry staggered into camp.

"Mr. Randall," he cried breathlessly, "Philip's gone. We got separated and I think he wandered off the trail. I waited for him, and called and called. He's lost out there. We've got to get help."

"Okay, Terry. Stay calm and let's think this through. It's getting dark now, and there's nothing we can do until daybreak. We might all get lost if we left camp. The thing to do is stay put. Philip knows where we are. Unless he's hurt, he'll meet us at the next checkpoint. He's got a map of the trails, and a good compass. And he knows how to use them. So now's the time . . . "

How should we use the Bible?

◆ **TAKE A LOOK / Psalm 119:105-112**

Philip's hope of reaching safety lay in the fact that he was properly equipped and thoroughly trained to use his equipment. He had to rely on his trail map and his compass to guide him into camp.

Our hope for safety on life's journey also lies in our preparation and equipment. God has given us His Word to equip and train us to stay on the path God intends for us to follow. The longest chapter in the Bible is about the Bible: Psalm 119. Most of its 176 verses mention God's Word by using words that describe it. As you read verses 105-112, pick the word in each verse that means the same thing as God's Word, the Bible.

A

The Bible shows me God's road map for my life.

▲ **TAKE A STEP**

Because God knows the path better than we do, the psalmist declares:

Your word is a lamp to my feet and a light for my path (Psalm 119:105).

Turn back to page 181 and reread the Key Verse on the Bible. This verse really tells how to use the wonderful "lamp" God has given you. The teaching of Scripture shows you the path God has mapped out; the rebukes warn you of dangerous detours to avoid; the corrections of Scripture bring you back if you leave the path; the training of Scripture prepares you to guide others over the same path.

Just as Philip had what he needed to find his way back to the trail, you have what you need on the "path of life." But do you know how to use it? Can you think of three ways to improve your skills in handling the lamp of God's Word?

*S*ix-year-old Betsy watched her older brother Mark—a Cub Scout—whittle on a stick. Thinking she could do that too, Betsy went to the kitchen and picked up a knife. Soon a loud scream brought her mother running to discover Betsy with a bad cut—and a bad case of hurt feelings.

"I only wanted to whittle like Mark's doing," Betsy explained between sobs.

"But Betsy, knives are sharp. You have to use them very carefully or they will cut you instead of the stick. When you're old enough, your daddy will teach you how to whittle, too."

"Okay," said Betsy, fighting back tears. Then her eyes brightened. "Mommy, can I join the Cub Scouts, too?"

◆ **TAKE A LOOK / Hebrews 4:12; Colossians 3:16-17**

Lots of things around your house are sharp: the lawnmower, knives, Dad's razor, Mom's scissors. Use them in the proper way, and those sharp tools can do great good; use them incorrectly, and they can do great harm. It is no accident that God's Word, the Bible, is called a sword.

The word of God is living and active. Sharper than any double-edged sword, it penetrates even to dividing soul and spirit, joints and marrow; it judges the thoughts and attitudes of the heart (Hebrews 4:12).

Just as a surgeon's knife can perform delicate operations, so God's Word can cut into your thoughts and motives, helping you to have the right attitude in the things you do and say. Turn to Colossians 3:16-17 to discover what else God's Word can do!

▲ **TAKE A STEP**

As your family reads God's Word together, you're developing a life-changing habit that will help you grow in your walk with God and in your relationships with other family members. It will also help you understand your world and the society you live in.

The Bible is more than a sword; it is also milk to nourish you (1 Peter 2:2), water to refresh you (Ephesians 5:26), and seed to cause your life to be fruitful (Luke 8:11) as you tell others about the good news of Jesus.

Nutrition . . . protection . . . refreshment . . . fruitfulness. No two ways about it, God's Word is good for you! Read this treasure daily, obey its directions, and watch what happens!

The Sword that inflicts the kindest cut of all

Q

How should we treat the Bible?

A

The Bible contains what I need to grow spiritually.

PARENT
This might be a good time to make sure each family member has an easy-to-read translation of the Bible. This book uses the NEW INTERNATIONAL VERSION, but there are others just as easy to understand.

FRIENDS

*O*h, how Tina dreaded that first day of school. Leaving her friends back home had been hard. Her dad's exciting new job and the family's move had seemed like an adventure—for awhile. But now the thrill was gone, and Tina felt all alone.

As she trudged slowly to the bus stop, she remembered the storybook she'd read to her five-year-old brother Benjie the night before. It was entitled, The Bunny Who Wanted a Friend.

"That's it!" she thought to herself. *"I'm just like bunny Charles. If I can be a friend, I'll find a friend."* With new determination she stepped onto the bus and smiled at the first girl her age.

"Hi, my name's Tina. This is my first day. What's your name?"

◆ THINKING ABOUT FRIENDS

David and Jonathan. Tom Sawyer and Huck Finn. Batman and Robin. Famous pairs of friends who stood by each other.

Is there someone you think of as your special friend? Someone who listens to you, is fun to be with, accepts you as you are, helps you do your best, **cares for you and shares your cares**? And are you a special friend like that in someone else's life?

Everybody needs and wants a friend. But sometimes friends are hard to find—and even harder to *be*. It's not easy because . . .

● KEY VERSE ON FRIENDS

A friend loves at all times (Proverbs 17:17).

▲ LOOKING AHEAD

As you start this week, ask Mom or Dad about their special childhood friends. How did they meet their friends, what did they like to do together, and how did they help those friendships grow?

Then read Proverbs 27:10 and Ecclesiastes 4:10. You'll see two reasons why you never outgrow the need for having friends—and being a friend.

"She said spell friend, and I put B-I-L-L-Y. What's wrong with that?"

*J*ust two more days, Mom!" Tim yelled excitedly. "This will be the best camping trip ever. Hiking . . . rafting . . . fishing. I can hardly wait. But it sure won't be the same without Chad there."

"Tim, you told me Chad wouldn't miss this trip for anything."

"That's what he said. But after his dad lost his job, there wasn't enough money for him to go. So Chad's got a summer job lined up next week."

"It sounds like Chad could really use the trip, Tim. Perhaps your father and I could help pay his way."

"It's too late, Mom. The park service only lets in a certain number of campers, and all the spaces are filled."

"Tim, if you think about it, there is a way. Someone else could give up his place so Chad could go instead."

◆ **TAKE A LOOK / 1 Samuel 18:1-9**

Caring for someone and sharing that person's cares. That's our definition of friendship. And you don't have to search very long in the Bible to find examples of people who cared and shared in each other's lives.

King Saul was losing the war with the Philistines when a young shepherd boy volunteered to fight the Philistine champion, Goliath. Saul finally consented to let David fight—and to the king's surprise and delight, David won!

When David returned with Goliath's head on a pole, Saul summoned him for a royal interview. There, for the first time, the king's son Jonathan saw David.

As you read about their meeting in 1 Samuel 18:1-9, ask yourself this: What did David, a humble shepherd, have in common with Jonathan, a royal prince?

▲ **TAKE A STEP**

No doubt Jonathan was listening as David told the king his life story—caring for the sheep, fighting lions and bears, composing songs, learning to love the Lord. David's spiritual vitality drew Jonathan like a magnet, and a friendship began that would last a lifetime.

Jonathan became one in spirit with David and he loved him as himself (1 Samuel 18:1).

Go back to the story of Tim and Chad. Tim faced a tough decision—with more at stake than a camping trip! If you were Tim, what would you do? Think twice before you answer. Friendship can be costly—as can anything of real value!

Who's number one around here anyway?

Q

Who is a true friend?

A

A friend puts others' needs above his own.

Friendship, the world's strongest glue

*I*n the locker room, the girls were dressing after drill team practice. As Debbie bent to put on her shoes, she overheard two other girls talking about her friend Tammy.

"You're right," one of them said. "Tammy's a snob. Ever since she was picked as a cheerleader, she won't have anything to do with us."

"Yeah, I guess she thinks she's too good to be seen with us. And she probably spends time with Debbie just because they ride to school together. I'll bet Debbie thinks Tammy's just as big a snob as we do! Everybody knows cheerleaders are like that!"

Q

Why do I need friends?

A

Friends stand with me when others are against me.

PARENT
Discuss some specific ways you can be a friend to your child and still maintain your authority as parent.

◆ TAKE A LOOK / 1 Samuel 18:28–19:9

When Debbie overheard unkind words about her friend Tammy, she had to make a decision. Should she tell Tammy what was being said? Or maybe she should speak up on behalf of her friend? Or should she do nothing?

Jonathan was faced with a similar decision, but the outcome would have far more serious consequences.

As King Saul saw David's popularity with the people, his jealousy exploded into violent action. Twice Saul hurled spears at David, but missed. He sent David into battle, hoping he would be killed; instead, David returned victorious.

Thinking that his daughter might help him trap David, Saul demanded that David kill 200 enemy soldiers in order to marry her; David did exactly that and won the king's daughter! Now continue the story by reading 1 Samuel 18:28–19:9. Do you think David really trusted Jonathan? Would you have trusted Jonathan?

▲ TAKE A STEP

Jonathan warned David of King Saul's anger; then he approached the king on David's behalf. Jonathan "spoke well of David" (19:4) and bravely faced Saul's fury in order to restore peace between his father and his friend. He was practicing the truth Jesus proclaimed:

"Greater love has no one than this, that he lay down his life for his friends" (John 15:13).

Jonathan put his life in danger to defend David. Think about the quality of Jonathan's friendship—loyal, supportive, brave. Would you want Jonathan for a friend? More important, would Jonathan have wanted you for a friend?

Girls are so silly," Mike exclaimed to his father. "All they ever do is talk, talk, talk. In the halls, in the cafeteria, on the phone. They just hang around and talk. Now Ellen and Mary are back in Ellen's room crying because another friend is moving away. They're taking turns talking to the other girl on the phone."

"Well, you and Matt talked on the phone a good bit, too, before he moved away," Mike's father interrupted.

"It's not the same, Dad. We talked about important things—baseball, and cars, and stuff like that. But Ellen and her friends just talk about whether they're happy or sad or lonely or angry. Can you believe it?"

"Yes," Mike's father mused, "I think I can."

◆ TAKE A LOOK / 1 Samuel 20:30-42

Mike noticed something important without even knowing it! Girls often seem more willing to share their inner feelings; guys like to share outward activities. But true friendship involves both. It means letting your friends see you as you really are: your thoughts and feelings, your joys and sorrows, your strengths and weaknesses. It's like opening a window to yourself and letting others look inside.

David and Jonathan built a close friendship because they were willing to talk about how they felt. In 1 Samuel 20:30-42, you'll read how David and Jonathan planned to find out just how angry the king was. The story's sad ending shows that the young men were not ashamed of their emotions. As you read, see if you can discover who cried the most—and why.

▲ TAKE A STEP

Why were David and Jonathan crying? They knew that David must run for his life. But even more painful was the thought that they might never see each other again. Perhaps David cried the most because Jonathan hurt the most. (After all, how would you feel if your father wanted to kill your best friend?) David's tears showed that he was willing to . . .

Rejoice with those who rejoice; mourn with those who mourn (Romans 12:15).

David's tears said "I really care" in a way no words could. Ellen's sadness at losing a girlfriend was just as real. Name two ways Mike could have helped Ellen feel better. How could he put Romans 12:15 into practice?

Share a feeling, find a friend— for life

Q
What helps friends stay close?

A
Friends grow closer when feelings are shared.

To have a friend, first be a friend

Q

How can I be a friend?

A

A friend shows God's love to others.

PARENT
Feelings are sometimes hard to identify and even harder to share. Discuss why people have a hard time sharing feelings, and let your child offer suggestions that might help your family "open up."

For a whole week Tina had sat beside Karen on the school bus, trying to be a friend so she could make a friend.

First, Tina asked Karen about her classes at school. The next day she asked about Karen's family and told her a little about her own. Now it was Friday, and Tina was beginning to wonder if Karen would ever open up and really tell her how she felt.

"I'm feeling pretty lonely today," Tina confessed. "It was hard moving here, and I'm really trying to make friends. But it just doesn't seem to be working."

"I know exactly how you feel," Karen said softly. "It's been almost two years since we moved here, and I still don't feel like I know anyone or belong anywhere . . . "

◆TAKE A LOOK / 1 Samuel 31:2; 2 Samuel 1:17, 25-27; 9:1, 3, 6-7

Someone who cares for you and shares your cares. Someone who loves you at all times. Each of us needs a friend like that. But don't stop there!

We also need to be people like that. You can start by reaching out to others—as Tina did and as Jonathan did.

Jonathan gave David his possessions and his attention. He also gave encouragement, support, and love. Their friendship got better day by day, but each one only got out of it what he was first willing to put into it.

Saul pursued David so long and so hard that David had to flee from his own country. But danger, distance, and even death could not destroy the friendship of David and Jonathan.

Read out loud the nine verses listed above (have members of the family take turns). Watch for the lasting effects of David's and Jonathan's friendship.

▲ TAKE A STEP

The name *Jonathan* means "the Lord has given." What a wonderful gift of love God gave to David in the friendship of Jonathan—a friendship in which each treated the other with . . .

Love [that] always protects, always trusts, always hopes, always perseveres (1 Corinthians 13:7).

Tina and Karen shared a common problem—loneliness. But only one girl was trying hard to find a solution.

Which one do you think was making friends—and why?

LIFE

*H*ey, *Lewis, can you come spelunking with us Saturday?" Chip asked as the boys climbed into the bus.*

"No, I think I'll pass," Lewis replied. "War of the Worlds is on TV and I don't want to miss it."

"Good grief, Lewis, how many times have you seen it already? It's like you were living in another world! What good is it?" Chip was clearly exasperated with his friend.

"I just like it, that's all," Lewis replied defensively. "It's fun to imagine all the different life forms that might be living in the universe. We might even discover some in our lifetime."

"You're so busy dreaming about life on other planets you're letting life pass you by on this one," Chip said in disgust. Then he turned his eyes skyward: "Beam me up, Scotty; there's no intelligent life down here!"

◆ THINKING ABOUT LIFE

Lewis and Chip had different views about life. Lewis was interested in biological life, even imagining that life forms might exist beyond earth. Chip was concerned with experiences that make up the quality of life here and now. And both aspects of "life" are important. Basically, life is **that state of being in which a person, plant, or animal functions in its environment.** But the Bible shows us that life has a much deeper meaning.

● KEY VERSE ON LIFE

Jesus answered: "I am the way and the truth and the life" (John 14:6).

▲ LOOKING AHEAD

"Choose life!" is a popular slogan you may have seen on bumper stickers or sweatshirts. Did you know that phrase is from the Bible? Read Deuteronomy 30:15-20. What do you think God means by "choosing life"? How do you and your family demonstrate that you choose life?

"I don't have any trouble understanding the concept of eternity. Eternity is forty-five minutes in math class."

Life is one thing everybody leaves behind

"*Look, he's scratched his face,*" Cindy exclaimed. "*How can his fingernails be so sharp when his fingers are so tiny?*" Nine-year-old Cindy was fascinated by her three-day-old brother. She examined the baby carefully while her mother gently bathed him. Cindy's eyes widened as her mother explained the reason for the soft spot on top of his head. She winced with her new brother when Mrs. Holmes carefully dressed the baby's navel where the umbilical cord had been clipped. "*It's okay,*" Cindy cooed. "*Now that you're born, you can breathe and eat by yourself. You don't need a 'lifeline' any more.*"

Then she giggled. "*Look, Mom. He's putting his thumb in his mouth and holding my finger with his other hand. Why does he know how to do that?*"

◆ TAKE A LOOK / Psalm 139:13

Just like Cindy's brother, you were a precious life even before you were born. Even though you were very tiny, you were not like anybody else, and the pattern for what you would become was already in your cells. You are, in fact, a miracle of life.

The Bible says a great deal about physical life. But the most important fact is that God is the Creator of all life. You'll discover God's interest in your physical life as you read Psalm 139:13. Then learn more about how God views life by matching the verses on the left with the phrases at the right:

Q

What does the Bible teach about physical life?

This verse shows me	that human life is:
Psalm 39:5	a. more precious than a sparrow's
Psalm 90:10	b. like a mist that vanishes
Isaiah 64:8	c. very short
Matthew 10:31	d. like clay in a potter's hand
James 4:14	e. limited by God

A

Life is a gift from God and should be respected.

▲ TAKE A STEP

God is the source of life. The Bible states: "*He himself gives all men life and breath and everything else*" (Acts 17:25).

We are to respect life—especially human life—because God made it. Based on what you've read, what do you think God's point of view is about: (1) Ending the life of an unborn baby through abortion? (2) Putting a critically ill or very old person to death so he or she won't be miserable anymore? (3) Treating a handicapped person as less important? Do your beliefs and actions reveal that you view life as God does?

ANSWERS
c, e, d, a, b

*T*humbing through newspapers and magazines you've probably seen and scoffed at ads like these:
- *Wash Gray Away with Vibrant Hue Color Shampoo.*
- *Consider Cryogenics—Put Life on Hold Until Cancer is Cured!*
- *Alleviate Stress! Wear New Perfect Bounce Aerobic Shoes.*
- *Bring Youth Back the Weight-Away Way!*
- *Be a New You! Contact the Body Sculpture Clinic.*
- *Stay Wrinkle-Free with Youth Dream Age-Control Creme.*
- *Be the Man You Once Were. Call Acme Hair Replacement Today!*
- *Take ABC Vitamins, the Liquid Answer to Concentration Problems*

◆**TAKE A LOOK / Psalm 103:15-19; Isaiah 40:6-7**
You might think such advertisements sound silly. But whether you're 16 or 60, you're the target for hundreds of products that claim to strengthen and/or lengthen physical life.

Scientists continue searching for that magical ingredient that will lengthen life. They interview senior citizens on every continent, hoping to discover their secret for long life.

And each year people spend billions of dollars trying to look younger, feel younger, and live longer! But only God, the Creator of life, has the secret to life. And He has limited the life span of human beings.

The length of our days is seventy years—or eighty, if we have the strength (Psalm 90:10).

As you read Psalm 103:15-19 and Isaiah 40:6-7, you'll see that whether a person's life stretches to a hundred years or lasts only a few short hours, it is always brief in God's sight.

▲ **TAKE A STEP**
Against the vastness of eternity, the length of human life seems insignificant. But it's not. In fact, the time we spend here on earth—and the choices we make—determine where and with whom we will spend eternity.

The products mentioned at the top of the page may seem crazy to you. But what do they tell us about how people view life?

Quickly list some ways your family spends time and money pampering your physical bodies. Do you spend as much time and money strengthening your spiritual life?

My life is one small tick on the clock of eternity

What does the Bible teach about long life?

A

Life on earth is brief, but it is long enough for me to choose where I will spend eternity— and with whom.

PARENT
Your view on abortion reveals a great deal about how you view all of life.

I'm living a life that's not my own

Q

What is eternal life?

A

My life becomes what God intended it to be when I believe in Jesus.

I magine that you are the best glassblower in the world. One day you begin to create a beautiful cut crystal globe. When it is finished, you plan to put an incredibly beautiful light inside, knowing that it will then be your most treasured possession.

Day after day you work on the crystal, creating facet after facet to catch and reflect the light you plan to put in it. In your mind's eye you can already see it shimmering like a living, radiant diamond. At last it is finished, and you tenderly place it on your workbench. Tomorrow you will install the light.

Then tragedy strikes. That night a thief comes and steals your crystal globe. But he doesn't really see much value in it and eventually throws it away. The beautiful globe finally ends up in the city dump, damaged and dirty, almost unrecognizable.

But one day you pass the dump and see the rim of the globe emerging through the rubbish. Eagerly you retrieve it and take it home. There you lovingly repair each chip and crack, and spend days cleaning it up. Soon it's a beautiful crystal globe again. But do you, the glassblower, have what you originally planned?

◆ TAKE A LOOK
John 1:4; 3:15-16, 35-36; 6:40; 10:10, 28

Of course the answer is no. Not until the light is inside will the globe truly become the glass-blower's masterpiece, showcasing his skill and casting light like living jewels.

In a similar way God created human beings to be His "crystal globes," containers that would hold His kind of life—eternal life. But before Adam received God's eternal life (which he would have done if he had eaten of the Tree of Life), God's enemy stole and damaged the container. At a terrible cost to Himself, God rescues man, cleans him up, and—for those who believe in His Son—God puts His own eternal life inside . . . as you'll learn when you read John 1:4; 3:15-16, 35-36; 6:40; 10:10, 28.

▲ TAKE A STEP

"Whoever believes in the Son has eternal life" (John 3:36).

When you believe in Jesus Christ as Savior, God puts His eternal life in you. Close your family time by thinking about what it means to walk around with God's life inside you. Do other people see the difference? If not, what needs to change in order for you to "let your light shine"?

*T*he master glassblower finally completed the last delicate repair on his crystal globe. Lovingly he took a bit of wax from his special supply and fashioned a candle. He knew that once he lit this unique candle, it would burn forever in the crystal globe.

Soon the great day arrived. Moving the globe to a prominent place in his shop, he anchored the candle inside and lit the wick. Instantly the flame was magnified, reflecting through the diamond facets of the crystal and breaking into a million shimmering dots of color. No light like this had ever been seen on earth.

Soon the glassblower's fame spread everywhere. Daily people asked how they could have a "Living Light" (which was what it came to be called). Sometimes other glassblowers tried to duplicate this wonder, but none had the talent, the skill, or the formula for the wax. The master glassblower remained the only source for the Living Light, but he gladly gave one to anyone who asked.

As the years passed, more and more people owned Living Lights. As they were placed in homes, businesses, and schools, the land grew more lovely, for the light had a powerful effect. It exposed dark corners of evil that were rapidly cleansed. It calmed children's fears. It melted hard hearts and created a warm climate in which people developed loving and caring relationships with one another as they never had before. And strangely enough old-timers began to remark wisely, "You know, a lot of people are beginning to resemble the master glassblower. You remember him, don't you—the one who gave us our Living Light years ago? Seems like the whole place is filled with his light. It's almost like he planned it that way."

◆ TAKE A LOOK / 2 Corinthians 4:6-18; 3:18

Like the parables Jesus told, the made-up story of the master glassblower shows a familiar truth from a fresh angle—and helps answer our question for today.

"What is the purpose of life?"—Remember the story of the glassmaker as you read 2 Corinthians 4:6-18 and 3:18.

▲ TAKE A STEP

God's purpose for human beings is not simply to save us from sin. His plan is to fill us with His kind of life—eternal life—so He will be glorified as His life shines through us. How does glory come to God through your life today? Choose a verse from 2 Corinthians 4:6-18 that you think best describes your reason for living.

"In Him was life, and that life was the light of men"

Q

What is the purpose of life?

A

My life fulfills its purpose when God is glorified as His life shines through me.

OBEDIENCE

Don't move! And don't say anything! I'll be right back." At her father's *urgent whisper, Lisa froze, already stretched out to climb to the next fork of the tree. She could not see her father; she did not know what was wrong. But she obeyed.*

For three long minutes she held her position. Then she heard her father whisper: "I've got the gun, Lisa. When I shoot, get down fast."

The noise of the shot nearly deafened her. But the large poisonous snake—a copperhead that was lying coiled in the fork of the tree—was dead. As the crying child reached the ground and was gathered into her father's arms, she heard him say again and again, "Oh, baby, I'm so thankful you obeyed!" Instant obedience had saved Lisa's life!

◆ THINKING ABOUT OBEDIENCE

Maybe you have never been in such a life-or-death situation. But from infancy you have been learning the importance of obeying those in authority over you.

Obedience is not just a good idea; it is a clear command from God. Everyone must obey someone. And everyone at times disobeys someone! There are penalties for disobedience. And when the Bible speaks of obedience, it is not simply talking about an outward action. True obedience involves an inward attitude.

" . . . Then I said, 'All right, Mom. I'll get up, but I won't get dressed for school.' "

● KEY VERSE ON OBEDIENCE

This is love for God: to obey his commands. And his commands are not burdensome (1 John 5:3).

▲ LOOKING AHEAD

Obedience is **gladly doing what pleases the one in authority over us.**

Read about Jonah's disobedience in Jonah 1. Think about the way you usually obey: quickly or slowly . . . gladly or grudgingly. If you had been up in the tree instead of Lisa, would the snake have bitten you? If you had been Jonah, would you have been dinner for a fish?

*A*nd so," the youth leader concluded, "God still expects you to honor and obey your parents, whether you're six or sixteen."

"You just don't know my mom," Katie blurted out. "She's impossible. She leaves me a list of chores to do every day when I come home from school. If I did it all, I'd just be a slave."

"Yeah," Mike chimed in. "My dad's just as strict. I never get to go anywhere with my friends because I have to help him around the house. And he's always yelling and cussing if I mess up. I don't think I should have to obey someone like that."

◆ TAKE A LOOK / Luke 2:41-52

It's easy to say with Katie and Mike, "Lord, I want to obey You." It's tougher when you realize that obeying God means obeying the authorities He has put over you. Because the fact is:

Everyone must submit himself to the governing authorities, for there is no authority except that which God has established (Romans 13:1).

When it comes to obedience, Jesus is our example. In fact, the only story in the Bible about Jesus' growing-up years is a story about His obedience to His earthly parents.

When Jesus was 12 years old, He stayed behind when Mary and Joseph left Jerusalem. Thinking Jesus was in the caravan, they headed home to Nazareth—65 miles away! But after a day's travel, Jesus was nowhere to be found.

Anxiously Mary and Joseph returned to Jerusalem to look for Jesus. Read Luke 2:41-52 to discover where they found Him.

▲ TAKE A STEP

After three days of frantic searching, Jesus' parents found Him in the temple (verse 46)—not just listening to the teachers, but teaching the teachers! Mary and Joseph were amazed. Clearly, they had much to learn about their special Son!

Jesus could have said, "You don't understand. I know what I'm doing." Instead, He went back to Nazareth. God had put Him under their authority, and in obedience to God, "He . . . was obedient to them" (verse 51).

Obedience is one of God's ways of guiding and protecting you. Think about the hardest thing you have to do to be obedient to those over you. Would your advice to Katie and Mike be the same advice you are willing to follow?

Me obey them? You've got to be kidding!

Q

Whom should I obey?

A

Obedience is my proper response to God and those He places over me.

If all else fails, follow the instructions!

Greg, Tom, and Eddie had a difficult time concentrating in class that morning. Their spacesuit project had won first prize in the regional science fair, and that afternoon they would be traveling to the state competition.

"I can't wait to get there!" Greg exclaimed. "I know we're gonna win. Mr. McFarlane says he's never seen a better project—and he's been a judge before."

"Yeah," Eddie replied. "I wish the bus would hurry up." At that moment, the school principal summoned Greg into the hall. He had a worried look on his face.

"Greg, there's a problem. I can't find your permission slip anywhere, and I can't let you go until I find it. Do you remember which day you brought it into my office?"

With a sinking feeling, Greg remembered the permission slip. It was still on his desk at home—stapled to the instruction sheet. Worse yet, Dad was away on a business trip, and Mom was gone for the day. If only he had followed instructions . . .

Q

How should I obey?

A

Obedience that is complete and cheerful brings God's blessing in my life.

◆ TAKE A LOOK / Genesis 6:9-22; 7:23-24

Greg missed the trip of a lifetime because he failed to follow the directions he had been given.

When Noah was almost 600 years old, he too was given a set of instructions—a blueprint for building an ark. Though Noah probably had never seen a boat that size, he obediently followed God's plan. He knew that when God spoke, he'd better listen. With the psalmist he could say:
You have laid down precepts that are to be fully obeyed (Psalm 119:4).

Noah didn't try to change God's plan ("Lord, don't You think we need more windows?") or find a shortcut ("Lord, don't You think one coat of tar will be enough?") or complain about the cargo the ark would carry ("Lord, do You know how smelly elephants are?"). As you'll discover by reading Genesis 6:9-22 and 7:23-24, Noah fully obeyed.

▲ TAKE A STEP

Would Noah have been safe in an ark only 75 percent waterproof? No, but he was fully protected because he "did everything just as God commanded him."

Close your time together with family members telling about a time when obedience kept them safe. Or, if someone learned more from a time when disobedience brought trouble, he or she might share that as well. You can learn a lot from another person's leaky boat!

*T*he five boys had grown up together in the same neighborhood, their friendships molded by 12 years of togetherness—school, camp, sports, Sunday school.

They had gone through dozens of tricycles, Big Wheels, and bicycles together. Time and again their moms had warned them, "Don't ride down the driveways and into the street; cars cannot see you in time to stop."

But in an instant, their lives would change—forever.

From the top of Mike's steep driveway, Brad gathered speed to cross the street and zoom up his own driveway. He neither saw nor heard the car accelerate around the corner. With a sickening thud Brad flipped high into the air and came down hard on the asphalt. Minutes later he lay in the hospital, while anxious friends wondered if he would walk again.

◆ TAKE A LOOK / 1 Samuel 15:1-23

In Brad's case, careless disobedience changed his life. In King Saul's case, deliberate disobedience also brought tragedy—to a king and his kingdom.

Through the prophet Samuel, God gave Saul a direct command: "Attack the Amalekites and totally destroy everything that belongs to them" (1 Samuel 15:3).

In response, Saul raised an army and attacked the Amalekites. But King Saul's obedience only went halfway; he chose to obey only the part of God's command that suited him. The next morning Samuel confronted Saul with his disobedience and with the Lord's displeasure.

Though Saul insisted he had done what the prophet told him to do, the mooing of cattle and the bleating of sheep told a different tale. Read that story right now in 1 Samuel 15:1-23.

▲ TAKE A STEP

Both Brad and Saul were only partially obedient, and discovered—too late—that incomplete obedience is really disobedience in disguise. That's why you're never too young, or old, to learn that . . .

"To obey is better than sacrifice. . . . For rebellion is like the sin of divination, and arrogance like the evil of idolatry" (1 Samuel 15:22-23).

Hard consequences came from Saul's disobedient action (1 Samuel 15:28)—and also from Brad's! But it didn't have to be that way.

Stop and think how each story could have ended happily instead of tragically. It's not hard to see why obedience is best!

That doesn't sound like obedience to me!

Q

What happens if I don't obey?

A

Obedience is disobedience if it's incomplete.

What do you do when chores become a chore?

Q
What if I don't want to obey?

A
Obedience is doing the right thing with the right attitude.

PARENT
Discuss with your child how chores, responsibilities, and rewards are assigned in your home. Ask what the child would do differently if he were assigning chores. Carefully listen to his answer.

"Tony, don't forget tomorrow is trash day," his mother called.

Slamming his books down, Tony stomped to where the trash cans were kept. "Can't somebody else do this just once?" he grumbled. "I do all the dirty work around here!"

Just then, Tony's neighbor Jeff walked by, cheerfully dragging the garbage cans to the curb. "Tony, you gripe all the time. Somebody's gotta do it, or the whole place would stink! Besides, you need the exercise."

"Very funny, Jeff. I just wish my folks would make my sister do this once in a while. That's fair, isn't it?"

"Well, do you ever fold clothes or help with dinner?"

"No, but that's different . . . sort of . . . "

◆ TAKE A LOOK / Philippians 2:12-16

The contrast between Jeff's willingness and Tony's grumbling shows the importance of your attitude in the matter of obedience. What if you really don't want to obey? What if you grumble and complain to let others know just how you feel?

The Bible says all such grumbling is a form of rebellion—and rebellion, as we learned yesterday, can be sin.

Do everything without complaining or arguing, so that you may become blameless and pure (Philippians 2:14).

The Bible is full of stories about people who were asked by God to do something they didn't want to do: Abraham didn't want to sacrifice his son Isaac; Moses didn't want to talk to Pharaoh; Jonah didn't want to preach in Nineveh. But they obeyed. The apostle Paul wrote about obedience in Philippians 2:12-16. As you read, look for the verse that explains why your attitude is an important part of obedience.

▲ TAKE A STEP

Obedience is "gladly doing what pleases the one in authority over you." So, even if you don't feel like it

. . . obey anyway, for God is working in you to do His will (v. 13).

. . . don't argue, for God wants you to be blameless (vv. 14-15).

. . . do what God has told you in His Word, for that is an example in your dark and crooked world (v. 15).

Is your normal response gladness or grumbling when you face an unpleasant chore or a difficult assignment? Starting today be glad to obey!

COMPASSION

*F*irst the cameras showed a little boy. His swollen stomach, broomstick-thin legs, and staring eyes indicated how close he was to starvation. The next pictures were of workers at an aid station forcing drops of liquid between a little girl's lips. But help had come too late. She died in her mother's arms.

Finally the cameras panned to the desolate surroundings. Thousands of people stood or squatted in hopelessness under the desert sun. There were no trees, no grass, no animals, no water—only the few tents that served as a hospital.

As Joyce watched the newscast of the famine, tears began to flow. "Dear God, please show me how I can help," she prayed.

The next week Joyce used her savings to pay for handbills explaining how aluminum cans could be turned into money. She gave one to each of the 472 children and teachers in her school. In eight months, Joyce and her classmates contributed $3,484 to famine relief.

◆ THINKING ABOUT COMPASSION

By starting a drive to collect cans, Joyce turned her feelings of pity and sorrow into caring concern and action.

And that's what compassion is. Many people feel pity and concern when they see the needs of others, but a compassionate person channels those feelings into action. Compassion is **caring enough to become involved in meeting someone's needs.**

Jesus was often moved by compassion. We can follow His example.

● KEY VERSE ON COMPASSION

Be sympathetic,
love as brothers,
be compassionate
and humble
(1 Peter 3:8).

▲ LOOKING AHEAD

As you read Mark 6:34-35 and 8:1-3, identify the needs to which Jesus was sensitive. How did He respond to them?

Pray right now that you will see and respond to the needs of those around you this week.

"He didn't take Visa or MasterCard. He did it for free!"

God's compassion means our salvation

Q

How does God show compassion to us?

A

Compassion was shown when Jesus paid for sin by His death on the cross.

*T*he pond was warm and shimmering in the September sun. The mother mallard had just finished her swim and had retreated to the meadow with her four ducklings.

It was then that Bowser, the hound dog, decided to have a bit of fun. With a howl he began the chase. As fast as she could, the mallard led her brood back toward the pond. There the ducklings would be safe. But Bowser was faster. Though it was only a few more feet to the pond, the mother mallard knew she wouldn't make it.

The mother duck could easily have flown to safety. But her ducklings were too young to fly. They were helpless. Quickly she spread her wings, tucked the ducklings close to her body, and turned to face the dog. In a few seconds the dog trotted away, leaving the dead mother duck. But safe under her wings were the four ducklings she had given her life to save.

◆ **TAKE A LOOK**
Psalm 103:8-17; Romans 5:6-8

The mallard mother could have saved herself and left her ducklings to the dog. Instead she sacrificed herself for them. In a way, human beings are as helpless as those little ducklings. We have no ability to save ourselves from the consequences of sin. But God had compassion on us. He saw our need and did something about it. As you read Psalm 103:8-17, list several ways God shows His compassion. Then read Romans 5:6-8. What action described there should go at the top of your list?

▲ **TAKE A STEP**

[He] has removed . . . our transgressions from us (Psalm 103:12).
While we were still sinners, Christ died for us (Romans 5:8).

Because people cannot pay the price for their own sins or avoid the consequences, the death of Jesus is God's most wonderful expression of compassion and love. Just as the mother mallard gave her life for her ducklings, Jesus gave His life for us. And just as the ducklings found safety under her wings, our safety from sin is in the cross of Jesus and what He accomplished there.

If one duckling had refused the safety of its mother's body, it too would have died. There was no other way. And in the matter of sin, Jesus is the only way to safety. But people must choose to accept the gift of salvation He offers.

*J*ohn and his tour group were in a market section of old Cairo, Egypt. Lining the street were dozens of stalls filled with unusual merchandise—everything from expensive gold jewelry to relics from the pyramids (or so the vendors claimed). John was glad he had enough money to buy nice souvenirs for his family and friends—and a gold bracelet for himself.

Just then a man grabbed his arm. "Dol-lar?" the man asked in heavily accented English. He was dressed in a ragged tunic and wore a dirty turban like most of the beggars John had seen in Egypt.

John jerked his arm away and brushed off the sleeve where the man had touched him. "Get away; I don't have anything for you!"

Just then John's friend Marcus handed the man some coins. The beggar nodded and turned away.

"What'd you do that for? Now we'll have every beggar on this side of Cairo coming after us," John accused.

"Maybe, maybe not," Marcus responded. "Anyway, I just had to help somehow."

◆ TAKE A LOOK / 1 John 3:16-24

Both young men were Christians, but only Marcus showed compassion to the beggar. John was more interested in his own wants than in the needs of others.

Jesus was always moved by the needy people around Him. He was not offended by ragged clothes. He did not shun the diseased. He understood that people sometimes can't help being poor. His heart was burdened for the sorrowful.

Following Jesus includes showing compassion as He did. Read 1 John 3:16-24 to see one way you can turn compassionate feelings into action. (By the way, what word in verse 17 means the same as compassion?)

▲ TAKE A STEP

The apostle John is very specific. As some might say, this is "where the rubber meets the road":

If anyone has material possessions and sees his brother in need but has no pity on him, how can the love of God be in him? (1 John 3:17).

Look closely at the people around you. Is there a dad who's out of a job? An older person who needs money for medicine? A child who needs shoes?

Pray that God will open your eyes and fill your heart with compassion. Discuss specific ways your family can help people in need.

How can I share and show I'm there?

Q

Why should I be compassionate?

A

God wants me to show compassion by using my possessions and money to help people who have needs.

Including the good, the bad, and the unlovely

For three years, Tom Perone hadn't stepped inside a church—not since the rumor that he was leaving his wife to marry his secretary had spread like wildfire through the church. Although that had almost happened, fortunately it did not. Tom, in fact, did stay with his family and he stopped seeing the secretary.

And finally Tom repented. He asked God to forgive him for the sin of adultery. He realized how steadfast his wife's love had been, and he asked for her forgiveness too. But the church members were different. As Tom sat in the pew for the first time in two years, he could faintly hear the whispering. "That's the trouble with living in a small town," he thought. "Everybody minds everybody else's business." But Tom was hurt too. He felt abandoned. He wondered if he would ever again feel a part of his church.

Just then, he felt a hand on his shoulder. It was Al Smith, his former Sunday school teacher. "Move over," Al whispered. "There's room for both of us on this pew."

Q

To whom should I show compassion?

A

Compassion in the form of forgiveness should be shown to anyone who repents of sin.

PARENT
Do you set an example by helping those in need? Your child will not learn compassion unless he or she sees it in action.

◆ **TAKE A LOOK / John 8:2-11; 13:37-38; Luke 22:61-62**

Showing compassion involves meeting physical and material needs. But what does a compassionate person do when feelings—not physical needs—are involved? How do we treat those who may have let us down or have hurt us badly? What about people who are grumpy or mean?

Those are hard questions, but looking at Jesus' life reveals the answers, as you'll see when you read John 8:2-11; 13:37-38; Luke 22:61-62; and John 21:17-19.

▲ **TAKE A STEP**

Jesus had compassion for the woman caught in adultery. He didn't require her to make up for her sin. He didn't condemn her. He simply offered forgiveness and acceptance.

But what happens when a Christian sins? Again, Jesus provides an answer. Peter was very sorry when he realized how he had hurt Jesus by his denial. Peter repented, and Jesus forgave and accepted him as He had before.

How do you treat a fellow believer who has sinned and repented? God's Word is very clear: *You ought to forgive and comfort him . . . [and] reaffirm your love for him (2 Corinthians 2:7-8).*

How would you treat Mr. Perone if you were a member of his church? Do you know someone who needs compassion in the form of forgiveness and acceptance?

A man visiting a mission station in a tropical country was startled to find the missionary going barefoot. As the two men entered the missionary's hut, the visitor commented, "I don't understand why you're not wearing shoes. Before I came here, my doctor cautioned me about two things: (1) Always boil my drinking water; and (2) Always wear shoes. Isn't there danger of getting hookworm from this soil?"

"Of course there is!" the missionary explained. "But years ago the traders who came here wore heavy boots. The native people hated the traders because they mistreated them and never hesitated to kick them with those boots. People with bare feet cannot kick others, and worms can be treated later. So I wear no shoes."*

◆ **TAKE A LOOK**
Matthew 9:35-36; 14:13-14; 15:32, 20:29-34
The missionary felt compassion for the islanders. He knew that above all else they needed to know Jesus as Savior. But his compassion also made him sensitive to their feelings. So he took a risk: To show that he cared and that he wasn't like the harsh traders, he went without shoes.

Eventually many island people accepted Jesus as their Savior. The missionary's concern for their feelings opened their hearts to the message of God's love.

Read the following verses to discover what kinds of needs Jesus was sensitive to as He moved among the crowds. Jot down those needs on the lines at the right.

Jesus was sensitive to these kinds of people:
Matthew 9:35-36   _____
Matthew 14:13-14   _____
Matthew 15:32   _____
Matthew 20:29-34   _____
Mark 1:40-41   _____

▲ **TAKE A STEP**
Sensitivity to others' hurts is the first step in showing compassion. Doing what you can about those needs makes compassion real. As you go through this day, concentrate on specific ways of being

. . . *kind and compassionate to one another* (Ephesians 4:32).

Open your eyes to see the needs of those around you!

*This story is adapted from the November 1984 issue of DECISION magazine. Copyright 1984 by the Billy Graham Evangelistic Association. Used by permission.

It's true— little things mean a lot!

What actions show that I am compassionate?

A

Compassion is sensing the hurts of others and then doing something about them.

PARENT
The parable of the Good Samaritan (Luke 10:30-37) is a good illustration of compassion. Read it together and discuss how the Samaritan put his compassion into practice.

SELF-ESTEEM

*H*ow was school today?" Greg's mother asked over dinner.
"The usual," Greg replied. He sounded very bored.

"Greg, your art teacher called me today."

"I didn't do anything, Mom. Mrs. Kirby always picks on me."

"She didn't accuse you of anything, Greg. She was concerned, that's all. She says you have some real talent in art—if you'd concentrate on your work instead of trying to be the class clown."

"Mom, the other guys think art is for wimps. They're just in the class for an easy A. If I told them I really liked that stuff—"

"Greg, why is it so important what your friends think? They could be wrong, you know."

"Yeah, I know. But if they don't like me, who will?"

◆ THINKING ABOUT SELF-ESTEEM

Each of us builds a picture of ourselves from the way others respond to us. But sadly, those opinions are often based on false ideas of what's important: looks, talent, intelligence. If someone doesn't measure up to the standards of others, he or she is made to feel unacceptable.

You won't find the term *self-esteem* in the Bible. But the concept is there—and so is the true standard for measuring self-esteem.

Self-esteem means that **you see yourself as valuable to God and to others.** You know that this verse is true:

"Okay, but it'll probably be wrong."

● KEY VERSE ON SELF-ESTEEM
We are God's workmanship, created in Christ Jesus to do good works (Ephesians 2:10).

▲ LOOKING AHEAD
When you read Psalm 139:13-16, you'll find that you are an important person because God made you. There is nobody else like you!

Have each family member complete this sentence five different ways: "I am . . ." You'll quickly see what an interesting person you are!

*F*or three years Stephen had played on the athletic field as captain of the football team. Many times his heart had raced to the cheering of fans as he crossed the goal line for a touchdown. But tonight there were no special cheers for Stephen. He was just one of 223 seniors graduating in the outdoor ceremony.

Edward's memories of the same field were far different. Painfully he recalled the shame he had often felt in P.E. classes as he slowly—and self-consciously—ran laps around the track, while faster classmates stopped to jeer: "Hey, it's the Pillsbury Doughboy!" Embarrassment, not excitement, was all Edward felt. That is, until he heard his name called and went forward to accept the award as the senior with the highest grade-point average.

"Thank you, Lord," Edward prayed silently, "for loving me and helping me to be the best student I could possibly be."

◆ TAKE A LOOK / 1 Samuel 17:28-37

Many of us can identify with Edward. When compared with friends, we just don't seem to measure up. Too many pimples, too tall, too short, too slow, too shy.

In the Old Testament, David, the caboose in a family of eight brothers, experienced the same feelings. Yes, the same David who would later kill a giant and become a king was often overlooked when there was important work to be done! But there came a time when David and big brother Eliab had an important conversation that showed how David had developed a healthy sense of self-worth. Read the account in 1 Samuel 17:28-37. As you do, can you discover why David felt so confident in his ability to fight the giant Goliath?

▲ TAKE A STEP

Obviously, David didn't get much encouragement from his brothers! But he had learned to measure his value by God's standard. Alone with his sheep, his slingshot, and his harp, David didn't feel sorry for himself. As he developed his mind, his musical talent, and his aim, David's self-confidence came from a close walk with his God.

You created my inmost being. . . . I praise you because I am fearfully and wonderfully made (Psalm 139:13-14).

With all his weaknesses and abilities, David was able to say, "I'm important to God because He made me." Close your family time today by turning Psalm 139:14 into your prayer of thanks!

I wonder how wonderful I really am . . .

Q

What is true self-esteem?

A

Self-esteem comes from knowing I am God's creation.

Be whatever you are (by the way, what are you?)

Q

Why do I need self-esteem?

A

Self-esteem helps me accept myself and love others.

PARENT
Take this time to share how you've come to accept something about yourself that bothered you. Be honest with your child and let him know that you sometimes hurt too.

*I*n one day, 11-year-old Karen heard all of the following comments:

Mother: *"If I've told you once, I've told you a hundred times—turn off the water in the sink! Can't you remember anything?"*

Older Sister: *"Will you get your junk out of my room? You're so sloppy."*

Teacher: *"You've got to concentrate, Karen. One more poor grade and you'll fail this class."*

Father: *"I'm afraid I can't make it to your recital this Saturday. I've got a golf game with my boss."*

It's no wonder Karen said to herself by day's end, *"I can't do anything right. I might as well give up."*

◆ TAKE A LOOK / Genesis 29:31-35

If others always seem "down" on us, it won't be long before we feel down on ourselves.

In the first book of the Bible you'll meet Leah, who had a beautiful younger sister named Rachel. Living with her homecoming-queen sister had made Leah feel that when it came to looks she just couldn't measure up.

Leah's own father doubted her. He tricked a man named Jacob into marrying Leah, even though Jacob loved her sister Rachel!

Leah knew she was unloved. But God knew it too, and did something about it. As you read Genesis 29:31-35, notice what finally brought happiness into Leah's life.

▲ TAKE A STEP

Even after the birth of three sons, Leah still felt unloved and unwanted. Why? Because she was still depending on the acceptance of others before she could accept herself. But Leah's story doesn't end there. After the birth of her fourth son, she exclaimed:

"This time I will praise the LORD" (Genesis 29:35).

Leah deliberately chose to accept God's unconditional love.

It's the same choice you can make—to recognize that God loves you just the way you are. You don't ever have to wonder again if you are important to someone, because you are eternally important to God.

By the way, did you notice the name of Leah's fourth son (verse 35)? Turn to Luke 3:33—the family tree of Jesus Christ—and see if you can find the name again! Aren't you glad God doesn't give up on "unlovely" people?

*J*ulie was crying as she ran to her room. "What's the matter?" her mother asked soothingly. "I thought you went over to Debbie's house to play." "I did, but Mom, Debbie's no fun anymore. Every game we played, Debbie won. And when I finally got ahead in one game, she quit playing. It was like she had to win every game. Why was she acting like that?"

Julie's mother gently stroked her daughter's hair. "Julie, Debbie's mommy and daddy have been separated for several weeks. I know that's hard for you to understand. But maybe Debbie just needs more attention. She wants to win all those games so she can feel important. She needs your friendship more than ever. Let's bake a batch of cookies to take to her house. Maybe that will show how much you still like her."

◆ TAKE A LOOK / John 4:4-26, 39-42

There are many ways you can try to build your self-esteem, but like Debbie's attempts to win at all costs, they can often produce more harm than good.

One day as Jesus sat alone by a well, a Samaritan woman came to draw water. Like Debbie, the woman had tried to fill her life with substitutes for real love and affection. She had been married to not one or two, but five husbands. And none of them had satisfied her need to feel loved and accepted.

As Jesus spoke to the woman about the need in her life, He told her He could provide "living water" that would satisfy her thirst like no water on earth. As you read John 4:4-26, 39-42, can you discover what that living water is?

▲ TAKE A STEP

People look everywhere for love and acceptance. They work to get recognition; they wear the nicest clothes; they compete with others to feel they are "better."

But as Jesus told the Samaritan woman, only His love lasts, for He is the only person whose love is a deep well that won't run dry. Close your time together by having one family member read aloud this timely verse on God's timeless love:

"For I am convinced that [nothing] will be able to separate us from the love of God that is in Christ Jesus our Lord" (Romans 8:38-39).

Now, personalize that verse by listing several things about yourself that you don't like—or feel others don't accept. Can those flaws separate you from God's love?

If I were you, I'd stay away from me!

Q

How can I build self-esteem?

A

Self-esteem is built by accepting God's unconditional love.

A pat on the back helps keep you on track!

Q

How can I help others develop self-esteem?

A

Self-esteem in others grows through encouragement.

PARENT
Think of some ways that your child builds your self-esteem. Then let him share ways that you build up his self-esteem. Have a time of mutual appreciation and encouragement!

*T*he graduation ceremony was over, and the students were laughing and sharing special memories.

"Hey, Einstein," Tony called to Edward, "it's terrific about your scholarship. Remember me when you're famous!"

"Yeah," Stephen chimed in, "it went to the right guy."

Edward felt good all over. It would be hard saying goodbye, but these friendships would last.

"Tony, do you remember that freshman P.E. class in track and field? You guys always beat me by miles, and I was out there all alone just trudging along. But the day the coach told me I had to do four extra laps, you slowed down and stayed with me the whole way. I never told you before, but that meant a lot. Thanks for being my friend."

◆ TAKE A LOOK / Acts 15:36-41

"Even if it takes you 20 minutes to run a mile, I'll stick with you. I accept you the way you are."

By sticking with his friend, Tony encouraged his self-conscious, overweight friend to keep trying. In Acts 15 we find another young man who needed encouragement. John Mark had accompanied Barnabas and Paul on a missionary journey but later left the team and returned home.

While they were preparing for a second journey, Paul didn't want to take John Mark. Barnabas, whose very name means "son of encouragement," wanted to give John Mark another chance. He was practicing this command:

Encourage one another and build each other up (1 Thessalonians 5:11).

Read about "The Case of the Runaway Missionary" in Acts 15:36-41. Then turn to 2 Timothy 4:11 and Colossians 4:10 to discover how encouragement made a new man of John Mark.

▲ TAKE A STEP

Like Tony and Edward, Barnabas stuck with John Mark. Encouragement at the crucial point helped John Mark grow spiritually and emotionally, so much so that years later Paul said, "He is helpful to me in my ministry."

There are people around you who, like John Mark, need a friend. The loner in the lunchroom . . . the person always picked last for the team . . . the new student. As you think about school, church, or neighborhood, who comes to mind as a person needing encouragement? What can you do to "encourage and build up" that person today?

PSALMS

*S*tanding backstage, butterflies in their stomachs, the cast of Newman
High waited for their cue.

This number would be spectacular. Long rehearsals would pay off in
the excitement of this opening song! The curtain parted . . . the director
motioned for the music to begin . . . the beautifully costumed chorus
marched onto the stage and started singing. But then members of the
audience began glancing around with puzzled expressions. Everyone was
confused as they heard unfamiliar words sung to a familiar tune!

"Seventy-six **sopars** led the big parade,
 With a hundred and ten **tsiltsils** close behind,
They were followed by rows and rows of the finest **kinnors**,
 The **tōps** of every famous band . . . "

◆ THINKING ABOUT PSALMS

Of course, they sang nothing of the kind. But if you had been
there as King David led the ark of God into Jerusalem (2 Samuel 16),
you would have been surrounded by music made by the sopar, tsilt-
sil, nebel, kinnor, and tōp—known today as the trumpet, cymbals,
harp, lyre, and tambourine. And they would have been playing
music from the book of Psalms—**majestic choruses of praise to God.**

● KEY VERSE ON PSALMS

Let everything that has breath praise the LORD. *Praise the* LORD
(Psalm 150:6).

▲ LOOKING AHEAD

This week we'll look at
four of the 150 songs in the
book of Psalms.

Read today's key verse
again. Is everyone around
you still breathing?

Good! That means the
Psalms are meant for you.
Begin your enjoyment by
reading Psalm 150. Then
unpack any musical instrument you can play and
close your family time playing and singing a hymn of
praise!

*"God called the light daytime, and the
darkness He called primetime."*

Ready, set, grow where you are planted

High in the Sequoia National Park of northern California stands a massive tree—a giant sequoia. Towering nearly 300 feet above the landscape (that's as high as a 30-story building), the tree is nicknamed "General Sherman" and contains enough timber to build forty 5-room houses.

Well watered and well rooted, this magnificent tree has grown in the same place for several thousand years. But perhaps the greatest miracle of all is the tiny seed from which it grew—weighing only 1/6000 of an ounce!

◆ TAKE A LOOK / Psalm 1

Have you ever seen a giant sequoia? If not, think instead of your favorite tree—maybe one in your yard, in a park, or along a road you travel often. Perhaps you like that tree because it is so tall and strong. Or its gnarled and twisted trunk makes it a favorite tree to climb. Or its spreading branches provide shade for you and a home for the birds.

Have you ever noticed that people are like trees? They draw their strength from the "soil" in which they are rooted. As you read the six short verses of Psalm 1, look for what makes the difference between a life that is as stable as a sequoia . . . or as windblown as chaff (the dusty husk from a grain of wheat).

Q

What is the best foundation on which to build my life?

▲ TAKE A STEP

As you read, did you discover the secret of the well rooted life, the one that can't be blown away by the storms of life? The answer lies in verse 2.

His delight is in the law of the LORD, and on his law he meditates day and night (Psalm 1:2).

Styles will change, fads will come and go, seasons will ebb and flow. But the law of the Lord never changes. And that unchanging law provides the best soil for your family to grow in. Regardless of whether you are rich or poor; black or white; educated or uneducated; living in a crowded city or a country farm, you can grow more like Jesus Christ each day as you plant your life in the rich soil of God's Word.

If time permits, visit your local nursery or garden center and buy a packet of seeds or a bulb to plant sometime this week. You might even enjoy choosing a shrub or small tree for your yard. Then every time you see your plants growing, you'll be reminded that God wants you to grow each day in your love and knowledge of Him.

A

The Psalms teach that God's Word is a sure foundation for my life.

*A*t age 10, Elliott is very much at home in his city—2 1/2 million people densely packed into buildings that seem to reach the sky. At night he admires the twinkling beauty of the brightly lit buildings. But he seldom sees the stars and rarely thinks about God.

Halfway around the world, another boy named Ismah has never seen a city. His village consists of fewer than 100 people, living in huts clustered around fields of manioc (sweet potatoes). But as he looks up into the night sky from the African countryside, he is awed by the millions of stars shining out of the blackness of the night. And he realizes Someone must have made those stars—and Someone must have made him.

◆ **TAKE A LOOK / Psalm 19**

Black holes . . . quasars . . . white dwarfs—through the use of more and more powerful telescopes, we are constantly expanding our knowledge of the universe.

We know that our galaxy, the Milky Way, is just one of millions of such galaxies, and that the next nearest galaxy, Andromeda, is over 700,000 light years away (that means traveling at the speed of light—186,000 miles per second—it would still take 700,000 years to get to Andromeda!).

So it is not surprising that the psalmist David, looking at the night sky over the hills of Judea, wrote these words:

The heavens declare the glory of God; the skies proclaim the work of his hands (Psalm 19:1).

The stars are there for a purpose. Their grandeur, beauty, and orderliness all speak of a powerful Creator—the same God who created you and gave you His Word, the Bible, so that you might learn more about Him.

As you read Psalm 19, notice how it is divided into three parts: the world of God (verses 1-6), the Word of God (verses 7-11), and a prayer to God (verses 12-14).

▲ **TAKE A STEP**

Tonight, weather permitting, take an outdoor walk and spend a few minutes doing what the psalmist loved to do—look at the stars. See if you can count them!

Look for the Big Dipper and the North Star, or other stars and constellations visible from where you live. Most important, let those stars remind you again of your Creator God who put the universe in place—and deserves the worship and praise of His creation!

Twinkle, twinkle, little star . . .

Q

Where are God's glory and power visible?

A

The Psalms teach me to look at God's handiwork and praise Him.

PARENT
Ask your child, "If you were a tree, what kind would you be, and why?" Listen carefully to the answer!

And everywhere that Mary went, her lamb wouldn't!

Q

How does God care for me?

A

The Psalms teach that God cares for me as a shepherd cares for his sheep.

Sheep are curious creatures. Because of their nervous nature it is almost impossible for them to lie down and rest unless four things are true:
1. They are free of all fear.
2. They are at peace with the other sheep.
3. They are free from pests and insects.
4. They are well supplied with food.

Sheep that are nervous, upset, or hungry refuse to lie down and rest. A careful shepherd sees that these needs are met so that his flock stays quiet and content.

◆ TAKE A LOOK / Psalm 23

It is no accident that the Bible compares people to sheep, because in many ways (some of which are not very flattering) people are just like sheep! The author of Psalm 23 is well qualified to speak of the Lord as his shepherd, for he is none other than the shepherd-turned-king from the pastures of Judea.

David knew from experience how difficult it is to look after sheep. As he provided tender, day-to-day care for his helpless sheep, David saw many similarities to the kind of care he received from his Shepherd Lord. And as David took his sheep through dark, stormy valleys, he was reminded of the guidance and protection the Lord supplied for him.

Do you know where to find the "Shepherd's Psalm"? Of course! It's Psalm 23. Turn there now, and as you read, see how many ways you can think of in which you are like a sheep and the Lord is like a shepherd to you.

▲ TAKE A STEP

The Lord has not changed. He still cares for His sheep, looking for those who are tired, anxious, and in danger.

"I am the good shepherd. The good shepherd lays down his life for the sheep" (John 10:11).

Make Psalm 23 your family's memory project today. Assign one or more verses to each family member. (If there are three people, each learns two verses; if four people, only two must learn a second verse.) Sound difficult? Try it!

The psalm will already be familiar to most, and with a few minutes of practice, you'll quickly know your part. If you find you need more practice, read your verse(s) several times during the next 24 hours. Decide on a time to recite the passage aloud together. Have fun!

Most of the time the milkman liked his job, especially the quiet of the city streets before the rush of morning traffic. But this morning the biting cold numbed his hands and feet as he shifted the crates of milk from his truck to the delivery dock of the grocery store.

As he stacked the final crate, he heard a strange noise coming from a nearby trash bin—a rustling sound like that of a rat or a cat rummaging through the garbage. But then the noise became very un-cat-like. It changed to a strange, thin cry, and the man decided to investigate.

Cautiously he poked a long stick into the litter and gently moved it aside. Imagine his surprise when he uncovered a tiny, shivering, newborn baby girl!

◆ TAKE A LOOK / Psalm 100

Within a few days the baby was adopted by loving parents. But as the little girl grew she wondered about her natural mother. She longed to know if she had brothers or sisters or other grandparents somewhere. She felt rootless because she didn't know where she "belonged."

Today many people are interested in studying their family tree and tracing their "roots." But there is something more important than discovering your human ancestry. Do you know what it is?

The writer of Psalm 100 asks and answers the questions, "Where did I come from in the first place? Who made me the way I am?" Take turns reading one verse at a time as you look for the answer!

▲ TAKE A STEP

Where did you come from? Are you a cosmic accident—the result of a big bang or eons of evolution?

Know that the LORD is God. It is he who made us (Psalm 100:3).

Two of the most important facts you can know are these:

1. God is really there, and
2. He is your Maker. You belong; you have roots!

Close your family time by putting one of the psalmist's commands to work: "Serve the Lord with gladness"—think of a kind deed you can do for someone in your neighborhood.

"Come before him with joyful songs"—sing a favorite hymn or chorus together.

"Give thanks to him and praise his name"— tell something you are especially grateful for today.

Q

What are the real facts about my "roots"?

A

The Psalms reveal that because God is my Maker, He cares for me.

PARENT
Surround your child with music of praise. He will like the melodies, and the words will reinforce important truths about God. Check the music section of your local Christian bookstore.

BIBLE LANDS

*T*his is the 'trip of a lifetime,' " Grandpa Mitchell declared—12 days in the Holy Land. And we want you and the children to go with us."

Wide-eyed, Jeffrey Mitchell listened to his parents and grandparents discuss visiting Israel next spring. "Why Israel?" he thought. If the choice were up to him, he'd pick Nepal any day! He could almost see himself tackling the foothills of the Himalayas . . .

But his daydreams ended as he vaguely heard the end of Grandpa's question: " . . . you'd like that, wouldn't you, Jeffrey?"

"Wha . . . uh . . . I guess so," he mumbled as his father glanced up sharply. To divert Dad's attention, Jeffrey continued: "Grandpa, why is it called the 'Holy Land'? Is one country more holy than all the others?"

◆ THINKING ABOUT THE HOLY LAND

Grandpa Mitchell must have been expecting the question: "It's not holy because the people there are better than other people, or even because the land is different. I think it's called the Holy Land because it's *set apart*—that's what the word *holy* means. It's the part of the earth that God set apart for Abraham and his descendants."

"We had a skit today. Bucky Sims was a Hittite and I was a Hittee."

● KEY VERSE ON BIBLE LANDS

The LORD *appeared to Abram and said, "To your offspring I will give this land" (Genesis 12:7).*

▲ LOOKING AHEAD

This week we want to look at **the place where the action of the Bible took place.**

Mesopotamia is often called the "Cradle of Civilization" because archaeologists have uncovered some of the world's oldest civilizations there. Can you identify the names of the two rivers of Mesopotamia mentioned in Genesis 2:8-14? Now find a map of the Holy Land in the back of your Bible or in a Bible atlas and locate those two rivers.

Ohh, Dad," Jeffrey moaned, "I know we're going to Israel, but why do we have to study Bible lands? I hate geography."

"I know you rank geography right up there with eating spinach," Mr. Mitchell chuckled. "But since we're going to Israel, Mom and I thought it would be a good idea for us to take a closer look at some of the places we'll be seeing. After all, geography can help us understand some of the events recorded in the Bible."

"How?" Jeffrey asked.

"Well, you remember the story of God's people battling for the land of Canaan, don't you? They had their hands full fighting the Philistines in the Jezreel Valley."

"Yeah? So what?" Jeff's interest was starting to spark.

"Well, the Jezreel Valley is flat and smooth. The Philistines could easily drive their chariots on the level ground," Mr. Mitchell explained. "But when the fight moved into the mountains, the Philistines couldn't maneuver their chariots, and the Israelites won. You see, geography does make a difference."

Jeff thought about that for a minute. "Dad, do you know any more neat stuff like that?"

◆ **TAKE A LOOK / Ezekiel 5:5**
You too may have wondered how studying the geography and history of Bible lands could possibly be important—or interesting. But you'll find one reason when you see what God says in Ezekiel 5:5 about the placement of Bible lands.

▲ **TAKE A STEP**
This is what the Sovereign LORD says: "This is Jerusalem, which I have set in the center of the nations" (Ezekiel 5:5).

Locate the Bible lands on a present-day world map or globe. First find the Mediterranean Sea; then locate the nation of Israel and the city of Jerusalem.

Can you find Lebanon, Syria, Jordan, Iraq, and Iran to the east and Egypt and Libya to the west? These are the lands where the world's oldest civilizations have been found—and where most of the action of the Bible takes place.

You'll find one clue as to why Israel is so important when you name the three continents that are linked by this tiny section of geography. Why do you think this area is sometimes referred to as a "bridge" between continents? What major event occurred there that makes it the spiritual center of the world as well?

The Holy Land is the center of the world!

Q

Why should I study Bible lands?

A

Bible lands help me understand past history and current events.

And the walls came tumblin' down!

Dad, I showed Ethan how the Israelites used military strategy to conquer Canaan," Jeff told his dad. "But he said the Bible is just a bunch of fairy tales some guys made up. What should I have told him?"

"Well, you could tell him about some of the exciting discoveries archaeologists have made," Mr. Mitchell replied. "Take the story, for instance, about the Battle of Jericho. The Bible says the walls of Jericho crumbled so that the Israelites could enter the city. For years unbelievers scoffed at the notion . . . that is until archaeologists unearthed Jericho. Guess what they found?"

A grin broke on Jeffrey's face. "I bet they found a heap of crumbled walls. Right?"

◆TAKE A LOOK / 2 Peter 1:19-21

Archaeology is the study of ancient peoples made by uncovering their cities, relics, and artifacts. Though some unbelieving scientists once scoffed at the biblical version of ancient history, archaeology has instead demonstrated that the historical accounts in the Bible are definitely reliable.

Take a look at what some critics said and what archaeologists later found.

Unbelieving critics said:
- "The Hittite people of the Old Testament never existed."
- "Moses didn't write the first books of the Bible because writing was unknown then."
- "The mention of a public census in Luke is fiction."

Archaeologists found:
- Hundreds of references to the Hittite civilization.
- Written characters on the "Black Stele" that date 300 years before Moses.
- Rome had a regular census every 14 years.

The apostle Peter explains why the Bible is accurate in 2 Peter 1:19-21. How would you put these verses in your own words?

▲ TAKE A STEP

Men spoke from God as they were [led] by the Holy Spirit (2 Peter 1:21).

The Bible is not a geography or history textbook. But it is trustworthy. Why? Because God is its Author. Let a volunteer go to the library and choose a recent book on archaeology in Bible lands. Then together make a list of archaeological discoveries that show the Bible's accuracy.

Q

How do we learn about Bible lands?

A

Bible lands can become more familiar as we study their geography, history, and archaeology.

PARENT
If you are able, invest in a good Bible atlas to make Bible places "come alive."

When I left for college, all you thought about was football. Now you've got your nose in a Bible atlas." Nicole was teasing her brother. "How'd you get from the practice field to being our resident geographer?"

"By way of the Sinai Peninsula," Jeff quipped. "They're both deserts." Then he was more serious. "I have learned a lot. But one thing still bothers me."

"What's that, Professor Mitchell?" Nicole asked.

"Well, when I checked on the map, I couldn't find some of the countries mentioned in the Bible."

"I know why," Nicole replied, "thanks to my ancient history course. Some of the names are the same, but a lot of them have changed. Historians can trace them through historical records to their Bible names. Like ancient Assyria is now part of Iraq. Persia is now Iran. But the most interesting one is Israel itself."

"Yeah, why's that?" Jeff could hardly believe his sister knew something useful.

"Down through history the Jewish people lost their land," Nicole explained. "But after World War II, the United Nations made Israel a nation again. Nothing like that had ever happened before. The nation of Israel really is a modern miracle."

◆ **TAKE A LOOK / Daniel 2:20-21; 5:1-7, 17-31**

Nicole was right. Over the centuries the nations mentioned in the Bible have changed names and boundaries. By New Testament times, Rome controlled most of the Bible lands. Eventually most of the Jewish people were deported to other countries, other empires conquered that area, and the name "Israel" disappeared from the world map. But in 1948, Israel became a nation again.

Since that time, the Bible lands have once again been in turmoil, and today that area (which we know as the Middle East) experiences almost constant tension and war. But just as in ancient times, nations rise and fall at God's will, as you'll see when you read Daniel 5:1-7, 17-31.

▲ **TAKE A STEP**

Daniel, a Jewish captive in Babylon, understood how God works in history:

He [God] sets up kings and deposes them (Daniel 2:21).

Based on the verses you read, why did God take the kingdom away from Belshazzar? Could God remove a modern nation today? Can you name a modern nation whose godless government has been removed? Why is that good?

The Hittites and the Hivites— where are they?

Q

Have the names of Bible lands changed?

A

Bible lands may have changed names, but they are still under God's control.

"Why do you stand looking into the sky?"

Q

What will happen to the Bible lands?

A

Bible lands are still part of God's plan for the world.

PARENT

With the aid of an encyclopedia, help your child compare maps of the Babylonian and Roman Empires with a modern map. You'll be surprised at the differences!

Dad," Jeffrey said one evening at dinner, "when Nicole was here, she said God isn't finished with the Bible lands. What did she mean?"

"Well, I'm not sure because I didn't hear the conversation," Mr. Mitchell replied.

"But what do you think?" Jeffrey asked eagerly. "Do the events in the Middle East have anything to do with Jesus coming back?"

Mr. Mitchell looked thoughtfully at Jeffrey. "You're old enough to realize that Christians have different views about the future," he said. "No one knows exactly what will happen in the Middle East. But I think the Bible makes one thing pretty clear: The Lord is going to return and plant His feet on the Mount of Olives near Jerusalem. When you consider that other ancient cultures have long since vanished, I think it's safe to say that Jerusalem is still 'center stage' in world history. God isn't finished yet. But beyond that we'll just have to wait and see."

◆ **TAKE A LOOK / Acts 1:9-11; Zechariah 14:1-9**

As Jeffrey prepared for the trip to the Holy Land, he began to read more of the Old Testament. It seemed to him that many of the prophecies about Jerusalem are still unfulfilled. He wondered if the territory occupied by ancient Bible lands still has a part to play in history.

As you read Acts 1:9-11 and Zechariah 14:1-9, see if Jeffrey's excitement rubs off on you too.

▲ **TAKE A STEP**

Six hundred years before the birth of Christ, the prophet Zechariah proclaimed that the Lord Himself would one day stand in Israel.

On that day his feet will stand on the Mount of Olives . . . and the Mount of Olives will be split in two (Zechariah 14:4).

Years later, the prophet John wrote that when Jesus returns "every eye will see him" (Revelation 1:7).

If Zechariah had predicted that Jesus would return to the Mayan civilization, we might have cause for concern. All that's left of the Mayan cities are uninhabited ruins in overgrown jungles. But in every way—geographically, politically, historically, and most of all spiritually—the lands of the Bible (and especially the city of Jerusalem) have remained at the center of world events.

Based on what you've learned this week, discuss why you think God is or isn't finished with Bible lands.

COMMUNICATION·

S moke signals rise from cliffs on either side of a canyon. Drums sound through dense jungle to warn of danger. Satellites send radio signals around the world and far into space. Telephones, telegraphs, televisions— there is hardly a place you can turn without finding the tools of communication.

But sometimes the greatest challenge is not spanning a continent, but simply spanning the distance between two people who are standing next to each other! Making yourself heard and understood is not an easy task.

◆ THINKING ABOUT COMMUNICATION

Our topic this week is communication—**the skill of sending and receiving messages.** When God communicated with the first man, Adam, He shared with man His mind, emotions, and desires. As He walked with Adam in the cool of the evening, God revealed many things about Himself.

In the same way, communication makes it possible for you to share yourself with others—and they with you. As you send and receive messages, you are able to "climb inside someone's skin" and get to know people from the inside out. A good communicator observes how feelings influence people's actions and how their attitudes affect the way they make decisions.

The Bible says this about communication:

● KEY VERSE ON COMMUNICATION
Everyone should be quick to listen, slow to speak and slow to become angry (James 1:19).

▲ LOOKING AHEAD
True communication involves sharing yourself with another person with understanding and love. Begin good communication in your family by rereading James 1:19 now. Let each person suggest reasons why God gave us two eyes, two ears, but only one mouth! Is it possible that listening is twice as important as speaking?

"I meant a <u>drink</u> of water, and you know it!"

When it comes to listening, I'm all ears

Q

What causes communication breakdown?

A

Communication breaks down when I fail to listen to others.

J udy arrived home two hours late, and her mother was obviously upset. "Judy, it's after 11:00. How could you be so late?"

"But Mom," Judy sobbed, "you don't understand. Cindy and I had to talk; it was our only chance to be together before—"

"And be tired and grumpy for school tomorrow? You two girls talk all the time. Now to bed with you."

The next morning Judy's mother learned from a neighbor that Cindy had just been diagnosed with bone cancer. She was going into the hospital for surgery the very next day.

That afternoon, Judy's mother came into her room to apologize. "Oh, honey, I'm so sorry. I didn't know. Can we talk about it?"

"Go away," Judy replied. "Just leave me alone."

◆ **TAKE A LOOK / Esther 6:1-13**

When communication between people breaks down, the result can be tragic.

One aspect of communication involves how you listen. The book of Proverbs describes a poor listener this way:

He who answers before listening—that is his folly and his shame (Proverbs 18:13).

The Old Testament book of Esther takes place during a time when God's people were living far away from their homeland. As the story unfolds, you will meet the villain, a man named Haman, who made the mistake of speaking without listening. Read Esther 6:1-13 to discover why Haman didn't listen—a dangerous practice when it's the king who's doing the talking!

▲ **TAKE A STEP**

Haman only heard what he wanted to hear. Like Judy's mom, he learned that what you don't hear can hurt you!

A good communicator listens carefully. (Do you?)

A good communicator is sensitive to the feelings of others. (Are you?)

A good communicator disagrees without getting angry. (Can you?)

A good communicator asks the speaker to repeat anything that is unclear. (Would you repeat that, please?)

Identify where Judy and her mom failed to practice the principles of good communication. Choose two family members to reenact the situation without causing hurt feelings.

*S*tanding in front of the kitchen cabinet, 16-month-old Jeremy jabbered meaningless syllables.

He thought he was telling his mother, "I want some apple juice, please." But the message wasn't getting through. Jeremy's frustration grew, and he began to cry—very loudly! Though his mother hadn't understood his words, she did understand his unspoken request. Patiently she lifted him up, opened the cabinet, and began pointing to one thing after another. As she pointed to the juice, Jeremy's eyes lit up and he held out his hand. Though he couldn't say many words, he had communicated!

◆ TAKE A LOOK / Philemon

Jeremy had learned what everyone needs to know: Feelings are an important part of the messages you send and receive. They often communicate as much as words!

The apostle Paul, in his letter to the church at Rome, shares the reason why feelings should—and can—be shared without fear.

In Christ we who are many form one body, and each member belongs to all the others (Romans 12:5).

Paul wasn't afraid to share part of himself by sharing his feelings. Explore some of those feelings by reading the 25 verses of Paul's "postcard" to Philemon (it's located just before the book of Hebrews in the New Testament). Here's the cast of characters to help you understand what you are reading: Philemon—a wealthy slaveowner in the city of Colosse; Onesimus—his runaway slave, newly converted to faith in Jesus Christ; Paul—apparently the means of Onesimus's conversion, and a close personal friend of Philemon.

▲ TAKE A STEP

A good way to practice the skill of communicating feelings is by interviewing the characters of this story. Have one family member be Paul, another Philemon, and a third Onesimus. Then ask these questions, and let the "characters" respond.

"Paul, why did you take the trouble to write to Philemon? Is one runaway slave really worth the effort?"

"Philemon, what did you think when you received Paul's letter? Do you think you can truly forgive Onesimus?"

"Onesimus, how does it make you feel to know Paul cares enough about you to write a letter to your master?"

When it comes to talking, say it with feeling

Q

How can I improve my communication skills?

A

Communication improves when I share feelings.

PARENT
Relate an incident from your own life when a failure to listen had unpleasant consequences. Don't be surprised if you have a good laugh together.

Words whisper, but actions shout!

Hudson Taylor was deep in thought as he looked at the Chinese faces around him. Although he spoke Chinese very well, the people still feared this foreigner. How could he communicate the love of God to them?

At last Mr. Taylor came up with an idea that would make it possible for him to travel into the unreached interior of China with the gospel message. He stopped dressing like an Englishman of 1860 and started dressing like a Chinese man. In addition to wearing a long blue gown and cloth shoes, he shaved his head so that only a single, long pigtail of hair remained.

The Chinese people felt that here was someone who understood their ways. They began to pay attention to Hudson Taylor's message rather than his strange Western clothing. Because of Hudson Taylor's effective communication, many people came to know Jesus Christ as Savior.

Q
Are words the only way to communicate?

A
Communication involves actions as well as words.

◆ **TAKE A LOOK / John 12:1-8**

Hudson Taylor learned that words are not the only way to communicate. The way you walk, dress, gesture, and smile speaks volumes.

During the week before Jesus was arrested and crucified, His followers recognized the danger He was in. Some of Jesus' closest friends held a special dinner in His honor, and during that meal showed how much they loved their Lord. As you read the story of that emotional dinner in John 12:1-8, notice how two women honored Jesus without ever saying a word.

▲ **TAKE A STEP**

Scene One: You are slumped over your desk, working on your homework, when your dad comes in and rumples your hair. What does that gesture tell you?

Scene Two: You have just tracked up the carpet with muddy shoes. Your mom stands at the door with her arms crossed, a stern look on her face. She doesn't say a word, but you get the message. What is it?

Even a child is known by his actions, by whether his conduct is pure and right (Proverbs 20:11).

Whether you are a child or a parent, your actions speak—loudly! Close your family time together by having each person complete this sentence for one other person in the room: "I appreciated what you did when you _____."

Then to show that your appreciation goes beyond words, give that person a big hug!

*T*here is nothing sharper than an unkind word:
"Mom, you need to dye your hair! Your gray is
showing and you look as old as Grandma."

"You know, your braces are really ugly. I wouldn't
even open my mouth if I were you."

"The results from your tests are back, and I'd like
to read how you did: Tony, A; Jennifer, B; Chad, F . . ."

"Why don't you just forget about applying for medical school? Your grades are too low and you can't possibly afford it. You'll never be accepted."

◆ **TAKE A LOOK / Ephesians 4:2-3, 11-16**
Already this week we've talked about three
communication skills—listening, sharing feelings,
and making sure your unspoken actions agree
with your spoken words. Today we want to examine another side of communication—"speaking
the truth in love."

Think back to the four statements you read at
the top of the page. All of them communicate. All
of them may be true. But none of the four tells the
truth in love.

Truth spoken lovingly is very different from
truth delivered thoughtlessly or with hurtful intent.
Ephesians 4:1-16 will encourage you to be humble,
gentle, patient—and to communicate the truth to
others in a way that is both kind and helpful. Read
those verses together as a family right now.

▲ **TAKE A STEP**
When the Bible speaks of truth in verse 15, it
means the truth about Jesus Christ—God's truth as
proclaimed by the apostles, prophets, evangelists,
pastors, and teachers (verse 11). Because we know
the truth about Jesus—God's "love gift" to the
world—we'll want to share that truth in the spirit
of love. Paul gives instructions for this in verse 29
of the same chapter:

Do not let any unwholesome talk come out
of your mouths, but only what is helpful for
building others up according to their needs
(Ephesians 4:29).

With that as your guide, how would you
change the statements at the top of this page to be
sure that the truth is given and received in love?
("Mom, for a mother of three, you've sure done a
great job of taking care of yourself! Wouldn't it be
fun to try a color rinse on your hair?")
You try the rest.

A spoon-ful of love helps the truth go down

Q

What does
speaking
the truth in
love mean?

A

Communi-
cation
involves
sharing the
truth in a
kind, helpful
way.

PARENT
This might be
a good time to
discuss what
clothes "say"
about the person
wearing them.
Let 1 Peter 2:3-4
shed some light
on the subject.

LONELINESS

"*Oh, Tim, I should have called your teacher,*" Mrs. Elliott responded as Tim told her about the class Christmas party. "*Bringing gifts for your friends sounded like a wonderful idea, but I wondered about the kids who were new or didn't have very many friends.*"

"*I wish you had called her, Mom, because it was awful. Some of the kids had a whole pile of presents—and Mike didn't get even one. When Miss Franklin read the name on the last gift, everybody started talking and cleaning up the wrapping paper—real nervous-like. And no one wanted to look at him. Mom, I don't think I'll ever forget it. Mike just sat there, like he was the loneliest guy in the world.*"

◆ THINKING ABOUT LONELINESS

Mike was not alone in his class—there were 27 other students. But he was lonely. He felt as you may have felt from time to time: "I don't belong . . . I've been left out . . . No one cares."

Loneliness is **an inner emptiness waiting to be filled.** Everybody gets lonely once in a while. Most people recover quickly, but sometimes it can lead to other problems. It can take the form of angry behavior, an "I-don't-care" attitude, trying too hard, or acting like a clown.

● LOOKING AHEAD

Two facts will help you deal with lonely moments: (1) Everyone experiences loneliness, so you're in good company; and (2) God has promised never to leave you, so you're in good hands!

▲ KEY VERSE ON LONELINESS

"*Do not be afraid or terrified . . . for the* LORD *your God goes with you; he will never leave you nor forsake you*" (Deuteronomy 31:6). Memorize that verse now to help you when you meet lonely moments in the future.

*A*w, Dad, can't we just wait and go next week? It's a long trip, and besides, we never stay very long. Why don't you and Mom go, and let Meredith and me stay home?"

"Brad, I know you don't like that long drive every Sunday to visit Grandma. But think how much it means to her. If she were home right now, she'd be baking cookies, putting up decorations, and making Christmas a special time for us. Well, this year we get to make it special for her. She must feel lonely being so far away from her home and family. What do you think, son?"

"I think," Brad said slowly, "you'd better let me drive."

◆ TAKE A LOOK / Lamentations 3:1-3, 13-26

What are lonely people like?

Sometimes they wear sad expressions. Other times they disguise loneliness with anger or bitterness. They may pretend to be happy-go-lucky. But you can spot them if you know where to look. Lonely people are all around you.

The man who feels he is little more than the family paycheck . . . the wife who thinks she's no more than the family maid . . . the child who can't express why he's afraid to go to school . . . the teenager whose parents don't take time to listen . . . the student who feels he doesn't fit in anywhere . . . the grandfather who no longer feels useful to the family—all are lonely people. They are looking for someone or something to fill the void.

The Bible, too, is filled with people who felt lonely. But their loneliness had something that is often missing in the lives of lonely people today.

Read the words of the prophet Jeremiah in Lamentations 3:1-3, 13-26. See if you can spot what made his loneliness bearable.

▲ TAKE A STEP

As Jeremiah watched an enemy army destroy his city and carry away his countrymen, he must have felt terribly lonely. But even in his loneliness, he still had hope.

Jeremiah's hope was not a "maybe" kind of hope. It was a sure confidence that God never leaves His children like orphans in a storm. So Jeremiah was able to say:

The LORD is good to those whose hope is in him (Lamentations 3:25).

If you were Brad or Meredith, what would you talk about with your grandmother to help her feel less lonely? Is there a lonely person you can visit sometime this week?

Do lonely people ever have a nice day?

Q

What are the symptoms of loneliness?

A

Loneliness may be expressed as sadness, but it is helped when I place my hope in God.

"**T**is the season to be jolly, Fa-la-la-la-la-la-la-la-la." The merry sound swirled around the last-minute shoppers, but not everyone felt the happiness it spoke of.

"If I see one more street-corner Santa," elderly Mr. Jenkins muttered to himself, "I'll just stay home till January. The world is sure a lonesome place now that Frances is gone."

Around the corner, a young soldier entered a bar. "Six weeks without a letter from Mom and Dad. I guess they don't even think about me now that I'm away."

Waiting for the bus, Miranda got angrier by the minute. " 'Peace on earth, good will to men'—hah! What do they know? There's no peace anywhere, especially around our house."

◆ **TAKE A LOOK / 2 Corinthians 1:3-7**

Christmas. Normally, it's a happy time. But for people like Mr. Jenkins whose wife recently died . . . or the young soldier far from home . . . or 15-year-old Miranda whose parents are on the verge of a divorce . . . Christmastime is anything but the season to be jolly.

Nothing can separate you from God's love. That's what Romans 8:38-39 says. And once you experience God's forever love, you can reach out to others who feel lonely and unloved.

The Bible says that our own sorrows make us able to help others in similar situations. Read 2 Corinthians 1:3-7 and discover whose comfort you really pass on when you reach out to someone who is lonesome.

▲ **TAKE A STEP**

Holidays are hard times for lonely people. But they are wonderful times for "comforters"! When you comfort another person, you are obeying this important command:

> Each of you should look not only to your own interests, but also to the interests of others (Philippians 2:4).

Comfort comes in many forms. You can encourage lonely people by including them in special Christmas activities, offering rides to church, taking them shopping, being a caring listener. Can you think of other ways your family might turn the holidays into happy days for a lonely person you know? And after you've done that, choose a person, and put some of those ideas into practice!

Q

When is loneliness most likely to strike?

A

Loneliness hits hard during the holiday season— and so does God's comfort.

PARENT
When was the last time you encouraged your child by showing that you are on his or her side? Even a child can feel like it's "me against the world."

*M*om, do you have to go to work today?" Lisa asked as her mother placed the bed tray across Lisa's lap. "Can't you just stay home and take care of me?"

"You know I would if I could," her mother replied. "But I'll call you in a little while to see how you're doing."

"I feel so sad, Mommy. Things aren't like they were when Dad was here, are they?"

"No, honey, they aren't. But that just means we have to stick together closer than ever. Now you try and get some rest. Your lunch is in the frig, and if you get bored you might try reading some good books—like your school books, for instance."

"Very funny. Hey, Mom?"

"Yes, Lisa."

"I love you."

"I love you too. Rest well, and don't be lonesome. I'll see you tonight."

◆ TAKE A LOOK / Romans 12:9-13

Like many people today, Lisa and her mother were making the best of a less than ideal situation. But just because Lisa was alone didn't mean she was lonely.

If you want to conquer loneliness, you need to know that there is something far more important than being surrounded by people. Do you know what it is? Being surrounded by love!

Lisa and her mother were separated for an entire day. But because they had expressed their love so clearly to each other—with a word, a touch, a hug—Lisa wouldn't feel lonely all day. (Well, maybe just a little bit!) They were practicing this important truth:

Be devoted to one another in brotherly love (Romans 12:10).

That goes for motherly . . . and sisterly . . . and fatherly love too! Read about that kind of love in Romans 12:9-13.

▲ TAKE A STEP

One of the best ways to dig yourself out of loneliness is to begin to love others. The lonely person who decides to show love to someone else is taking the first—and biggest—step out of loneliness.

Loneliness is relieved as love is released. Try it right now as a family! All it takes is a hug and three heartfelt words: "I love you." Then ask God to bring another person into your life today who will be less lonely after you express your love.

When you're away, your love can keep me company

Q

How can I overcome loneliness?

A

Loneliness leaves when I reach out in love to someone else.

What does it take to turn "lonely" into "lovely"?

How can I help someone who is lonely?

A

Lonely people need to experience God's unconditional love.

PARENT
A long-distance call or family letter brings distant relatives closer. Try one this weekend!

*T*he following prayer was written by a teenager who, though not lonely herself, learned a painful lesson about loneliness.

"Lord, I never really said nasty things about her, but I didn't really accept her either. She reminded me of a scrawny cat that was afraid to let you pet it—maybe because it had been abused as a kitten. She seemed like that to me, wanting to be accepted, but shying away from everyone. Her face was all bones and she wouldn't look straight into your eyes. Once in the mall I ducked into a store so she wouldn't see me.

"Lord, I'm so ashamed. I didn't even try to be her friend. Please forgive me for feeling—and acting—so superior. I know I'm not. I know that I could have been kinder and nicer in the cafeteria and in chorus, everywhere. Maybe then she wouldn't have felt so alone and gotten pregnant. And maybe the baby wouldn't be so sick right now and her life wouldn't be hanging by a thread if she'd seen more of You in me. Well, if she'd seen anything of You in me. I'm so sorry."

◆ TAKE A LOOK / 1 John 4:14-21

Rejection, failure, insecurity—the inner emptiness of the lonely person cries out to be filled with love. Person-to-person love helps, but even that can be a fickle and fair-weather love. What is needed is perfect, never-failing love—the kind only God can provide.

As you read 1 John 4:14-21, look for the answer to our question: "How can I help someone who is lonely?"

▲ TAKE A STEP

People are lonely because they are separated from each other. Most of all, they are lonely because they're separated from God.

What a lonely person needs more than anything is to know that he or she is truly loved, forgiven, and accepted by the One who taught us about love in the first place!

We love because he first loved us (1 John 4:19).

Think back to the first time you heard about God's love for you. Were you perfect? Of course not, but God loved you just the same! Now He is calling upon you to demonstrate that kind of love to someone else.

Reread the last verse of today's Scripture passage. Then have a family "powwow" to discuss the who, what, when, and where of putting God's kind of love to work in your family and then in your neighborhood.

·· THANKSGIVING ·· ·

I *f you sat down at a Thanksgiving dinner and were given the following menu, which meal would you choose?*

Sukkot Smorgasbord—*thin barley cakes, brushed with olive oil and topped with herbs and spices; served with your choice of cheeses accompanied by pomegranates, figs, dates, and melons.*

Jamestown Jambalaya—*wild venison and roasted boar; accompanied by maize (corn), wild rice, and fresh berries.*

Turkey-Day Traditional—*roast turkey and dressing with giblet gravy; mashed potatoes, green beans, summer squash, stewed tomatoes, cranberry sauce; for dessert, pumpkin and mincemeat pies.*

◆ THINKING ABOUT THANKSGIVING

Every Fall, Americans celebrate a national day of thanksgiving. But the idea didn't start in the United States.

In Old Testament times, each year's crop was a sign of God's blessing. So God Himself established a special time of thanksgiving to be held at the end of the harvest season. The Feast of Booths or Tabernacles (*Sukkot* was its Hebrew name) lasted an entire week!

Thanksgiving is our **grateful response to the goodness of God.** This week let's concentrate on learning how we can . . .

● KEY VERSE ON THANKSGIVING

Give thanks in all circumstances, for this is God's will for you in Christ Jesus (1 Thessalonians 5:18).

▲ LOOKING AHEAD

In addition to offering a prayer of thanksgiving *before* your meals this week, follow the instruction of Deuteronomy 8:10 and pray *after* you've eaten as well.

Focus those prayers of thanksgiving on something about your country that you really appreciate—the opportunities, the beauty, the freedoms you have. Begin right now by letting each family member share two things he or she is thankful for at this very moment!

"They were thankful for a bountiful harvest? You mean the whole thing was about vegetables?"

Grumbling sends you tumbling every time

"Please get it for me, Mom," Cindy pleaded as her mother turned from the racks of colorful blouses. "It'll go with so many things."

"I know, Cindy. It is a cute blouse, but you really don't need it and I can't afford it today. Since Grandma always sends you clothes for Christmas, I'm sure you'll get some nice things then."

"Well, I don't think it's fair. You bought Chad that new shirt last week, and I didn't get anything."

"Cindy, that's not how things work in this family. Chad needed the shirt for choir, so we bought it. You don't need this blouse. Stop comparing what we spend on you and Chad. We love you both equally, and want you to be grateful for what you have."

◆ **TAKE A LOOK / Numbers 11:4-10**

God wants you to thank Him for what you have.

Let them give thanks to the LORD for his unfailing love and his wonderful deeds for men (Psalm 107:21).

The people of Israel had much to be thankful for. After being miraculously freed from slavery in Egypt, they were moving toward the land God had promised them. Each day God was providing food and water. Not one of the millions of people in the camp lacked anything that was really needed.

But a few people began to complain about the menu. They thought the flat cakes made from manna needed some garlic and onions from Egypt —sort of an Old Testament pizza! And their complaints became contagious. As you read the results of their grumbling in Numbers 11:4-10, you'll discover what God thinks about ungratefulness.

▲ **TAKE A STEP**

Did you notice where these events occurred? It was a place called Kibroth Hattaavah (Numbers 11:34), which means "graves of craving." And that's exactly where those who refuse to give thanks will find themselves.

When you continually crave things you do not or cannot have, you lose the joy of the things you already have. Cindy's problem was not so much with the blouse she didn't get, as it was with the blouses she already owned. How might she have used Psalm 107:21 to change her grumbling into gratefulness?

Can you identify areas of gloomy grumbling or ungratefulness in your life? What can you do to change?

Q

What should I be thankful for?

A

Be thankful for what you have already, and grateful for all you receive.

*T*hough he didn't show it outwardly, Charles was discouraged. It had always been difficult for him to make friends. Sitting down with a good book or challenging his dad to a game of chess was his idea of a good time.

"Dad, why is it nobody likes me? Just because I like to read and study a lot, does that make me so strange?"

"Charles, there are lots of people who like you. God has given you a good mind—and you're using it in ways that please Him. That makes your mother and me very happy. We like you, Charles. In fact, we love you. And we'd love you just as much even if you got C's and B's . . . like your dear old dad!"

"Thanks, Dad. I'm glad you're on my side. Hey, time to hit the books. I've got an algebra exam tomorrow."

◆TAKE A LOOK / Revelation 4:6-11

Charles might have done well in his studies without his father's encouragement. But words of praise really lifted his spirit.

In a similar way, thanksgiving means something special to God. As the mighty Creator of the universe, He does not need anything from us. But as the Creator, He deserves our praise and thanks—and that is one thing we can give Him that brings delight to His heart.

Revelation, the last book of the Bible, paints a word picture of God's heavenly home. As one person reads Revelation 4:6-11 aloud, close your eyes and picture what is happening.

▲ TAKE A STEP

Thanksgiving is more than a good idea. We are commanded to come before God with that attitude.

Enter his gates with thanksgiving and his courts with praise; give thanks to him and praise his name (Psalm 100:4).

The mighty Creator of the world is also the God who loves you as a father loves his own children. When you thank Him, you are doing what the angels around His throne always do: praising Him for His greatness!

As you think about the God who is worthy of your thanks every day of the year, pick a day next month when you can celebrate an unofficial Thanksgiving Day as a family. Mark it on your calendar right now and call it "Psalm 100:4 Day." On that occasion, simply read the verse and do what the psalmist has suggested!

Do you know the password to heaven?

Q

What does thanksgiving mean to God?

A

Thanksgiving gives God the same place in my heart that He holds in the universe.

PARENT
Be sure to let your child help with preparations for festive holiday meals. How about a special centerpiece or flower arrangement for your table? (And don't forget a hearty "thanks" for your child's best efforts.)

What can you give the God who has everything?

Mike and Mindy had often grumbled about how late their father came home from work, but they nodded in agreement as their mother explained:

"Daddy's project is nearly finished, and he's very tired. I know it's been difficult having him away so much, but he's been working hard so we can have the things we need. He just called, and tonight he's coming home early! I'm preparing his favorite dessert, and I thought you might like to do something special too."

The house became a beehive of activity. An hour later, Mike and Mindy's father was greeted with a thank-you poem, a silly cartoon, a banner proclaiming "You're Tops, Pops," and the aroma of a hot meal and warm apple pie.

◆ TAKE A LOOK / Luke 17:11-17

Yesterday we asked the question, "What does thanksgiving mean to God?" It honors God by giving Him the same place in your heart that He enjoys in the universe.

Today we want to answer this question: "What does thanksgiving mean to us?"

In Luke 17 you'll read the story of the ten lepers. Because of their disease, they were forced to live apart from other people. No one would have anything to do with them. No one, that is, until Jesus came along. Taking pity on them, He told the ten to go show themselves to the priest. And on the way, they were wonderfully and totally healed!

Ten were cleansed . . . but only one returned to say thank you. And that was the only one of the ten who felt the loving touch of the Savior.

Read about "The Case of the Forgetful Lepers" in Luke 17:11-17.

▲ TAKE A STEP

What does thanksgiving do for you? God Himself has said:

"He who sacrifices thank offerings honors me, and he prepares the way so that I may show him the salvation of God" (Psalm 50:23).

Do you want to see God do mighty things? Reach out and touch Him often by thanking Him.

Close your family time today by holding hands in a circle and taking turns thanking God for the things you can see right from where you are sitting or standing: your house, food, pets, swingset, parents, brothers and sisters.

There's no better habit than the habit of saying, "Thank You, God!"

Q
What does thanksgiving mean to me?

A
Thanksgiving helps me respond properly to God.

*S*even-year-old Ellen enjoyed watching her two-year-old cousin Eric feed himself. He made such a wonderful mess!

As Eric pointed to each item he wanted, Aunt Nancy would tell him, "Say 'please.' Then Mommy will give it to you." And Eric would hold out his hand and say, "Pwease." Then as Aunt Nancy handed him the toast, she would tell him again, "Now say 'thank you,' " and Eric would repeat, "Tank oou, Mommy."

"Aunt Nancy," Ellen finally asked, "why do you make him say please and thank you? Isn't he too little to understand?"

"Perhaps," Aunt Nancy replied. "But it's never too soon to learn the habit of thanksgiving. It's one of the most important lessons Eric will ever learn."

◆ TAKE A LOOK / 1 Samuel 25:14-25, 35-38
Aunt Nancy was teaching Eric manners, but she also was teaching him to be grateful. The Old Testament records the sad story of Nabal, a man who refused to be grateful. He lived during the time of King David.

As David and his men were roaming the desert, fleeing from King Saul, they stopped long enough to protect the flocks of Nabal from attack. And what "thanks" did they get? Read about it in 1 Samuel 25:14-25, 35-38.

▲ TAKE A STEP
"I can make it on my own. I don't need God." Very few people actually say those words, but by holding onto proud, ungrateful attitudes—refusing to be thankful—they express the rebelliousness this verse describes:

For although they knew God, they neither glorified him as God nor gave thanks to him (Romans 1:21).

God knows that thanksgiving is the way for you to say, "You are the One who takes care of me."

So sing it, say it, show it. Try putting these words to the familiar melody, "Are You Sleeping, Brother John?"

Are you thankful, are you thankful,
	Child of God, child of God?
God in heaven loves you,
	Does so much to keep you
In His care, in His care.

Now compose your own song of thanksgiving to that same tune. You'll feel your spirit lift in joy.

A helpful habit for this life and the next

Q
What if I refuse to give thanks?

A
By refusing to give thanks, I withhold from God the glory that He deserves.

PARENT
Psalm 136 is a wonderful pattern for giving thanks to God in big and little things. Read it responsively, with your child echoing the thought in the last half of each verse.

JESUS, GOD'S SON

indy and Peter looked forward each night to that favorite time when Daddy would read aloud to them. Even though Peter was learning to read by himself and Cindy knew all the stories by heart, it was wonderful to snuggle down on each side of their father and listen to his deep, gentle voice as he read about animals and adventures and faraway places.

Tonight as Daddy finished the story of Cinderella, Cindy looked up at him and said, "That was pretend, wasn't it, Daddy? But Jesus isn't pretend. He's real! Let's read a story about Him now."

◆ THINKING ABOUT JESUS, GOD'S SON

Four-year-old Cindy knew that Jesus is not a "pretend person" like the ones she read about in her storybooks. But many people today do not believe that Jesus actually lived, or that what the Bible says about His life is really true.

The account of Jesus' earthly life is found in four books of the Bible called the Gospels: Matthew, Mark, Luke, and John. The men who wrote those accounts were *not* writing fairy tales. They knew what they were writing was true because it came from God Himself.

Three of the writers knew Jesus personally, and the fourth investigated His life carefully. So you can be sure the Bible is correct when it says that . . .

"No, dear, it's Christianity that's lasted two thousand years. Not that sermon."

● KEY VERSE ON JESUS, GOD'S SON

[Jesus] being in very nature God . . . made himself nothing, taking the very nature of a servant, being made in human likeness (Philippians 2:6-7).

▲ LOOKING AHEAD

Jesus was more than a man. He was **God Himself in a human body,** and He came to earth for a very specific reason.

The good news about Jesus is better than just a good story! Can you discover why by reading His own words in John 10:10 and 14:6?

Alan was deep in thought as he approached his grandfather. "Grandpa, isn't everybody a citizen of the country where they were born?"

"That's right, Alan."

"Well, I heard you talking about my cousin Jason being an American citizen, but he was born in Saudi Arabia—and he's always lived there. I don't understand."

"Jason is a Saudi Arabian citizen because he was born there and his birth is registered there. But because his parents are Americans, he is an American citizen too. Right now he has 'dual citizenship'—he belongs to both countries. When he turns 18, Jason will have to choose which identity to keep."

"Oh, I see," said Alan. "He can't be an American and be something else at the same time!"

◆ **TAKE A LOOK / Hebrews 2:14-17**
Very few people actually belong to two countries, but the idea of dual citizenship can help you better understand the role of Jesus when He came to earth.

As God's Son, Jesus lived with the Father before the world began (John 17:5). When He came to earth, Jesus didn't come in a disguise, nor did He just pretend to be a man; He became a real, flesh-and-blood person. He got tired and sleepy, hungry and thirsty—just like any man. But at the same time He was able to perform miracles and forgive sins—things only God can do. "Dual identity"—God and man together in one person!

Why was it necessary for Jesus to become the God-man? Hebrews 2:14-17 answers that important question.

▲ **TAKE A STEP**
Do you remember the story of Adam and Eve (Genesis 3) and the tragic result of their sin? Romans 6:23 clearly explains that their sin meant death for every person who would ever be born. But . . .

> [Jesus] too shared in their humanity so that by his death he might destroy him who holds the power of death (Hebrews 2:14).

In the next three days we'll learn more about how Jesus can set people free from the power of death. But right now, look up Colossians 1:13-14 and Philippians 3:20-21. There you'll discover some privileges you will enjoy when you become a "citizen of heaven." What privilege of citizenship will be yours only when Jesus returns?

"Jesus, where is the place you call 'home'?"

Q

Why did Jesus come to earth?

A

Jesus came to earth as the God-man to destroy the power of death.

It's not easy to prove you're the greatest!

Q

Why did Jesus do the things He did?

A

Jesus acted as He did to prove He is the promised Savior.

M *om, don't forget I've got to have a copy of my birth certificate by Friday so I can play in the tournament."*

Mrs. Johnson nodded. "Don't worry, Eric. I haven't forgotten."

"Seems kinda silly, though," Eric said. "The coaches know me. Why do they need to know my birthday?"

"Because your team will be playing in a tournament for 12- and 13-year-olds. Some of the players look older than that—including you! Suppose someone were to question your age? Having a copy of the birth certificate to prove your age is a rule that safeguards all the teams. So don't worry, champ. You'll have your proof!"

◆ TAKE A LOOK / Isaiah 61:1-2; Luke 4:14-21

Having the right credentials—including proof of your identity—is important. (That is why your parents probably keep your birth certificate in a deposit box or other safe place.) Before you can enter school, get a driver's license, or travel in a foreign country, you must be able to prove you are who you say you are.

Jesus, too, had something to prove. In Old Testament times, God promised the Jewish people that a Messiah (Savior) would come. God even told them in advance the kinds of things the Messiah would do. Centuries later Jesus claimed to be that person! The proof? He did the things God had said the Messiah would do!

Prove that to yourself by reading two passages: first, the promise from the Old Testament (Isaiah 61:1-2); then, the claim of Jesus in the New Testament (Luke 4:14-21).

▲ TAKE A STEP

As Jesus' words and actions proved that He was in fact the Messiah of God, the people were faced with a choice. They could either deny His claim or accept it—but they could not ignore it.

Today you too must make a choice. Looking at the same evidence He has left behind—His "birth certificate" as the Son of God—what will you believe about Jesus?

"Whoever believes in the Son has eternal life, but whoever rejects the Son will not see life, for God's wrath remains on him" (John 3:36).

Do you believe Jesus is really who He claimed to be? Then tell Him so right now in a short prayer. Talk to Him just as you would talk to a member of the family, because that's what you are in Christ— a part of the family of God!

*L*isten, Todd, I'm telling you the truth. Dennis told me exactly what happened."

"Oh, c'mon, Andy, you must've heard it wrong. Nobody takes a spanking for somebody else—especially when that 'somebody' is your kid sister."

"It's true. Dennis was teasing his sister really bad, and she got mad and threw a baseball at him. But it missed him and broke a window in the garage door. Their dad was going to spank her for doing it, but Dennis asked his dad to give him the spanking instead. And his dad did! That's the part I don't understand. His dad went ahead and spanked Dennis, even though he didn't break the window."

◆ TAKE A LOOK / John 1:29

Like Todd, you might find it hard to imagine that anyone would be willing to take someone else's punishment. (If your parents punished you for something your brother or sister did, would you think that was fair?) Yet that is what happened when Jesus died on the cross!

According to God's law, sin is so terrible that its punishment is not just a spanking, but death (Romans 6:23). Only Jesus Christ, who had no sin of His own, could take that punishment for us and pay the penalty for our sins.

In Old Testament times God commanded the high priest to sacrifice a lamb once a year in order to "cover" the sins of the people. Those yearly sacrifices were symbols of the Lamb of God who would one day come to give His life in payment for sin.

Read John 1:29 to discover why the lamb is an appropriate symbol for Jesus Christ.

▲ TAKE A STEP

"God so loved the world that he gave his one and only Son" (John 3:16).

Jesus' death paid the penalty for sin. But John 3:16 says there is a response God expects in return: belief in His Son. You can personalize the good news of John 3:16 by putting your name in place of the pronouns:

"God loved _____ so much that He gave his one and only Son, that if _____ believes in Him, _____ shall not perish but have eternal life." Let each family member read the verse aloud that way.

Aren't you glad Jesus Christ said, "I'll take your place"? Close your family time with a prayer of thanks to the Lamb of God who was sacrificed in your place.

You can't say "Love" any louder than that!

Q

Why did Jesus have to die?

A

Jesus' death paid the penalty for sin.

What's so great about an empty grave?

*T*he first time Gary quietly bowed his head before he began to eat lunch, several kids snickered. But later they just kept on talking whenever Gary prayed. That is, until Derek transferred to Gary's school. Then each lunchtime became an ordeal as Derek drew attention to Gary's daily habit of mealtime prayer.

"Look, ol' Gary fell asleep again. I'll bet he's going to wake up with his face in the mashed potatoes one of these days! Hey, Holy Joe, how come you're always bowing your head? Nobody's listening to you."

"You're wrong, Derek. God's listening. I just like to talk to Him and tell Him thanks for the food."

"Well, I like to talk to George Washington myself," Derek mocked. "At least I know what he looks like."

◆ TAKE A LOOK / 1 Corinthians 15:12-20

Q

Why is the Resurrection so important?

If Derek is right, then Gary is foolish for thinking that God hears his prayers. But if Gary is right, what then?

It is possible today to visit the tombs of many famous leaders from the past: Napoleon, Lincoln, Lenin, Buddha, Mohammed. (And yes, Derek, even Washington.) In each and every case, the tomb is still occupied.

But the tomb of Jesus Christ is different from all other tombs. Three days after Jesus was buried, He arose from the grave. Over His tomb could be hung the words: "Empty, just as He promised!"

As you read 1 Corinthians 15:12-20, ask yourself this question: "How important is it that Jesus' tomb is empty?"

▲ TAKE A STEP

A

Jesus' resurrection proves that He is the Son of God.

What if Jesus had not risen from the dead? Would it really make that much difference? Take away the Resurrection and what have you lost?

According to Paul, plenty! In fact, you would be the most hopeless, pitiful person in the world if Jesus' body were still in the tomb. But the facts prove otherwise.

[Jesus] was declared with power to be the Son of God by his resurrection from the dead (Romans 1:4).

The Resurrection is the final proof that Jesus is who He claimed to be. The tomb is empty; God is alive; your faith is real!

PARENT
Your older child may have questions about the Resurrection, or other important teachings from the Bible. Why not "team up" to study a helpful book such as Paul Little's WHY I BELIEVE.

Derek thought Jesus Christ was only a man like George Washington. What might Gary tell Derek to convince him that Jesus is far more than a famous person?

TRADITIONS

A s the foreign visitor entered the Czar's palace, he noticed a guard standing in the middle of a grassy lawn. Curious as to why the sentry stood in such an unusual place, he asked the Czar. The Czar didn't know, so he asked his chief advisor. The advisor asked the commander of the palace guard.

Eventually the answer came back. The sentry stood on that spot because of an ancient tradition:

It seems that 100 years earlier, Catherine the Great had seen a bright spring flower blooming amid the melting snow. To prevent its destruction, she ordered a sentry to guard it. Years passed and another ruler came to power, but no one canceled Catherine's original command. So there a guard stood—day after day, year after year—though the flower had long since died!

◆ THINKING ABOUT TRADITIONS

This month families around the world celebrate Christ's birth—a historical fact—not a tradition. But as the years have gone by, some ways of celebrating Christmas have turned into traditions, **customs handed down from one generation to the next.**

Christmas means many things to many people. But all those rich traditions are empty if they do not point to Jesus Christ.

● KEY VERSE ON TRADITIONS

He is the beginning and the firstborn from among the dead, so that in everything he might have the supremacy (Colossians 1:18).

▲ LOOKING AHEAD

This week we will explore four Christmas traditions that help us understand the true meaning of Christmas. You'll discover that the real purpose for Christmas traditions is to help you celebrate Jesus' birth and give Him first place in your life.

As you read Colossians 1:15-20, the passage of Scripture where this week's key verse is found, list as many reasons as you can why Jesus is first!

"Why are you sending it to the North Pole? He's over at the mall."

You can celebrate even while you wait

Never before had seven-year-old Erica been so excited. Her mother was due to go into the hospital any day now, and then Erica's dream would come true. The BABY would be born!

Erica had enjoyed the time of preparation. She helped decorate the nursery, select clothes and toys, and had even gone to a baby shower with her mother. But now she was ready for the real thing—the baby brother or sister she had waited for so long.

Every day was one of anticipation. Erica knew she would just jump for joy when at last she could tell her friends, neighbors, and the whole world, "We have a new baby at our house!"

Q

What does "Advent" mean?

A

Advent represents the "coming" of Christ into the world.

◆ TAKE A LOOK / Luke 2:25-38

In Old Testament times, God had promised that a Savior would be born in the little town of Bethlehem.

Many years passed and nothing happened. But still people waited and watched, knowing that God never lies. They were looking for the coming of the Christ child, the Messiah, into the world.

Advent means "coming." The 24 days leading up to Christmas are called Advent. Christians use this time to prepare to celebrate Christ's birth.

Mary and Joseph took Jesus to the temple when He was eight days old. There they met two people who were waiting for the advent of the Messiah. As you read about Simeon and Anna in Luke 2:25-38, compare the way they waited for Jesus with the way you prepare for Christmas.

▲ TAKE A STEP

Waiting for God to keep His promise—that's what Simeon and Anna were doing. And the Advent season can help you do that as well.

Many families begin an Advent calendar on December 1, and open one "window" in the calendar each day before Christmas. Others celebrate with an Advent wreath, lighting one of the four red candles on each of the four Sundays before Christmas, and then lighting the central white candle on Christmas Eve.

This year, let the days before Christmas remind you that your faith is built upon God's promises—those He has kept in the past, and those He will keep in the future.

For no matter how many promises God has made, they are "Yes" in Christ (2 Corinthians 1:20).

*T*he bright lights, the decorations, the carolers, and the crowds added to Mandy's excitement. Christmas shopping was fun!

But one thing didn't quite make sense to Mandy. Mother had promised that if Mandy was a good helper she could go through the department store's Winter Fairyland (third floor, toy department) and sit on Santa's lap. Mandy was looking forward to that—but for a very different reason than her mother expected!

"At last," Mandy thought to herself, "I can ask Santa how he can be in so many stores at the same time!"

◆ TAKE A LOOK / Exodus 20:1-5

Another name for Santa Claus is "Saint Nick." It may surprise you to learn there really was a person by that name, Nicholas of Myra.

Nicholas was a wealthy young man who loved the Lord and was so concerned about the poor that he gave away a great deal of his money. For his generosity he was called a saint—Saint Nicholas. Many years later, Dutch settlers in America pronounced his name "Santa Nikalaus." Eventually it was shortened to "Santa Klaus."

In 1922 a professor made up a story about a jolly, red-capped man with twinkling eyes who gave gifts at Christmas. The Santa in the professor's story could be many places at once; he knew whether boys and girls had been naughty or nice. But he was only a "pretend" person.

By contrast, turn to Exodus 20:1-5 in your Bible; there you'll read about a real Person who can do all those things—and much, much more!

▲ TAKE A STEP

There's something exciting about sitting on "Santa's" lap and then finding what you asked for in your stocking or under the tree on Christmas morning. But that doesn't make Santa Claus real.

Before many weeks have passed, all the Santa suits will be folded up and put away for another year. But God, whose love moved Him to send His Son that first Christmas, never changes.

Every good and perfect gift is from above, coming down from the Father of the heavenly lights, who does not change like shifting shadows (James 1:17).

Knowing that, how would you answer Mandy's question about Santa Claus?

"Santa, didn't I just see you across the street?"

Q

Is there really a Santa Claus?

A

Saint Nicholas was real; Santa Claus is make-believe; but God is the Giver of every good gift.

PARENT
Do you remember the joys and anxieties you faced as you awaited the birth of your first child? Share a few memories with your firstborn!

It's just not Christmas if the tree's made of tin

But Daddy, we can't have an artificial tree. Every year we go with you to pick out a real tree, and it just wouldn't be Christmas if we didn't."

"Mama, you've got to fix the turkey like you always do. No one can do it as well, and besides, ham or roast beef just wouldn't seem like Christmas."

"Can we bake gingersnaps . . . please? The house looks so bare without a cookie jar full of good things to munch. And besides, it's almost Christmas—and what would the holidays be without the aroma of cookies?"

◆ TAKE A LOOK / 1 Peter 2:21-24

Traditions seem to grow as families grow. At the Christmas season every family seems to have its "traditional" way of celebrating. One of those traditions usually centers around a tree—the Christmas tree—that adorns a room in many homes.

What does the tradition of the Christmas tree mean?

More than 400 years ago, Martin Luther, a great preacher in Germany, was walking home one cold December night. In the crisp night air it seemed as though the heavens were ablaze with stars, their radiance reflecting off the frosty boughs of pine trees.

Luther was so touched by this beauty that he cut down a small evergreen tree, took it home, and decorated it with candles so that his family might share its beauty. Within 50 years, the custom of bringing a tree into the house at Christmastime was well established in Germany.

A

The Christmas tree reminds us of the cross of Calvary.

God too has beauty He wants to share with you. It is beauty found by gazing at another "tree"—the tree on which His Son Jesus was crucified, where the price for sins was paid and eternal life was purchased. You can read about God's "Christmas tree" in 1 Peter 2:21-24 and Colossians 2:13-14.

▲ TAKE A STEP

This year as you turn an evergreen tree into a glittering thing of beauty with tinsel, lights, and ornaments, remember that on another tree—the cross of Calvary—Jesus made it possible for those who believe in Him . . .

" . . . to eat from the tree of life, which is in the paradise of God (Revelation 2:7).

Why not turn your Christmas tree into a "Christ tree" this year by making or purchasing at least one ornament that reminds you of the cross of Calvary.

H ere is a list of traditional things associated with a Christmas celebration. If you can tell what they all have in common, you may go to the head of the class!

Mincemeat pie
The Magi (wise men)
The song "The Twelve Days of Christmas"
Kings, crowns, and feasts
Give up? Well, keep reading and you'll soon find out!

◆ **TAKE A LOOK / Matthew 2:1-12**
In traditional nativity scenes you often find three wise men sitting on camels or kneeling by the manger, offering their gifts to the Christ child.

Not much is really known about the wise men, or Magi as they were called. We don't know where they came from, how many there were, whether they rode camels, or exactly when they arrived in Bethlehem. But their story is wonderful!

As you read about the wise men in Matthew 2:1-12, notice how little is actually said about them—except for the reason they came all those miles.

▲ **TAKE A STEP**
The coming of the Magi is traditionally celebrated on January 6—twelve nights after Christmas. From the year 567 until the 17th century, people feasted all twelve days, with the greatest celebration reserved for the last night, the night known as Epiphany.

The word *epiphany* comes from a Greek word meaning "appearance," and this feast celebrates the appearance of God on earth. In particular, it marks the arrival of the wise men to worship Jesus—a sign that Jesus had come to bring salvation to all people, Jews and Gentiles alike.

This grace was given us in Christ Jesus before the beginning of time, but it has now been revealed through the appearing of our Savior, Christ Jesus (2 Timothy 1:9-10).

This season celebrate Epiphany by inviting another family for dinner. Share the changes that have taken place since Jesus Christ made His "appearance" in your home.

For dessert, serve mincemeat pie. For centuries it was made in an oblong shape to symbolize the manger of the baby Jesus. Mincemeat represents the spices the wise men offered Jesus. Serve it on Epiphany and revive an old tradition by starting a new one in your family.

When Christmas is over, the best is yet to come

Q

Why do we celebrate Epiphany?

A

Epiphany celebrates the appearing of the Savior, Jesus Christ.

PARENT
Gift-giving is a skill even a young child can learn. Discuss with your child what makes a gift special, either to give or to receive.

FAMILY

"**G**randma, I'm here," *five-year-old Kimberly sang out happily as she skipped into her grandmother's kitchen. "To help you with the violets, like I promised."*

"Well, I'm ready, too," Grandma laughed as she gave Kimberly a quick hug. "Let's move the violets here to the table."

That afternoon Kimberly learned a lot. She learned there are many beautiful varieties of violets; that violets like sunlight; that violets can be rooted in water and then transplanted. More important, Kimberly was reminded of what it means to belong to a family where you are loved.

◆ THINKING ABOUT FAMILY

Violets need special attention. Light, temperature, food, water—all are necessary for strong plants and colorful blooms. Like a fragile young violet, Kimberly was also growing in the environment best suited for her—the love and care of her family.

A family is **a group of people related by blood, marriage, and/or adoption.** A family includes people of all ages who help and care for each other. The best thing about a family is the love and support you find there.

"Hello, Mrs. Horton? Could you please stop by school this afternoon?"

● KEY VERSE ON FAMILY

Children's children are a crown to the aged, and parents are the pride of their children (Proverbs 17:6).

▲ LOOKING AHEAD

Read Psalm 68:5-6 together to discover one reason why God puts people in families. Then make a list to see just who your family includes. With the help of Mom or Dad (or both), see how far and wide you can trace both sides of your family tree: grandparents, aunts, uncles, cousins, nieces, nephews. Pull out a family photo album for some help!

*T*he Olympic Trials for track and field were in full swing with activities of all kinds: shot put, discus throw, pole vault. Ken's parents saw none of these. Their attention was focused solely on their son, crouched in the starting block for the mile relay. If his team won today, he and his three teammates would represent their country at the Olympic Games.

As they prepared for the longest—and shortest— three minutes of their lives, Ken's parents couldn't help but think of their son's years of intense training. The lonely runs in all kinds of weather . . . the victories and defeats . . . the injuries and sore muscles. Their thoughts were interrupted by the sound of the starter's gun as Ken sprang smoothly from the block.

◆ TAKE A LOOK
Genesis 18:18-19; Deuteronomy 6:4-9
A swift start, a determined run, a sure pass of the baton—these are the elements of a winning relay. In a similar way, the Christian family plays an important role on God's "relay team."

Think of God's changeless truth as the baton to be passed from generation to generation. As parents train their children in God's principles for right living, the "handoff" is smoothly accomplished.

This was the plan God gave to Abraham even before Abraham had a family. You'll find it set forth in Genesis 18:18-19 (and expanded in Deuteronomy 6:4-9). It's a plan needed just as much today as when it was first given more than 4,000 years ago!

▲ TAKE A STEP
God's purpose for the family has never changed. He wants individuals of every generation to know His love and forgiveness.

The family always has been, and will continue to be, God's perfect laboratory in which to instruct the next generation.

Impress [God's truths] on your children. Talk about them when you sit at home and when you walk along the road, when you lie down and when you get up (Deuteronomy 6:7).

Find an empty cardboard tube (like the one in a roll of paper towels) or perhaps purchase an 8-inch length of dowel rod and decorate it as your family "baton." Keep it near your family Bible to remind you often of the importance of passing on God's priceless truths . . . truths more valuable than any Olympic gold medal!

You can't drop the baton and win the race

Q

What is God's plan for the family?

A

The family exists to pass God's truths on to the next generation.

The kind of infection everyone should catch

It was Jason's first time away from home, and his mother was doing her best to see that it went smoothly.

"You'll really have a good time," she assured him while packing his clothes, some favorite books, and a few toys. "You can play with Aunt Cathy's dog and see the birds and squirrels in her yard. I hear her car. She must be here now."

At last, the moment of truth had arrived. "I love you, Jason. Be a good boy for Aunt Cathy," his mother said as she kissed him goodby. Both mother and aunt were hoping for a fearless, tearless parting . . . and Jason seemed calm enough as he climbed into his aunt's car. But suddenly he bolted from the car and ran back to his mom on the porch. After a few whispered words, Jason returned to his aunt, who was wearing a worried look. "It's okay, Auntie. I just forgot to tell Mommy, 'I love you.' "

◆ TAKE A LOOK / 2 Timothy 1:2-9; 3:14-15

It's no secret that love is easier caught than taught. Jason's mother was rewarded with a spontaneous expression of love because her son had "caught" her manner of expressing affection.

What is true of affection is also true of faith. It's contagious—you can catch it from other people. In the New Testament a young man named Timothy was infected with the same faith in God that characterized his mother and grandmother.

As you read 2 Timothy 1:2-9 and 3:14-15, try to imagine some ways Timothy learned to have faith in God.

▲ TAKE A STEP

God's goal for the family is that it become a transmitter of His truth. Lois and Eunice (from the first century) set examples of godliness and obedience for their children. Years later Paul would say to Timothy:

> From infancy you have known the holy
> Scriptures, which are able to make you wise
> for salvation through faith in Christ Jesus
> (2 Timothy 3:15).

Kids, what are you learning "from infancy" that your parents are trying to teach you about the God they know and love? Are you learning the lesson? And parents, what is it you should be passing on to your children through a consistent, godly model? Loving, caring, sharing, reading God's Word—all are models to be caught, and taught, in the home. That's God's plan!

Q

How can the family fulfill God's plan?

A

The family helps fulfill God's plan by modeling God's truth.

PARENT
Discuss with your child something you learned from your parents or grandparents —a funny saying, mannerism, or important lesson.

B reathlessly, 14-year-old Donna phoned her mother's office on Friday afternoon. "Mom, the Taylors invited me to spend the weekend at their cabin. Is it all right if I go?"

"Donna, I don't think so. Not this weekend."

"But Mom, why not? You've let me go before."

"I know, but this time I haven't talked with Mrs. Taylor. Dad may have other plans. You can go another time. I'll see you when I get home about 6:00. I love you. Gotta run."

Arriving home that evening, Mrs. Stephens greeted her husband and looked for Donna. She was nowhere to be found.

"Honey, where's Donna?" Mrs. Stephens inquired.

"Oh, she asked if she could spend the weekend with the Taylors at their cabin. I told her I thought it would be all right with you . . . "

◆ TAKE A LOOK / Colossians 3:12-21

Children learn at an early age who is in charge. Wise parents make the chain of command clear and accept their responsibility to guide and guard the family.

"Who's in charge here?" Parents are! The Bible makes it clear that God is honored when parents assume their proper role.

Children, obey your parents in everything, for this pleases the Lord (Colossians 3:20).

That command is found in the middle of what might well be called a "recipe" for family living: Colossians 3:12-21.

Verses 12-17 give a list of "ingredients" for happy home life (have Mom or Dad read this section).

Verses 18-21 give the "mixing and baking" instructions for each family member.

▲ TAKE A STEP

Put the proper ingredients together in exactly the right amounts, cook at the appropriate temperature, and you have something delicious to eat. The same is true of the family. Following God's recipe as set forth in the Bible is the responsibility of every family member.

Has your family ever been in a situation similar to that of Donna and her parents? What do you think Donna might have said to her dad when she asked permission to spend the night away? What should she have told him? What do you think Mr. and Mrs. Stephens should do now? What should Donna do?

"But she said that you said that I said . . . "

Q

Who's in charge of the family?

A

Parents are God's appointed leaders of the family.

The gift that keeps on (for-) giving

Q

How can I have a happier family?

A

Families are happy when every member is quick to forgive.

PARENT
Share from your own life an occasion when you had a hard time forgiving someone else. Honestly relate what happened and how the situation worked out.

I just won't live here anymore!"

Banished to his room, seven-year-old Greg planned to run away from home. Dad had spanked him yesterday, and now Mom was being unfair. Well, he'd show them! When lunchtime came and he wasn't there, Mom would be worried sick about him.

With his plan in mind, Greg sneaked out of the house, trudged down the street, sat under a stop sign, and waited. And waited. And waited.

But then it began to get dark, and Greg grew cold and hungry—not to mention a little bit lonely. He slowly walked home and arrived just in time for dinner.

"Mom," he blurted out, "I ran away and you didn't even notice!"

"Oh, yes I did," his mother replied. "I knew exactly where you were. But you had to decide to come back, Greg. Only you could make that choice."

 TAKE A LOOK / Luke 15:17-32

Jesus once told a parable about another family in which the younger son ran away from home. It wasn't long before he too landed in trouble and longed to return to his family. That's not so surprising. But what is surprising is the reaction of the son's father and brother.

Turn to Luke 15:17-32 and read the last part of the story, which some have called "The Wayward Lad and the Waiting Dad."

What do you think was the key to restoring happiness in their home?

▲ **TAKE A STEP**

Families aren't perfect because families are made up of imperfect people. That means there will be problems, misunderstandings, hurt feelings, and wrong attitudes from time to time. The family that can weather these storms is a family that is quick to forgive.

Bear with each other and forgive whatever grievances you may have against one another. Forgive as the Lord forgave you (Colossians 3:13).

The older brother in the parable needed to understand that his harsh attitude toward his younger brother made happiness and harmony impossible in his home. Is there a family member you have mistreated or are harboring hurtful thoughts against? Then the Bible is clear: Forgive that person just as God has forgiven you. Colossians 3:13 shows you how!

NATIVITY

O little town of Bethlehem, how still we see thee lie!
Above thy deep and dreamless sleep the silent stars go by.
Yet in thy dark streets shineth the everlasting Light;
The hopes and fears of all the years are met in thee tonight.
For Christ is born of Mary and gathered all above,
While mortals sleep, the angels keep their watch of wondering love.
O morning stars together proclaim the holy birth!
And praises sing to God the King, and peace to men on earth.

◆ THINKING ABOUT THE NATIVITY

During the Christmas season we see nativity scenes of every size and description. This week we want to focus on the event those scenes depict: the Nativity, **the miraculous birth of Jesus Christ,** which was foretold by the Hebrew prophet Isaiah in these words:

● KEY VERSE ON THE NATIVITY

For to us a child is born, to us a son is given, and the government will be on his shoulders. And he will be called Wonderful Counselor, Mighty God, Everlasting Father, Prince of Peace (Isaiah 9:6).

▲ LOOKING AHEAD

The Nativity—a birth and a gift. The Eternal God came to earth as a baby in a feeding trough.

Each day this week we'll accompany a 12-year-old boy named Joel on a journey back through time and history, back to the place where the first Christmas happened. Through the magic of imagination we'll view the Nativity through the eyes of the shepherds . . . angels . . . wise men . . . and even Mary and Joseph.

It's going to be an exciting week! But for today, close your time by singing together the familiar Christmas carol at the top of the page—and another favorite or two if you have time.

"Then the baby was born in a place called Bethlehem. It means 'The House of Bread.'"

The Boy who was King before He was born

Did it really happen . . . or was I dreaming?" Joel wondered as he gazed at the night sky over the fields of Bethlehem. Three years ago this same sky had blazed with the brilliance of a million torches and had swelled with the sound of angel choirs. He would never forget the sheer terror of that moment.

Yet, the angel had told the shepherds, "Do not be afraid. . . . Today in the town of David a Savior has been born to you; he is Christ the Lord" (Luke 2:10-11).

But when the shepherds hurried to the starlit inn, all they found was a tiny baby—in a feeding trough, of all places! Surely this couldn't be what all the fuss was about . . . could it?

◆ TAKE A LOOK / Luke 2:8-20

Bethlehem was a tiny village about five miles south of the city of Jerusalem. Kings ruled from Jerusalem, but only simple folks lived in Bethlehem. Yet it was there the Christ child was born. (Tomorrow you'll learn why.)

After the angel appeared to the shepherds, they left their sheep in the fields and went to the place where Jesus lay. They could hardly wait to see this wonderful baby!

Put yourself in their sandals as you read Luke 2:8-20. What would you think as you walked from the country to the village for the first look at the Christ child?

▲ TAKE A STEP

As the shepherds gazed into the manger, they saw a tiny, newborn baby boy. What they probably didn't realize was that Jesus existed long before He was born!

"But you, Bethlehem . . . , though you are small . . . , out of you will come for me one who will be ruler over Israel, whose origins are from of old, from ancient times" (Micah 5:2).

The phrase *from ancient times* literally means "from days of eternity." Jesus existed eternally before He ever came to earth! That's why He prayed to God in heaven, "Father, glorify me . . . with the glory I had with you before the world began" (John 17:5). The Christmas Baby existed even before the world was created!

The angel's announcement was all the proof the shepherds needed that this was Jesus Christ the Lord. And so they worshiped Him. You can do the same right now by quietly singing these words:

"O come, let us adore Him, O come, let us adore Him, O come, let us adore Him, Christ the Lord."

Q

Where was Jesus before He was born?

A

Jesus existed with God before He was born in Bethlehem.

*T*hree years earlier, when the shepherds had reported all they had seen and heard, the whole village buzzed with the news: the Messiah has been born! Joel remembered the excitement that filled the air.

Of course, there had been some doubters—those who refused to believe that such a wonderful thing could happen in an out-of-the-way country town. "If the Messiah is going to be King," they argued, "He'll be born in Jerusalem, the royal city."

But they overlooked one important fact, a fact that should have made it clear to everyone living in Joel's day—and yours—exactly where the Christ child would be born.

◆ TAKE A LOOK / Jeremiah 23:5; Micah 5:2-3

Centuries earlier, God, through His prophets, had given "road signs" pointing to the place of the Messiah's birth. It would not be in the capital city of Jerusalem, where the kingly palace was located. It would not be in Nazareth, home town of Mary and Joseph.

Rather, the Messiah would be born in the birthplace of a famous king of Israel. (Look up Jeremiah 23:5 and write his name here: _____)

That birthplace would be a village whose name means "house of bread." (Look up Micah 5:2-3 and write the name of the town here: _____)

▲ TAKE A STEP

With all the great cities of the world to choose from—Rome, Jerusalem, Alexandria—God chose the tiny village of Bethlehem as the birthplace for His Son. And He made that choice clear in the pages of the Old Testament.

When you think about it, "house of bread" is a very appropriate birthplace for the One who would later describe Himself this way:

"I am the bread of life. He who comes to me will never go hungry, and he who believes in me will never be thirsty" (John 6:35).

One way to share the Christmas message with others this year is by giving them some "Bethlehem Bread."

Make a batch or two of your favorite bread or coffee cake. Before you gift-wrap each loaf, add a card explaining the significance of Bethlehem as the birthplace of Christ. Be sure to include the words of John 6:35 on the card.

What better Christmas present could you give than an introduction to the Bread of Life!

The Baby who was born in the House of Bread

Why was Jesus born in Bethlehem?

Jesus was born in Bethlehem because God had promised centuries before that He would be.

PARENT
Set aside a few minutes with each of your children to be sure he or she understands the "heart" of Christmas— the birthday of the Savior.

The jigsaw puzzle that took centuries to solve

*T*o Joel, one of the most amazing things about the baby Jesus was the way news of Him spread like wildfire.

There were no newspapers or television broadcasts in those days. Everything was passed along by word of mouth. News about Jesus quickly spread through the entire village. And the more Joel listened, the more excited he became. Why? Because the reports he was hearing sounded remarkably like the words Joel had heard his rabbi read from the scrolls of the Scriptures.

Those words were hundreds of years old and had been written at different times by different prophets. Yet they described in detail the Messiah who was to come!

◆ TAKE A LOOK / Matthew 1:18-25

Do you enjoy jigsaw puzzles? Then you will enjoy this activity. For the next few minutes, let's put together some pieces of the puzzle about the infant Jesus.

Using two Bibles, let one family member be the Old Testament reader, another the New Testament reader. Take turns looking up the Old Testament prophecies (promises), and the New Testament fulfillments about the Messiah:

How was Jesus different from any other baby ever born?

Jesus came to earth as Immanuel, "God with us."

Prophecy	Fulfillment
1. He would be a descendant of Abraham (Genesis 12:1-3).	Matthew 1:1
2. He would be born of a virgin (Isaiah 7:14).	Luke 1:26-31; 2:7
3. He would flee to Egypt for safety (Hosea 11:1).	Matthew 2:14-15
4. Children would be murdered in an attempt to kill him (Jeremiah 31:15).	Matthew 2:16-18

▲ TAKE A STEP

How was Jesus different from any other baby born into the world? All the Old Testament prophecies about the Messiah were fulfilled in Him. Isaiah was right when he proclaimed more than 2,500 years ago:

The virgin will be with child and will give birth to a son, and will call him Immanuel (Isaiah 7:14).

The name *Immanuel* means "God with us" (Matthew 1:23). One important question remains: Is Jesus your Immanuel? Only you can make that choice. Wouldn't today be a wonderful time to say, "Jesus, be King of my life"?

A year had passed since the most terrifying day of Joel's life—a day even more frightening than the angel's visit announcing the Savior's birth. For this had been a day of death, not life.

It had started quietly enough with a bit of news. (Rumor might be a better word for it!) Someone had seen Mary and Joseph and little Jesus leaving the city—not headed north for their hometown of Nazareth—but journeying south along the road to Egypt. The marketplace was astir: "Took the baby and left in the night, did they? That family won't be back for sure. You'll see."

But no one had time to think about it, for terror had suddenly arrived. Without warning, Herod's soldiers swept into the village and began to kill every baby boy under two years of age. Never would Joel forget the horrible sight as his little brother Micah was torn from his mother's arms—and killed before their eyes.

◆ **TAKE A LOOK / Matthew 2:13-18; Romans 6:23**
The story is tragic for two reasons. First, it is based on a true account, though Joel and his family are make-believe; and second, even those who survived the terror of Herod's soldiers would one day die nonetheless.

As you read this often-forgotten portion of the Christmas story in Matthew 2:13-18, think about this verse:

> The wages of sin is death, but the gift of God is eternal life in Christ Jesus our Lord (Romans 6:23).

No one likes to talk about death, but everyone likes to talk about gifts. And that's what Christmas is all about. It is the celebration of God's priceless gift to us in the person of His Son—the One who paid the "wages of sin" and now offers us eternal life.

▲ **TAKE A STEP**
Look at the letters in the word **GIFT**. When a **G**-ift is freely given, you must respond. You can **I**-gnore it, pretend you didn't see it, or you can **F**-orget it and never use it. But that wouldn't be showing much appreciation, would it? How much better to **T**-ake it gratefully and say thanks to the One whose love prompted Him to give it to you in the first place.

Gifts are expressions of love—so if a gift is especially meaningful to you, be sure to tell the giver. Take some time right now and tell God how grateful you are to Him for the original Christmas present, His only Son Jesus.

The original Christmas present from heaven

Q

What makes Jesus' birth so important?

A

Jesus came as God's gift of love that we might have eternal life.

PARENT
A gift of stationery and stamps to your child will encourage thank-you notes after Christmas.

TIME

I f you've been reading through this book consecutively, you're in the homestretch. Now it's time to look back over the 52 weeks just completed, and plan for the next 52 just ahead. A time to think about time.

This week we'll look at the one thing everyone has the same amount of, but no one seems to have enough of—TIME.

◆ THINKING ABOUT TIME

Time is difficult to define. Sometimes it flys; other times it drags. Always it marches on. It can be wasted, saved, managed, measured, lost, stretched, and spent.

It can be divided into seconds, minutes, hours, days, weeks, months, or years. It can be past, present, or future. Everyone has a lifetime supply, but not everyone has exactly the same amount. No two people use it quite the same way.

Some of us feel like the Mad Hatter in *Alice In Wonderland:*

Alice sighed wearily, "I think you might do something better with time . . . than wasting it asking riddles with no answers."

"If you knew Time as well as I do," said the Hatter, "you wouldn't talk about wasting it."

Although you may not fully understand time, you need to learn to use it wisely, for time is **one dimension of the world in which God has placed you.** And just as He expects you to use your material resources well, He also wants you to use your time in ways that honor Him.

● KEY VERSE ON TIME
He has made everything beautiful in its time. He has also set eternity in the hearts of men (Ecclesiastes 3:11).

▲ LOOKING AHEAD
Plan your family schedule right now so you will have time for God's Word each day this week.

"It was Monday morning, he kept hitting the snooze button, and before he knew it, it had been twenty years . . ."

*T*he trip to Ohio to see the grandparents had been fun—and full of surprises.

"This sure isn't what I expected Gramps to give me for Christmas," Eric remarked as he took his new rod and reel out of the trunk. "Were you surprised when he gave you one too, Dad?"

"Well, I'll admit I was puzzled at first," Mr. Wilson replied as he unpacked the car. "But then it began to make sense. You see, Eric, when I was growing up in Ohio, some of the best times I ever had with my dad were the times we spent together fishing. Grandpa remembers those times too. I guess he wants you and me to be sure we don't get too busy for the 'good stuff.' You can bet he'll be calling one Saturday night soon to ask where we went fishing, how many we caught, and who let the big one get away!"

◆ TAKE A LOOK / Proverbs 3:13-26

Eric and his dad understood the reason for the fishing equipment because they understood Grandpa Wilson's thinking. In a similar way, you can understand time better when you realize that God made it—and gave it to you—for a reason.

When God created the heavens and the earth in the beginning, He also created time. He is the One who "invented" mornings and evenings; seasons and tides; days, weeks, and years. And He is the One who inspired Moses to pray this prayer:

Teach us to number our days aright, that we may gain a heart of wisdom (Psalm 90:12).

By using time as God intended, we gain a "heart of wisdom," something very precious in God's sight. Discover just how precious by reading Proverbs 3:13-26.

▲ TAKE A STEP

Moses' prayer is timely indeed! Everybody, get some paper and pencils, and spend a few minutes numbering your days. Start by calculating how many days there are in 70 years (70 x 365 = ?). Next, figure how many days you have lived already (365 x your age in years). Now subtract your days from the days you will have if you live to be 70. (But remember, 70 is just an average age that Moses uses. You have no guarantee you'll live that long!)

Now think of one important goal you want to reach in the remaining days God gives you. What will you want to make time for in the coming year? Plan now how you can reach that goal, and mark your calendar accordingly.

There's more to life than playing "Beat the Clock"

Q

Why is it so important to see time as a gift from God?

A

Time is one of the tools God uses to teach us wisdom.

PARENT
Can your child tell time on both a digital and a dial watch? It's a skill he or she will use for a lifetime.

Morning people are hard to love at sunrise

"**M**aria is one of my best friends," Kelly commented to her mother, "but her family sure is different from ours."

"Why, Kelly, I'm not sure what you mean. They don't seem all that different to me."

"Well, you know how Dad is—always worried we're going to be late for something. Every time we take a vacation, he plans it months in advance: where we're going, what we're going to see, how long it will take to get there. But Maria's dad doesn't seem to know there is such a thing as a clock! Her family is always so relaxed. They're never in a hurry . . . "

" . . . and never on time?" Kelly's mother broke in.

"Well, yes. But you know, Mom, it's fun being in their house. It's like they have all the time in the world for me!"

◆ TAKE A LOOK / Ephesians 5:15-20

What Kelly was noticing in her friend Maria is that different people view time differently.

Some are morning people. They spring from bed at dawn, ready to face whatever life may bring. Others are night people. Their day doesn't really begin until 9 or 10 o'clock in the morning. But long after morning people have gone to bed, night people are full of energy and enthusiasm!

Regardless of which time temperament you have, God wants you to live your life wisely.

[Make] the most of every opportunity, because the days are evil. Therefore do not be foolish, but understand what the Lord's will is (Ephesians 5:16-17).

Today read Ephesians 5:15-20. Watch for two phrases that tell you what wise living is all about.

▲ TAKE A STEP

In many ways we are all governed by clock time, the hours that we must measure and manage. The school bus comes at 7:25 . . . Dad has to be at work by 8:00 . . . Sunday worship begins at 11:00 . . . band practice starts at 3:00 P.M.—regardless of how you feel about those times!

But each of us also has a "body clock," an internal rhythm that causes us to use clock time differently. And wise is the family that encourages snooze alarms for night people . . . and early bedtimes for day people.

Spend a few minutes discussing the time temperaments of each person in your family. What problems arise because of the differences? What does the family do to solve them?

Q

✓ Why do people see and use time differently?

A

Time is used differently because people have different "time temperaments."

*H*ow does this schedule compare with a busy day in your home?

7:15 A.M. — Tony, early band practice
7:45 A.M. — Mom, car pool (all week)
9:15 A.M. — Susan, orthodontist appointment
10:00 A.M.— Mom, take Buster to the vet for shots
12:00 P.M.— Mom, PTA planning committee
3:15 P.M. — Mom, car pool
4:30 P.M. — Susan, piano lesson
5:30 P.M. — Dad, pick up Susan from piano lesson
6:00 P.M. — Dinner (turkey hash)
7:30 P.M. — Dad, finance committee at church
8:00 P.M. — Take Tony to the library
9:30 P.M. — Mom, pick up Tony
10:00 P.M.— Everyone home . . . at last!

◆ TAKE A LOOK / Ecclesiastes 3:1-8, 12-14

A problem in many homes today is not so much a tight budget, or the TV, or the telephone. Instead, it's the maze of activities and appointments called the "daily schedule."

Sometimes it seems that there aren't enough hours in a 24-hour day to do all that a 24-hour day demands. But is that really true? Do you run the calendar, or does the calendar run you?

In thinking about how you can manage your time wisely, the place to begin is not with your schedule as it is now, but with a blank calendar. Ecclesiastes 3:1-8, 12-14 will give you encouragement as your family tackles the tyranny of time.

▲ TAKE A STEP

There is a time for everything, and a season for every activity under heaven (Ecclesiastes 3:1).

As you read the Scripture passage above, did you notice that nearly all the activities mentioned involve person-to-person contact?

As you begin to fill your family calendar for the coming year, keep these important tips in mind:

1. Schedule time with each child (or parent) in the family each week.

2. Watch out for too many activities or not enough variety. Break up busy schedules with fun family outings.

3. Meet as a family at the beginning of the year to talk about the "big things" and pray together about the new year.

4. Above all, keep eternity in view. Committees, jobs, and sports will one day pass away. What will you have left to show for your time when they are gone?

"I'd like to get organized, but I can't find the time"

Q

How can I use my time wisely?

A

Time, wisely used, gives priority to relationships.

Where do you turn when it all starts to burn?

As dense black smoke billowed above the treetops and flames leaped high into the air, the Morgans' house turned from a stately old home into a burned-out shell.

For more than 120 years, Morgans had lived in that house. Then in a matter of minutes it was all gone: the house, furniture (much of it three generations old), family heirlooms, and all the Morgans' personal belongings.

Nothing could be saved. The nearest help, 15 miles away, arrived just in time to inspect a pile of smoldering ashes and ugly black rubble. For the Morgans, one chapter in their lives had ended; another was about to begin.

When will time as we know it come to an end?

◆ **TAKE A LOOK / 2 Peter 3:3-13**

Most of us can recall times when life seemed to turn a corner. We reached a goal . . . won a trophy . . . completed a project . . . graduated . . . lost a job . . . moved to a new city . . . lost a loved one. We may not remember the exact date, but we vividly remember the event because, though life went on, it was never quite the same again.

The Bible speaks of another "turning point" in life—one more dramatic than anyone has ever experienced—an event which, like the Morgans' house fire, will mark both an end and a beginning.

No one knows for sure which houses will be destroyed by fire in the next year. But the Bible says that one day fire will destroy the whole earth! And the best use of your time is to be sure you and those you love are ready for that day. Read about "the time when time will be no more" in 2 Peter 3:3-13.

A

Time as we know it will end when God destroys the world by fire.

▲ **TAKE A STEP**

Although some people scoff and say the world will never end, they are in for a surprise! God has assured us that one day life as we know it will end. But why is He waiting? His Word gives the answer.

[God] is patient with you, not wanting anyone to perish, but everyone to come to repentance (2 Peter 3:9).

No amount of fire insurance could save the Morgans' house from perishing. And nothing but repentance can save people from a similar fate. As this new year begins, it's a good time to come to God in repentance and childlike faith. After all, a life is a terrible thing to waste—especially if it's yours!